'A GOOD JEW
and
A GOOD ENGLISHMAN'

'A GOOD JEW
and
A GOOD ENGLISHMAN':
The Jewish Lads' & Girls' Brigade
1895–1995

SHARMAN KADISH

VALLENTINE MITCHELL
LONDON

First published in 1995 in Great Britain by
VALLENTINE MITCHELL & CO. LTD
Newbury House, 900 Eastern Avenue,
London IG2 7HH

and in the United States of America by
VALLENTINE MITCHELL
c/o ISBS, 5804 N.E. Hassalo Street, Portland, Oregon 97213-3644

British Library Cataloguing in Publication Data
Kadish, Sharman
  Good Jew and a Good Englishman: Jewish
  Lads' and Girls' Brigade, 1895–1995
  I. Title
  369.40941

  ISBN 0-85303-300-5 (cloth)
  ISBN 0-85303-306-4 (paperback)

Library of Congress Cataloging-in-Publication Data
Kadish Sharman, 1959–
  'A good Jew and a good Englishman' : the Jewish Lads' & Girls'
  Brigade, 1895–1995 / Sharman Kadish.
    p.   cm.
  Includes bibliographical references and index.
  ISBN 0-85303-300-5 — ISBN 0-85303-306-4 (pbk.)
  1. Jewish Lads' & Girls' Brigade (Great Britain)—History.
  2. Jewish youth—Great Britain—Societies and clubs.   3. Jews—Great
  Britain—Social life and customs.   I. Title.
  DS135.E5K335   1995
  369.42'089'924041—dc20   94-48167
                                                                    CIP

Typeset by Vitaset, Paddock Wood, Kent
Printed in Great Britain by
Bookcraft (Bath) Ltd

Contents

List of Illustrations

Tables

Abbreviations

ACF	Army Cadet Force
AJ	Anglo-Jewish Archives, Hartley Library, Southampton University
AJY	Association for Jewish Youth
ARP	Air-Raid Precautions
ATC	Air Training Corps
ATS	Auxiliary Territorial Service (women)
AYZS	Association of Young Zionist Societies
BB	Boys' Brigade
BBYO/A	B'nai Brith Youth Organisation/Young Adults
BNCA	British National Cadet Association
BUF	British Union of Fascists
CAJEX	Magazine of the Cardiff Jewish Ex-servicemen's Association
CLB	Church Lads' Brigade
CPGB	Communist Party of Great Britain
DEA	Duke of Edinburgh Award Scheme
EJ	*Encyclopaedia Judaica*
EZF	English Zionist Federation
FZY	Federation of Zionist Youth
GLC	Greater London Council
JC	*Jewish Chronicle*
JFS	Jews' Free School
JG	*Jewish Guardian*
JLB	Jewish Lads' Brigade
JLGB	Jewish Lads' & Girls' Brigade
JPC	Jewish People's Council
JW	*Jewish World*
LCC	London County Council
MCRL	Manchester Central Reference Library
NSPCC	National Society for the Prevention of Cruelty to Children
OCA	(JLB) Old Comrades' Association

PZ	Poale Tsion
TA	Territorial Army
TJHSE	*Transactions of the Jewish Historical Society of England*
WIZO	Women's International Zionist Organisation
YCL	Young Communist League
YMCA	Young Men's Christian Association
YPZ	Young Poale Tsion

Foreword by the Brigade Commandant, Sir Peter Lazarus, KCB

A FAMILY WITHIN THE COMMUNITY – THE MAGIC
THAT CONTINUES TO WORK

As we think about the past of our people in this country, we are bound to reflect on the changing problems and pressures which have confronted us, as citizens and as Jews. This history sets out with great clarity just how our predecessors reacted to those pressures and challenges 100 years ago. We should never forget to be grateful for the liberty which has allowed us, in this country, to choose for ourselves how we are to live.

I am delighted that we now know, more than any member of the Brigade has known for nearly a century, what really happened 100 years ago. We now know why our founders started the Brigade in 1895, what they tried to achieve, the problems they faced and how nearly it all went wrong. But the Brigade survived, and grew, and we have inherited it to do our bit, in our turn, for our Jewish young people.

It will help and encourage us all to know how well our predecessors built, and how they overcame their problems of money, people, rows, disaffection and so on. As our author makes clear, there is some special mystery at the heart of the Brigade. Even the elderly, if they have once become active members, rarely wholly retire. The spell is too strong. I knew this from what I had heard from my great uncle, Ernest Halsted, who was Commandant from 1924 to 1944, and later from my father Kenneth Lazarus, when he was Treasurer. I visited two Summer Camps for a couple of days as the guest of Ernest's son, Victor, when I was in the army in the late

1940s and he first gave me my taste for the Brigade. But I never fully experienced it myself until I became Commandant.

When I think about the achievements of our past, I remember too the crowds of happy, tired, young people as they boarded their buses after the Summer Camp I commanded at East Mersea in 1993, bidding me and one another farewell for a year. For them, life without the Brigade would have lost all its savour.

Many of my colleagues have much longer memories of our past. There are those who still remember with affection Ernest Joseph who, with his great friend Ernest Halsted, was devoted to the Brigade for the whole of his life. I recall Sir Louis (Luigi) Gluckstein, Commandant and Council Chairman, whose son Roy still serves as a Trustee of Camperdown House. The names of our cups and medals recall the great names of the past. The Brigade is essentially a family affair. Wherever I visit, I meet the sons and daughters, and grandchildren, of past members. Even our oldest members never wholly retire. The Old Comrades are a constant source of strength.

We are shaped by the past – our family traditions give us added strength – and we are well poised, at the end of our first 100 years of service, to co-operate with the other communal efforts to halt the decline in the Jewish community; and to rebuild for the future, a future of service to Jewry and of service to the country. That is what our founders strove to achieve, a Brigade which requires the saying of the *Shema* at every parade, and stands with equal pride for the playing of *Hatikva* and the playing of the National Anthem, as we do at the close of every formal public parade. The uniform, and the discipline, however unimportant in themselves, represent our chosen and effective way to self-discipline, and a life of service to others.

There are of course ever more difficult problems to face. After two world wars, the *Shoah*, and the present Balkan disaster, none of us can be confident of finding the right way forward. The complexities of science and technology make it difficult to retain the simple piety and faith of our ancestors. The doctrinaire approach of some parts of Jewry makes co-operation in our kind of widespread family ever more difficult. Many of our young people have a far higher standard of living than 100 years ago, but there is less faith, less certainty, more doubts about the possibility of finding worthwhile work opportunities, and there are more broken homes and more cynicism. Our founders were inspired by the traditional values of Jewry when they saw the suffering of the new, impoverished immigrants and decided that they must help. It has been the tradition in this country for those already here to help the newcomers and to encourage them to play a full part in the life of the country that has given them shelter. That was the aim of our founders, that – as this history shows – is what they achieved, and it is this that we shall continue to try to do.

Looking back to the end of the last century, it is remarkable how many Jews were saved from persecution and death in their own countries, and how well those who came served their new country. Many of today's most cherished pillars – including, for example, Marks & Spencer – started as an effort by one of the new immigrants. The Brigade is proud to have played some part in helping so many Jews, when they reached sanctuary in this country, to recover their dignity as human beings, to learn how to serve as good citizens, to retain their precious identity as Jews and to teach their own families to continue the traditions of service which some of them learnt from the Brigade.

Great Britain must have seemed very strange to the parents of the youngsters who were our first members. Our founders gave these young people and their parents the knowledge that other Jews cared about them; the opportunity to look out from the confines of the sweat shops of the East End of London, and from the miserable houses and jobs of London, Liverpool, Manchester and Glasgow, to a wider horizon; some wholesome food at Summer Camp; and the belief that life in this country would give real opportunities to those who tried for them. We rejoice that, often with help from the Brigade and other youth organisations, so many succeeded.

There are new dragons to slay. We have to continue to show that British Jews can play a full part in striving for the peace, security and growth of Israel, without in any way prejudicing their loyalty to this country. There is still real poverty. There are insufficient jobs. Many of our young people still lack any real faith in God, themselves, or the future. We have to find the volunteers and other resources to enable us to help them to overcome all these dangers and difficulties.

I hope that this history of our first 100 years will give us strength and confidence to continue with undiminished fervour and enthusiasm for the next century. I want to see ever larger numbers of happy and committed Jewish boys and girls coming to our parades and camps, finding there new friends, and often future husbands and wives, learning how to be better members of Jewry and citizens of this country and encouraging their own children, in due time, to join the Brigade family and to maintain our traditions of service to others. That is I believe an objective worthy of our founders, and I confidently hope for support from everyone to achieve this.

Peter Lazarus

Preface

The Jewish Lads' & Girls' Brigade (JLGB) is the oldest surviving Jewish youth organisation in Britain, and indeed in the British Commonwealth, and celebrates its centenary in 1995. It was founded by Colonel Albert Goldsmid, an Army officer born in India, who discovered his Jewish roots and became a convert to Orthodox Judaism and *Chovevei Tsion* Zionism. To mark the centenary, I was commissioned to write the official history of the Brigade. In 1992–93, the Camperdown House Trust, an independent trust fund closely linked with the JLGB, sponsored the Camperdown House Fellowship at Royal Holloway College, University of London, to enable a professional historian to devote one year full-time to researching and writing the history. I was invited to undertake the task. It was a 'tall order' – from sorting the extensive archive – which the JLGB is fortunate in possessing – to delivery of the finished manuscript to the publishers. I managed to complete the task in just over a year. Time imposed the greatest limitation and readers are asked for their indulgence for any omissions of individuals (especially of oral history material) and events which inevitably occur in the text as a result.

This book is the first serious history of an Anglo-Jewish youth organisation to be published.[1] However, there is a precedent for it, which is not without relevance. The original Jewish Lads' Brigade (JLB) owed its inspiration to the example of Christian uniformed youth movements, a peculiarly British phenomenon, which sprang up in the 1880s and 1890s. The oldest of these, the Boys' Brigade, celebrated its own centenary in 1983 and commissioned John Springhall, of the New University of Ulster at Coleraine, and a leading authority on British youth movements, to write their history, in association with two Brigade 'insiders', Brian Fraser and Michael Hoare. Springhall writes in his introduction as follows:

> Because histories of youth organizations are generally written by 'insiders', self-congratulation is often their dominant characteristic. Research into episodes in their past which might point to adversely critical conclusions have seldom been undertaken, while systematic efforts to set youth organizations in their full social, economic and political contexts usually remain unattempted. The Boys' Brigade, therefore, demonstrated a certain amount of courage (or foolhardiness!) in commissioning a professional historian, an 'outsider' with no previous affiliation to the Brigade.[2]

The same might be said of the Jewish Lads' & Girls' Brigade.

A Good Jew and a Good Englishman sets out to be an honest appraisal of the first 100 years of the JLGB and to place the movement in its rightful context, as an integral part of English Jewish and British social history. As one would expect from a centenary history, this book gives a general account of the origins and development of the JLGB and examines the character and influence of its founders (especially Colonel Goldsmid), funders and Commanding Officers. The JLB was the first organised youth club for Jewish boys and remains today one of the most popular Jewish youth movements in Britain. Its traditional formula of military style discipline and rank, drill, uniform, and Summer Camp, remains attractive to the young, despite changes in society which might have rendered it 'old-fashioned'. What is the secret of the JLB's survival and success?

This book, however, also sets out to examine the Brigade critically. It shows how the original JLB was closely modelled on the uniformed youth groups started by the churches and how it shared with them an increasing preoccupation with militarism, national defence and social control in the years down to the First World War. The JLB, however, was also a product of peculiarly Jewish circumstances. It functioned chiefly as an agent of anglicisation, aimed at the Yiddish-speaking east European immigrants – and their children – who flooded into the country after 1881. The middle-class Anglo-Jewish gentlemen who ran the Brigade sought to transform foreign-born, working-class Jewish youth into respectable 'Englishmen of the Mosaic persuasion', moulded in the best traditions of the English public school, universities and officers' mess. As such, the Brigade may be regarded as an expression of 'native' Jewry's patriotic faith in the so-called Emancipation Contract and was, at bottom, a defensive response to rising anti-alienism and ultimately to anti-Semitism.

How far did the Brigade succeed in fulfilling its mission amongst the immigrants? How did they, both the boys themselves and their parents, react to the Brigade? The ambiguous – and sometimes controversial – relationship of the JLB with both Judaism and Political Zionism is explored as well as its changing role in the Jewish community over the years. The late arrival of girls on the scene (1963), and the reasons for it, is examined in the final chapter. As an organisation conscious of its own tradition, how much is today's JLGB influenced by its past?

I am grateful to a large number of people who have, in one way or another, facilitated the writing of this book. The Brigade Secretary, Charles Kay, and other members of the Brigade Staff in South Woodford have been most helpful and courteous throughout, giving me free access to all the archives and answering all of my questions. I have had many interesting conversations, both in person and on the telephone, with Charles Kay, whose long experience of working with youth has given me valuable insight into the psychology of the Brigade.

I must also thank the Academic Advisory Panel, its chairman Dr Tony Kushner and members Professor Geoffrey Alderman, Clemens Nathan and Bill Williams for their conscientious reading of the various drafts and many useful comments and criticisms at every stage of this project. Likewise, I am grateful to Anne Kershen, who did some preliminary research on the JLB, and who has given me unerring advice throughout. Thanks again to Tony and to Rosalyn Livshin and their families for their kind hospitality when I made research trips to Southampton University and Manchester during 1993. The British Academy kindly funded my attendance at the World Congress of Jewish Studies in Jerusalem in June 1993, where I gave a paper on the history of the JLB. The trip to Israel provided an opportunity to exchange ideas with academic colleagues from an entirely different perspective: Professors Richard Cohen,

Harold Fisch, Gideon Shimoni and David Mendelsson. David, Matthew Kalman and Rosalyn Livshin all kindly made available their unpublished dissertations on subjects bearing on the history of Jewish youth movements in Britain. As always, Professor Avraham Greenbaum and his wife Miriam made me very welcome at their home in Jerusalem.

I owe a debt of gratitude to Motel Robins who willingly took upon himself the task of Brigade Archivist many years ago and who collected a great deal of material upon which I have been able to draw. Motel and his sister Bina kindly agreed to be interviewed at their home in Hove. Beatrice Harris, daughter of pre-war Brigade Commmandant Ernest Halsted (formerly Hallenstein), and Josh Manches, Commandant in the 1970s and early 1980s, also granted interviews. Other Brigade people have provided material: Sidney Davis (Manchester), Jonathan Dubow (Cardiff), Cyril Goodman, Alex Jacob, Harvey Livingston (Glasgow), Clive Nagus (Liverpool) and David Spector. Others who have been helpful include: Percy Gourgey, David Jacobs (Manchester), Harvey Kaplan and Dr Kenneth Collins (Glasgow), Joe Wolfman (Liverpool) and Anne Yardley (Cardiff). Thanks also to research student Mark Connelly for sharing his ideas on the concept of Armistice Day and its commemoration, and to John Simon for taking the trouble to send me material on the turn-of-the-century South African JLB all the way from Cape Town. Thanks are also due to Spectrum Radio for inviting me onto their Jewish programme to talk about the history of the JLGB. The response to the phone-in was tremendous and provided me with some useful material which I have kept on tape. Last, but by no means least, I want to thank my husband Syd (Dr Sydney Greenberg) for initiating me into the complex mysteries of word processing! Without the aid of technology it would have been impossible to produce this book in the little time available.

In 1986, Motel Robins wrote:

> I am at the present collating as much information as possible, so that eventually, the Brigade will find an interesting person, very much like 'Boswell', who will be able to write a true unlaundered history of the J.L.& G.B., as it was, and as it is now.[3]

I may not exactly be 'Boswell', but I do hope that this history of the JLGB will not disappoint its readers, whether 'Brigade Boys' (or girls), academics or simply members of the general public interested in the sociology of the Jewish community or in the history of a very British youth movement.

Sharman Kadish
London
Tevet 5754
January 1994

Introduction

To mark the centenary in 1995 of the foundation of the Jewish Lads' Brigade (now known as the Jewish Lads' & Girls' Brigade), the Trustees of Camperdown House gladly acceded to the request of the Brigade that it should sponsor a volume setting out the history of the movement founded by Colonel Albert E.W. Goldsmid.

On the advice of Dr Martin Goodman, Reader in Jewish Studies at the University of Oxford, and of Dr Tony Kushner, Parkes Lecturer in Jewish Studies at the University of Southampton, the Trustees commissioned Dr Sharman Kadish to write the history. To this end, the Trustees provided the funds to establish the Camperdown House Research Fellowship which was held for one year by Dr Kadish at Royal Holloway and Bedford New College, University of London.

The Camperdown House Trustees likewise funded an Academic Advisory Panel set up under the chairmanship of Dr Kushner, the members of which formed a most valuable link with the Brigade and with the Trust at all stages of the writing.

The result is this volume in which Dr Kadish has provided a centenary history which, I venture to suggest, will become indispensable reading to researchers studying the Jewish youth movement in this country during the twentieth century.

The Camperdown House Trust was established by a Deed dated 4 April 1913. It declared that the new building, then in course of erection in Half Moon Passage, Whitechapel, should be used 'primarily for the purpose of providing accommodation for such philanthropic institutions having for their object the welfare of the lads of the poorer classes resident or employed in the Parish of Whitechapel or in any neighbouring Parish'. The Declaration of Trust specified that preference as regards accommodation should be given to the Hutchison House Club for Working Lads and to the Jewish Lads' Brigade so long as these bodies existed. The Club, in fact, eventually ceased functioning.

The new building was named Camperdown House, it having been erected on the site of the town house of Admiral Viscount Duncan of Camperdown who died in 1804. The Architect was Ernest Joseph, and it was generally acclaimed to be one of the finest purpose-built boys' clubs and recreational centres in the country.

The first Trustees of Camperdown House to be appointed were Lionel Nathan de Rothschild (the Member of Parliament for the Aylesbury Division of Buckinghamshire) as Chairman, Sir Max J. Bonn, merchant banker, and Frank Goldsmith (the Member of Parliament for the Stowmarket Division of Suffolk).

From 1913 to the outbreak of the Second World War in 1939 Camperdown House served as the Headquarters of the Jewish Lads' Brigade, and provided facilities for an infinite variety of activities. The building survived the bombing of London; during the war it had been used as a Fire Brigade Headquarters. However, after the end of the war in 1945, and with the movement away from the East End of much of the Jewish population, Camperdown House never recaptured its place as the heart of the Brigade. It was leased by the Trustees to the Territorial Army, then as rehearsal studios to the impresario Harold Fielding, and subsequently to the English National Opera Company.

Eventually in 1973 the Trustees sold the freehold interest. The building was demolished, and an office block erected in its place with a plaque affixed at pavement level recording that on the site had stood the Headquarters of the Jewish Lads' Brigade.

In 1983 the Trust acquired the freehold of the relatively modest property at South Woodford now serving as the administrative Headquarters of the Brigade, it being named 'Camperdown' for sentimental reasons.

The Camperdown House Trust is governed by Schemes of the Charity Commission. Although the primary beneficiary is declared to be the Jewish Lads' & Girls' Brigade countrywide, the Trustees are additionally empowered, subject always to the primary Trust, to advance funds for the benefit of young persons of the Jewish faith resident in Greater London who are not members of the Brigade. In practice, the Camperdown House Trust has for very many years provided the greater part of the funds required to run the Brigade, the Trustees receiving at their meetings detailed reports on every aspect of Brigade activities.

As a stripling, I was introduced to the Brigade in 1935 at one of the 'recruitment of officers' suppers held at Camperdown House. I was intrigued and, somewhat hesitantly, attended a few weeks later the camp held at Raynes Park on the outskirts of London to commemorate the Silver Jubilee of the succession of King George V.

This is now approaching 60 years ago, but I still vividly recollect the inspection carried out in full ceremonial uniform by Field-Marshal Viscount Allenby, of Megiddo and of Felixstowe, the Commander-in-Chief throughout the Palestine Campaign in 1917. I was then posted as a Second Lieutenant to Stoke Newington Company which paraded weekly with an attendance of 100 boys.

In the following year, at the Summer Camp at Walmer, Rufus Isaacs, first Marquess of Reading, inspected the Brigade at Walmer Castle where he resided as Lord Warden of the Cinque Ports.

It was in the early 1950s that I was invited by Ernest Joseph to become a Trustee of Camperdown House, he being the then Chairman. On the death of his successor Sir Louis Gluckstein in 1979, I was elected Chairman of the Trustees.

The Charity Commission Scheme regulating the Camperdown House Trust provides for a body of five Trustees. At the present time, the longest-serving Trustee is Edmund Leopold de Rothschild (the son of Lionel, the first Chairman), who is also the President of the Brigade. The remaining Trustees are Roy J. Gluckstein (son of Sir Louis), John R. Leffman, Dame Simone Prendergast and the writer of this Introduction. The Brigade has been fortunate to be commanded in the years preceding its centenary by Sir Peter Lazarus, an inspiring and dedicated leader. The Trustees are confident that the Brigade, as the senior Jewish youth movement in the country, will continue its outstanding work as, in good heart, it enters into its second century.

Cyril J. Goodman
Chairman of the Trustees of Camperdown House
January 1994

1 · 'General Gordon' Goldsmid: Origins and Early Years 1895–1914

The second Lady Swaythling, née Gladys Rachel Goldsmid, re-counted a story about her father Colonel Albert E.W. Goldsmid, which has come to assume legendary status. As a girl in the 1890s she 'was out riding with him in South Wales where he had been inspecting Church Lads' Brigade. He said to me "something similar would do Jewish lads good". That is where the idea of the Jewish Lads' Brigade was born.'[1]

There is little reason to doubt the accuracy of Lady Swaythling's recollection made over half a century later. We know that Colonel Goldsmid was appointed Colonel-in-Chief of the 41st or 'Welch' Regimental District at Cardiff in 1894. Indeed, he was the first pro-fessing Jew to achieve this rank. He remained in that city until 1897 where he formed close links with the Cardiff Jewish community. It is also the case that the Church Lads' Brigade (CLB) had been formed four years previously (1891) by Walter Mallock Gee in London. The Church Lads' Brigade was the Anglican answer to the Boys' Brigade, set up in 1883 by a Scottish Presbyterian Sunday School teacher, William Smith, in Glasgow. The Boys' Brigade became the role model for a whole clutch of uniformed youth movements which mushroomed in Britain in the last decade of the nineteenth century.[2] Common to them all was a potent mixture of Christian mission and military method. The combination of religion and uniform had originated with the Salvation Army (1878), an evangelical missionary society for adults. In the youth movements, parade ground drill and strict discipline reinforced the Gospel. Their youthful recruits, drawn from the 'better' working classes, were kitted out in the essential uniform of pillbox cap, leather belt and white haversack. It is safe to assume that the Jewish Lads' Brigade (JLB) of 1895 – and indeed the Catholic Lads' Brigade of 1896 – were sectarian variations on the theme.

Nevertheless, some recent research has shown that the idea of creating a Jewish boys' brigade did not originate with Colonel Goldsmid.[3] In April 1891 the *Jewish Chronicle*, self-styled 'organ of British Jewry', published a letter from the Revd Francis Lyon Cohen headed 'But what about the boys?' in which he called for the creation of a Jewish youth group, modelled on the Boys' Brigade, to channel the energies of working-class youth in the East End of London at that crucial period 'between their leaving school and the attainment of manhood'.[4] Perhaps surprisingly, Jewish girls were already catered for. The Jewish Girls' Club had been founded by Lady Magnus in 1886 and the West Central Jewish Girls' Club was to be established by Lily Montagu in 1893. Yet this apparent attention to female needs on the part of the Jewish community should not be misinterpreted as an early example of 'feminism'. Whilst Magnus and Montagu undoubtedly entertained 'progressive views' about the role of women, the underlying motivation for their activities was the 'protection' of their young charges from the dangers of the street, crime and prostitution. Young women were deemed to be more 'at risk' than their male counterparts who were presumed to be at school, *yeshiva* or work.[5] Even so, the girls' clubs encountered opposition from those traditional elements within the Jewish community who wanted to keep their women at home.

Revd Cohen suggested that adolescent boys, too, needed protection from presumably unhealthy 'influences' which assailed them in the less-than-salubrious surroundings of the East End and the working-class quarters of other industrial cities. He felt that the existing Jewish Working Men's Club and Lads' Institute (1874) did not answer this specific need. He appealed to Anglo-Jewry for personal assistance, financial aid and the provision of suitable premises for the establishment of a uniformed youth movement for Jewish boys. Such an organisation would 'utilise drill and a quasi-military organisation' with the aim of promoting 'a true God fearing manliness'. Indeed, the drill and other physical activity was intended merely 'to attract' the boys; once involved, religious instruction, as in the case of the Christian Boys' Brigade, was the

real aim: 'On the spiritual side . . . instruction in Hebrew, the fostering of Sabbath observance, of attendance at Public Worship, and so
on. These last, indeed, are the *cooking* of the hare, the drill and
exercise are but the *catching* of it.'

Despite the 'unkosher' choice of imagery, this approach came
naturally to Cohen, an educationalist and product of Jews' College,
an institution devoted to the training of 'a native Jewish ministry'.
Born in Aldershot, he had taken it upon himself in 1891 to assume
the role of Chaplain to the Jewish soldiers stationed there. Indeed,
Francis Cohen was the first Jewish Army Chaplain to be officially
appointed anywhere in the world in October 1892. The 1886 Queen's
Regulations had recognised Judaism as a separate denomination in
the British Army for the purposes of chaplaincy in the forces.[6]

Cohen came up with the idea of forming a Jewish Company
attached to the general Boys' Brigade and he wrote to William Smith
himself. The response was not encouraging. Smith felt that he 'could
not enroll a Company on other than a Christian basis which is an
essential feature of our organisation'.[7] But he did go on record as
saying that he would be glad to help in the creation of any distinctly
Jewish youth movement.

Nevertheless, the fact remains that it was Colonel Goldsmid who
brought the idea to fruition in the form of the Jewish Lads' Brigade.
Goldsmid's intriguing life story is worth telling for the light it sheds
on the origins of the JLB.[8]

Colonel Albert Edward Williamson Goldsmid was born at Poona
in India in 1846, the son of Henry Edward Goldsmid, a distinguished member of the British Imperial civil service in the Raj.
Henry Goldsmid was responsible for a reform of the Indian tax
system, 'Goldsmid's Survey', which was adopted by the Bombay
legislature in 1865. He was promoted to Chief Secretary to the
Governor of Bombay, but died, reputedly through overwork, at the
early age of 42 in 1855 in Egypt. His son was only eight years old.

Albert was sent to England where he received an education befit-
ting a son of the upper classes: private tuition at home followed by
Sandhurst military academy. He became a professional soldier,
returning to India to serve as an ensign in the 104th Foot (Bengal
Fusiliers, later the Royal Munster Fusiliers) in June 1866. He quickly
rose through the ranks, becoming a colonel in 1894. From 1879

3

onwards, he was attached to General Staff and was posted at various times to Belfast (1879–84), London (1884–92), Cardiff (1894–97), Chatham and Aldershot (1897–1902). He saw active service in South Africa during the Boer War. At the Battle of Paardeberg his horse was shot from under him, and, on his return, he was decorated for his bravery with the Royal Victorian Order by King Edward VII at Balmoral.

It was a conventional, if distinguished, military career. But there was more to Goldsmid than that as, indeed, his very surname implied. To look at, the Colonel was 'medium height, small black moustache, anglicized Jewish face with good, shrewd, dark eyes'.[9] Goldsmid's parents, Henry and his wife Jessie Sarah Goldsmid, may have been married at Trinity Church, Marylebone in 1845, but they were both of Jewish origin. Indeed, they were both descendants of Aaron Goldsmid (1715–82), the progenitor of the Goldsmid banking family in Britain. Two of Aaron's sons, Benjamin and Abraham, the Goldsmid brothers, made fortunes out of loan contracting during the Napoleonic Wars and fitted themselves up with country seats to match their new-found status in life. Strangely, despite making good, the brothers each committed suicide: Benjamin in 1808 and Abraham in 1810. Four years after his death (1812) Benjamin's widow Jessie, daughter of Israel Levien Salomons, a prominent East India merchant and reputedly worth a fortune, 'deserted together with her [seven] children, . . . the Jewish faith and was baptised at St Vedast's, Foster Lane'.[10]

According to Jewish law (*halakha*), even an apostate remains a Jew in terms of personal status, because Jewish identity is traditionally passed through the female line. Nevertheless, it is questionable whether the Jewish link was maintained in this case. Jessie's youngest son, Lionel Prager Goldsmid, married Eliza Campbell, the daughter of William Campbell of Philadelphia. Campbell's wife Mary was a daughter of David Salisbury (or Salesbury) Franks of the well-documented Jewish Franks family, with branches in Hanover, London and Philadelphia. David Salisbury Franks was born in Philadelphia, became a prosperous merchant and achieved prominence as an officer in the American Revolutionary Wars. It is recorded that he was a one time *parnas* of the congregation Shearith Yisrael in Montreal and contributed to the funds of Mikveh Yisrael in Philadelphia. However, when he died suddenly of yellow fever in 1793 he was interred in a Philadelphia churchyard 'to prevent [a] pauper's burial'. More significantly, nothing is known about the identity of his wife. It would be a fair guess that Franks had left the Jewish community upon marrying a non-Jewish woman, and had therefore surrendered burial rights in the communal cemetery. He could hardly have been 'a pauper', given that he had been appointed Assistant Cashier to the Bank of the United States three years before his death. It is also known that his older cousin David Franks had married a Christian in 1743 and that their children were baptised at the same Christ Episcopal Church in Philadelphia where David Salisbury Franks was later buried.[11]

Lionel Prager Goldsmid and Eliza Campbell's daughter, also called Jessie after her grandmother, became the mother of Colonel Goldsmid. Technically speaking therefore, Goldsmid's Jewish status through the all-crucial maternal line is unproven.

On the other hand, the Jewish status of Colonel Goldsmid's father is not in dispute. Henry was a grandson, through the female line, of Esther Goldsmid (174?–1811), an older sister of Benjamin. Esther's daughter Rose Joachim married Edward Moses of Dover who subsequently adopted the name Goldsmid. Henry was their fifth child.

Finally, whilst on the subject of Colonel Goldsmid's genealogy, we should also mention the fact that his wife, Ida Hendriks Stewart (they were married in 1879), was a great-great-granddaughter of the same Esther Goldsmid. However, in her case, the Jewish line was broken by her father Frederick Hendriks who had taken a non-Jewish wife, Hortense Littler, daughter of General Sir John Hunter Littler. Theodore Herzl, the Zionist leader, described Ida as 'a slender, refined Englishwoman' when he met her in 1895.

Clearly, it is doubtful whether Colonel Goldsmid passed *halakhic* muster by birth and his wife undoubtedly did not. On his own admission, 'I was born a Christian. My mother and father were baptized Jews.'[12] Nevertheless, he certainly had Jewish ancestry – and a somewhat 'incestuous' Jewish ancestry at that, typical of the 'Cousinhood' of families which became the aristocracy of Anglo-Jewry in the nineteenth century. Whatever his precise status, however, Goldsmid's reversal of the seemingly inexorable process of assimilation which characterised his social class is remarkable.

TABLE 1

GOLDSMID FAMILY TREE

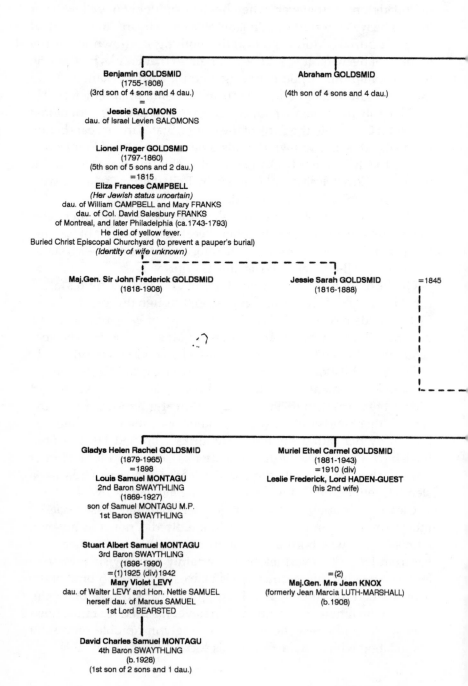

Benjamin GOLDSMID
(1755-1808)
(3rd son of 4 sons and 4 dau.)
=
Jessie SALOMONS
dau. of Israel Levien SALOMONS

Abraham GOLDSMID
(4th son of 4 sons and 4 dau.)

Lionel Prager GOLDSMID
(1797-1860)
(5th son of 5 sons and 2 dau.)
=1815
Eliza Frances CAMPBELL
(Her Jewish status uncertain)
dau. of William CAMPBELL and Mary FRANKS
dau. of Col. David Salesbury FRANKS
of Montreal, and later Philadelphia (ca.1743-1793)
He died of yellow fever.
Buried Christ Episcopal Churchyard (to prevent a pauper's burial)
(Identity of wife unknown)

Maj.Gen. Sir John Frederick GOLDSMID
(1818-1908)

Jessie Sarah GOLDSMID
(1816-1888)

=1845

Gladys Helen Rachel GOLDSMID
(1879-1965)
=1898
Louis Samuel MONTAGU
2nd Baron SWAYTHLING
(1869-1927)
son of Samuel MONTAGU M.P.
1st Baron SWAYTHLING

Muriel Ethel Carmel GOLDSMID
(1881-1943)
=1910 (div)
Leslie Frederick, Lord HADEN-GUEST
(his 2nd wife)

Stuart Albert Samuel MONTAGU
3rd Baron SWAYTHLING
(1898-1990)
=(1)1925 (div)1942
Mary Violet LEVY
dau. of Walter LEVY and Hon. Nettie SAMUEL
herself dau. of Marcus SAMUEL
1st Lord BEARSTED

=(2)
Maj.Gen. Mrs Jean KNOX
(formerly Jean Marcia LUTH-MARSHALL)
(b.1908)

David Charles Samuel MONTAGU
4th Baron SWAYTHLING
(b.1928)
(1st son of 2 sons and 1 dau.)

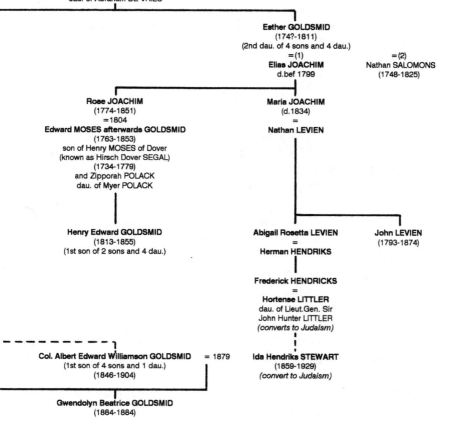

Aaron GOLDSMIT (GOLDSMID)
(1715-1782)
of Holland
Originally from Cassel and Frankfurt
Settled in London by 1742
=1740
Catherine DE VRIES
dau. of Abraham DE VRIES

Esther GOLDSMID
(174?-1811)
(2nd dau. of 4 sons and 4 dau.)
=(1)   =(2)
Elias JOACHIM   Nathan SALOMONS
d.bef 1799   (1748-1825)

Rose JOACHIM   **Maria JOACHIM**
(1774-1851)   (d.1834)
=1804   =
Edward MOSES afterwards GOLDSMID   **Nathan LEVIEN**
(1763-1853)
son of Henry MOSES of Dover
(known as Hirsch Dover SEGAL)
(1734-1779)
and Zipporah POLACK
dau. of Myer POLACK

Henry Edward GOLDSMID   **Abigail Rosetta LEVIEN**   **John LEVIEN**
(1813-1855)   =   (1793-1874)
(1st son of 2 sons and 4 dau.)   **Herman HENDRIKS**

Frederick HENDRICKS
=
Hortense LITTLER
dau. of Lieut.Gen. Sir
John Hunter LITTLER
(converts to Judaism)

Col. Albert Edward Williamson GOLDSMID   = 1879   **Ida Hendriks STEWART**
(1st son of 4 sons and 1 dau.)   (1859-1929)
(1846-1904)   *(convert to Judaism)*

Gwendolyn Beatrice GOLDSMID
(1884-1884)

Jewish line	————————
Halakhic Jewish line broken *(Jewish status passes through mother)*	– – – – –

Drawn by David Weingott of The Jewish Genealogical Society
of Great Britain

Acknowledgements to Anthony Joseph

©Sharman Kadish 1994

Goldsmid grew up ignorant of his origins. According to his daughter, Lady Swaythling,

It was by accident that he heard he had Jewish blood when in his teens and the idea came to him that he would like to become a Jew. When, in the Army in India, he told his brother officers of his intentions and said that he would send in his papers (i.e. leave the Army), his brother officers (who liked him immensely) said, 'certainly not – be anything you like !' With the help of the Sassoons, whilst in India, he became a Jew.[13]

However, his obituary in the *Jewish Chronicle* in 1904 states that Goldsmid was 'received into the Abrahamic Covenant at Aldershot' by Dr Asher. This expression means that he underwent *brit mila* (circumcision). It would be interesting to discover whether or not this was accompanied by the other rite associated with formal conversion, *tevila* (immersion) in the *mikva*. According to other sources, Goldsmid returned to Judaism in 1870, at the age of 24. Certainly, the official rite of initiation must have taken place before his marriage in 1879 because Lady Swaythling notes: 'My grandfather [General Littler] forbade my mother to marry my father because he became a Jew – but my mother ran away and married him'.

Goldsmid himself told Herzl about his conversion to Judaism: 'My family were indignant. The woman I loved was also a Christian of Jewish stock. I eloped with her to Scotland where, to begin with, we had a civil marriage. Then she had to become a Jewess, and we were married in a synagogue.'

Albert and Ida were zealous proselytes. A one-time member of the West London Reform Synagogue, Upper Berkeley Street, Colonel Goldsmid defected to the New West End Synagogue, St Petersburgh Place, a pillar of the Orthodox establishment, under the spiritual guidance of the Chief Rabbi. The move was in protest against the decision of the Reform in 1888 to introduce *Haftarot* recited in English instead of Hebrew.[14] 'I am an orthodox Jew. It has not prejudiced my position in England,' Goldsmid proudly informed Herzl. In Cardiff, he was a prime mover in the building of the Cathedral Road Synagogue. Goldsmid also became a champion of Hebrew as a living language (his father had been an outstanding scholar of oriental languages, Hindi and Persian, before going out to India). Albert and Ida's two surviving daughters, Gladys Rachel and Carmel, 'received a strict religious upbringing and learned Hebrew at an early age'.

'I am Daniel Deronda' said Goldsmid in the famous meeting with Theodore Herzl in Cardiff in 1895. He was a self-confessed Jewish nationalist, 'convinced that the time would come, sooner or later, when the Jews would by [sic, be] a nation among nations, and Israel would be represented on the council of nations'.[15] Back in 1891, Goldsmid was a founder of the British branch of the *Chovevei Tsion* (Lovers of Zion), a proto-Zionist organisation, originating in eastern Europe, which advocated Jewish colonisation in Palestine. As he declared in an (unsigned) interview with Lucien Wolf for the *Daily Graphic* in 1892: 'The Jewish question will never be solved until a Jewish state guaranteed by the Powers is established in the Land of Israel.'[16]

Goldsmid was probably the first to advocate security arrangements for the protection of the 'Bilu' settlements in 1882, saying that 'It is a task I should not hesitate to undertake were it confided to me, and it would be to me a labour of love'.[17]

He first visited Palestine in 1883 and was to go there again in 1891. Having once (1882) turned down an invitation by the Russo-Jewish Committee to work with Laurence Oliphant in Galicia aiding refugees from the Russian pogroms, in 1892 Goldsmid obtained leave of absence from his military duties in England to supervise the work of Baron Edmund de Hirsch's Jewish colonies in the Argentine. It seems that he was recommended for this task by no less a personage than the Prince of Wales (Edward VII). The British press hailed him as 'The Joshua of the new Exodus'. Goldsmid remained in South America for just under two years, gaining practical experience of settling about 700 Jewish families in four great colonies. According to one family story, Goldsmid's 'tenure of office [in South America] was rather limited because he had to be recalled hastily having misjudged a William Tell performance to the detriment of his human target. He is also reported as riding a white horse on his visits to the Hirsch settlements.'[18]

On his return to England, Goldsmid encouraged the *Chovevei Tsion* to adopt a written constitution and proceeded, with the first President and his distant relative from India, Elim Henry d'Avigdor, to draw up plans which were 'a cross between standard military practice and his own understanding of the framework employed by the Children of Israel in the wilderness of Sinai'.[19] He duly became Commander-in-Chief of the *Chovevei Tsion*, at the top of an organisational pyramid comprising 'tents' (local societies) and cadet tents (junior societies), led by 'commanders' under the overall control of 'headquarters' in London. He designed the *Chovevei Tsion* banner, based on the emblems of the Twelve Tribes of Israel.

However, Goldmid's involvement with the Hirsch colonies in Argentina had excited controversy within the international *Chovevei Tsion* who regarded the enterprise as a betrayal of the main aim of colonisation of Palestine. On the contrary, he declared that he 'look[ed] upon the Argentine as a nursery ground for Palestine', and that 'Everything has a beginning – even the alphabet; it begins with A(rgentine) and ends with Z(ion)'.[20] Indeed, the first English edition of Leon Pinsker's influential pamphlet *Autoemancipation* (Pinsker had become the leader of the international *Chovevei Tsion* in 1884) was 'dedicated to Lieutenant-Colonel A. Goldsmid as a token of esteem for his zealous championship of Palestine colonisation'.

However, the arrival of Herzl on the scene led to a parting of the ways. Despite the initial success of their first meeting in Cardiff (Herzl confided to his diary that Goldsmid 'has already grown dear to me – like a brother') the relationship soon cooled. Goldsmid was convinced by Herzl's case for the creation of a Jewish state. However, he could not accept the strategy he adopted to achieve this end. Political Zionism, as formulated in the Basle Programme at the First Zionist Congress (1897), entailed securing a public charter from the Great Powers which recognised the right of Jews to settle en masse in Palestine. Goldsmid, in other words, sided with the 'practical' Zionists against the full-blooded political programme outlined by Herzl. The *Chovevei Tsion* in London and Paris found themselves under threat and were very soon overtaken by the new Zionist organisation. Goldsmid distrusted Herzl's appeal to popular support and refused to chair the great mass meeting at the Jewish Working Men's Club in Whitechapel in 1896. Nor did he attend the Basle Congress; his excuse being that, as a professional soldier, he could not get mixed up in politics; nor did he participate in the Anglo-Jewish 'Pilgrimage' to Palestine in 1897.

Nevertheless, Goldsmid was a member of the El Arish Commission in 1903 which investigated the possibilities of Jewish settlement in the vicinity of Palestine, with both the British and Egyptian governments. By this time, of course, the English Zionist Federation (1899) had entirely eclipsed the *Chovevei Tsion*. No longer rivals, relations between Goldsmid and Herzl improved again. The Colonel worked closely with Herzl as secretary to the El Arish Commission and finally attended the Sixth Zionist Congress in 1903, a few months before his death in March 1904. Herzl himself died in the summer of 1904.

In 1902 Goldsmid became president of the Maccabaeans Society, having been a vice-president since its inception in September 1891. The Maccabaeans started life as a kind of Anglo-Jewish gentlemen's club which, to this day, holds dinners, lectures and socials for its very select membership. (Women were admitted in 1951.) The Maccabaeans were the brainchild of barrister Herman Cohen and the painter Solomon J. Solomon; members were co-opted from the ranks of the Jewish professional classes. The society 'was reserved for Jews in the literary and learned professions and the arts, to the exclusion of those engaged in commerce, a Jewish reflection of Victorian prejudice'.[21] It aimed to 'focus the Jewish men of brains', promoting appreciation of Jewish culture amongst the sophisticated post-emancipation generation. Colonel Goldsmid was a founder member, along with such luminaries as the writer Israel Zangwill and scholars Elkan Adler and Israel Abrahams.

In 1894 Goldsmid was instrumental in instituting the Maccabaeans' Physical Education Sub-committee 'to consider the best means of ameliorating the physical conditions of our East End coreligionists'.[22] In the 1894-95 Session, he delivered a lecture to the Society advocating the establishment of a Jewish Boys' Brigade to improve both the physical and moral health of Anglo-Jewish youth – health and morality being inextricably linked in the prevailing educational theory of the day. The proposal was taken up with enthusiasm by the Maccabaeans and the inaugural meeting of the 'Jewish Working Lads' Brigade' took place at the Jews' Free School, Bell Lane on 16 February 1895. About 120 boys turned up for enrolment, many 'undersized' but sturdy and of good appearance, according to the *Jewish Chronicle*. They were 'drawn in about equal numbers from recent pupils of the Jews' Hospital [Norwood], apprentices under the care of the Board of Guardians and scholars at East End schools'. Colonel Goldsmid addressed the assembled company

> in terms of martial simplicity and directness explaining that the objects of the movement were to cultivate the sound spirit in the sound body which marked the well-trained and disciplined soldier, to encourage self-respect and self-reliance, while checking opinionated self-esteem, and to spread among Jewish working lads the habits of smartness and obedience, while augmenting their growth and general vigour.[23]

His conception was soon translated into the official 'Object' of the movement: 'to instil into the rising generation, from earliest youth, habits of orderliness, cleanliness, and honour, so that in learning to respect themselves they will do credit to their Community.'

For a subscription of 1d per week, boys were eligible to become members between the ages of 12 and 16 and to remain up to the rank of Sergeant until aged 18. Those reaching that age without being commissioned as officers or staff-sergeants were to receive a certificate of discharge.

The JLB was from the outset conceived as a quasi-military organisation, and the debt to the Boys' Brigade and Church Lads' Brigade was overtly acknowledged. Revd Cohen was present at the inaugural meeting, but the JLB was to differ in one essential respect from his original idea and from the Christian models which inspired it. The *Jewish Chronicle* spotted this difference immediately, namely 'the elimination of the religious, or rather devotional, element peculiar to the older organisations [the Boys' Brigade and the Church Lads' Brigade]'.[24] The JLB has been seen as the Jewish equivalent of the 'muscular Christianity' fashionable in the late Victorian period. But if this was indeed the case, the Judaism which it was supposed to espouse was of an essentially secular nature. This is an issue to which we will return later.

The original JLB pocket book, later called the 'Blue Book' and sold to members for 2d a copy, declared that 'The Brigade is organised and drilled as a military body' with special emphasis placed on parade ground discipline and physical fitness. Swimming, cricket, football and athletics events were to be encouraged. Local Companies could join together on special occasions for camps, parades and sports tournaments, forming Battalions and National and Provincial Regiments, the whole to be administered centrally by Headquarters in London. However, uniform was kept to a minimum: regulation cap, belt and haversack to be worn over the member's everyday clothes. This served an educative purpose; the pocket book stated that 'the lads, knowing that they have to attend parade in their ordinary clothes, are led to take greater care of them, and thus are made neater and more cleanly in their daily life'.

Nevertheless, economy was the chief criterion: 'Expenses must be kept down to the lowest possible limit', the pocket book noted in italics. Ranks were differentiated by variations in caps, sashes and badges. Officers were expected to wear 'a blue serge suit'. The Brigade adopted as its motto the verse *yukhlu makhyil el khyil*, 'They go from strength to strength' (Psalm 84).[25]

On 1 April 1895 the first weekly drill was held at the Gravel Lane Board School in Whitechapel.[26] The one original Company soon expanded so that the school playground was filled to capacity. Within a year, the JLB had outgrown its first home and was offered more spacious premises at the Jews' Free School. This was appropriate given that the first recruits were for the most part drawn from the JFS, totalling 142 boys by 1898. They were divided into two Companies because the space problem had not been entirely solved. (The school's assembly hall was only available to the JLB for two hours on a Tuesday evening, until the erection of a new Drill Hall as part of the school's Rothschild memorial wing extension in 1898.) The officers of the Free School Battalion included 'Lieutenant-Colonel Commandant' David de Lara Cohen and 'Captains' Ernest M. Hallenstein and J.S. Marks. The use of military titles became *de rigueur*. Their 'Chaplain' was Revd Simeon Singer, better known as the editor of the *Singer's Prayer Book*, still the 'authorised' *siddur* used by the United Synagogue and like-minded congregations throughout Britain. Singer was known to be keen on military training for the young. In July 1897 he presided over the first JLB synagogue parade held at the Great Synagogue in Duke's Place and attended by the 'cream' of West End Jewry. The performance was repeated a year later, this time at the New West End Synagogue. It being a *Shabbat*, 100 boys marched to Bayswater from the East End and back again in honour of the occasion.

In the summer of 1896 the first JLB camp was held at Deal. This event apparently secured for the Brigade its first 'press notice'. The *Star* announced that 'twenty gutter-snipes today left London for their annual camp at Deal'.[27] The annual Summer Camp was to become, and still remains, a focal activity of the Brigade. Holidays for city boys under canvas had been made fashionable by the Boys' Brigade, the London Diocesan Council for the Welfare of Young Men (forerunner of the Church Lads' Brigade), and the Children's Country Holiday Fund. Eighteen to 20 boys participated in the first JLB camp under the supervision of Cecil Sebag-Montefiore and Algernon Lesser. It was held on a site at Sandhills taken over from the Boys' Brigade. The farmer who owned the field, Mr C.H. Page JP, happened to be a captain in the Boys' Brigade, and the field was taken over from the West Kent Battalion of that organisation.[28] Assistance was also on hand from the Volunteers, not least from Sergeant-Major James Brock of the Inns of Court (Devil's Own) Rifles who put the lads through their paces on the parade ground.

The camp was run on highly disciplined and spartan lines, and a vivid account is provided by an intrepid *Jewish Chronicle* reporter.[29] The campers were housed in white bell tents; four for the boys, accommodating four or five each, and two for the officers. The latest in tent technology – 'green "tortoise" marquees with windows and ventilation shafts' – served as the mess. There were two mess tents, one for the officers and the second, kitted out with tin trestle tables arranged along three sides of a square, for the lads. There was also a guards tent which had to be manned 24 hours a day by sentries who, if found guilty of dereliction of duty by falling asleep, ran the risk of court martial! Outside stood a wooden canteen from which lads could purchase 'ginger beer, lemonade, shandy-gaff and biscuits' (supply was very soon outstripped by demand), and 'Four large tubs of water stood near the cooking apparatus, two being for drinking purposes and two for washing'. The require-ments of hygiene were largely met, however, by the early morning dip in the sea (7.30am) unless the weather was inclement. This, if our correspondent is to be believed, was 'an intense delight. Some of the lads have never seen the sea before, the majority had only spent a day at Clacton.' This was not surprising given that they were 'all from very poor families', school-leavers who were forced to go out to work in the sweatshops and warehouses of the East End.

The discipline began even before the campers got to Deal. Orders were issued army-style, under which lads were expected to form up at Cannon Street Station with the requisite equipment: 'a kit bag, containing two towels, brush and comb, extra shirt, extra pair of boots, extra pair of socks, and extra pair of trousers.' Over and above this they had to turn out with their 'cap, belt, badge of rank, and uniform [swagger]stick'. Regulations became more exacting. By 1899, Brigade Orders stated

considerable difference in the wearing of caps and haversacks having been observed, the following orders are to be strictly adhered to: CAPS (OFFICERS AND LADS). To be worn cocked on the right side of the head, and the edge to be one inch above the junction of the right ear with the head, chin straps to be on the point of the chin. HAVERSACKS. Sling to be worn over the right shoulder and under waist belt in front and rear. The top of the haversack to be one inch below the belt, and the haversack to be neatly folded up when empty.[30]

A dummy rifle was issued to each boy. On arrival at Deal station, the lads were marched in formation, the Norwood Band at their head, through the town to the campsite. Thereon, it was a healthy regime of fresh air and exercise. Our reporter waxed lyrical about the delights of camping in 1896:

During the day, the sleeping tents are . . . brailed up, so that the sweet, fresh breeezes which blow from Deal Downs on the one side, and straight away, without interruption, from Minster and Sandwich on the other, are sweeping through them for nine or ten hours out of the twenty four. Each boy's bed consists of a waterproof sheet laid upon the grass, a mattress stuffed with straw, and a double brown blanket. No healthier or warmer bedroom could any lad in fine weather desire.[31]

Unless, of course, if the weather turned foul. At the 1898 camp driving rain and gale force winds forced the campers to repair to quarters in the town overnight.

Each day of the holiday was highly structured, punctuated by a

15

bugle call at regular intervals. The day was a long one, beginning at 6.00am in 1896, and subsequently at 5.30am and ending at 10.15pm (later 9.45pm). In 1896 the weekday timetable was as follows:

6.00 am	Reveille
6.30 am	Prayers
7.00 am	Parade, coffee and biscuits
7.30 am	Bathing in the sea followed by physical drill
8.30 am	Breakfast, 'porridge, tea and coffee, bread and butter, marmalade and eggs'
9.00 – 11.00 am	Drill with rifles
12 noon – 1.00 pm	Free
1.00 pm	Dinner, 'roast beef and two vegetables'
(pm)	'Play' e.g. cricket, chess, rowing, some lads given permission to go into town
5.30 pm	Tea, 'tea, bread and butter, jam and cake'
9.00 pm	Supper, 'This is a light meal of bread and butter, and jam or cheese'
9.20 pm	Prayers
9.30 pm	First Post
10.00 pm	Last Post
10.15 pm	Lights Out

By the following year the numbers participating in camp had increased to 96, and in 1898 to 459 when the total strength of the Brigade had reached some 800. The JLB now consisted of four Companies: the two original JFS Companies together with those of Bayswater (formed March 1897) and Brady Street (April 1897). The latter was so named because its members were recruited almost entirely from the recently founded (1896) pioneer Brady Street Boys' Club under the patronage of Lady Rothschild. Indeed, it is claimed that, in its early years, 'approximately one-third of [its] members also belonged to the Jewish Lads' Brigade'. There was not enough space in the club to hold drill and 'so a bugle band was formed to march us round to the Whitechapel Foundation School to drill in the huge playground'.[32] But the popularly held view that the JLB was created exclusively for the benefit of the East End Jewish immigrants is called into question by the appearance of the first West End Company as early as 1897, drawn from pupils and ex-pupils of the Bayswater Jewish Schools. In reality, many of these children,

JEWISH LADS' BRIGADE,

COMMANDANT: COLONEL A. E. GOLDSMID, A.A.G.

Chief Staff Officer:
CAPTAIN CECIL SEBAG-MONTEFIORE.

HEAD-QUARTERS:—

63, Finsbury Pavement,

London, June 11 1898

Cheques to be crossed "Capital & Counties Bank," a/c Jewish Lads' Brigade.

To the Members of the Jewish Community.

The Executive Committee of the Jewish Lads' Brigade invite your earnest attention to their first annual Report and trust that you will respond liberally to their appeal.

Unless substantial financial help is forthcoming, the Movement, which has spread by leaps and bounds, must inevitably collapse.

All, who are so disposed, are cordially invited to visit the seaside camps at Deal, between August 8th & 15th, where may be seen the results of the training of some hundreds of Jewish Lads in manliness, discipline, and a high sense of honour. All visitors will be welcomed and a limited number can by arrangement be accommodated a day or two under canvas.

Pray help us for our Lads' sakes to raise the thousand pounds necessary to place the Brigade on a sound financial footing,

Albert E.W. Goldsmid Col
Brigade Commandant

To Mrs Louis Samuel Montagu,

---

1. Circular appeal for funds in Colonel Goldsmid's own hand. This copy is addressed to Mrs Louis Samuel Montagu – his daughter, Gladys (later the second Lady Swaythling) – and is dated 11 June 1898

From the *Jewish World.*   1

Jewish Lads' Brigade Display at Queen's Hall.

2. Sketches of the JLB Display at the Queen's Hall on 11 November 1905, from *Jewish World*, 17 November 1905. Drawn by M. Weinberg

too, came from poor homes. Pockets of the Jewish working class existed in Soho as well as in Whitechapel. By the end of 1898 five more Companies had been formed in the East End: Old Castle Street, Chicksand Street (May 1898, revived October 1907), Bow, Hanbury and Deal Street (June 1898) and Stepney (July 1898). Another, Gravel Lane and Swan Street came into being in February 1899. Companies in north London (meeting at Dalston Synagogue) and south London (Borough Jewish Schools) were also established.

The first Company outside London was set up at Liverpool in January 1898 with 78 members under the command of Captain Ellis Keyser Yates, scion of an old Liverpool Jewish family, who served as warden of the Princes Road Synagogue, on the Jewish Board of Guardians, Hebrew Philanthropic Society, and Jewish Association for the Protection of Girls and Women (i.e., from prostitution) in that city. The Company paraded at the drill hall in Shaw Street belonging to the 4th Volunteer Battalion, the King's Liverpool Regiment to which Yates was attached. Forty-one members of the Liverpool JLB joined the London Camp at Deal in August 1899. In 1907 Yates was promoted by London HQ to the rank of Commandant Provincial Regiment in succession to Cecil Sebag-Montefiore. His brother, Montagu Solomon Yates, who had joined the JLB in 1901, now became Commanding Officer of the Liverpool Company. The younger Yates, who was rejected on volunteering in 1914, kept the Brigade in being until January 1917, by which time 'numbers had become so small that it was no longer possible to carry on, and the Company was disbanded'.[33]

Already in 1897 the first Colonial Company had been established at Montreal, Canada. It was set up on independent local initiative by Captain W.H. Baker, a local headmaster and a non-Jew. The existence of the Montreal Company was announced in what was probably the first Brigade Order published in the Jewish press, on 16 April 1897. Further information on its activities was subsequently reported to HQ in London in a communication dated 6 August 1898. During the winter of 1898–99 the Company was visited by George A. Cohen from London at the request of Colonel Goldsmid. He reported back that the Canadian Company consisted of 70–80 working lads as well as a Cadet Corps for boys still at school: 50 strong. Facilities for drill were kindly provided by the Colonel of the

17

local garrison who also regularly inspected the Company. 'The inclemency of the climate' in winter posed a particular problem for the Canadian Company, it being found to be 'indispensable to wear a fur cap'. This being the case, Baker complained that 'the expense of providing suitable uniform caps would be too great'.[34] Nevertheless, it appears that his requests to London for supplies of ordinary caps, belts and badges were met. By December 1899 the Montreal Battalion had spawned three Companies: Companies A and B designated the Hirsch Cadets, under the aegis of the Baron Edmund de Hirsch Institute in the city, and Company C, followed in April 1901 by Company D, the Zion Cadets. The latter Companies were formed after a public meeting at the Hirsch Institute on 14 October 1900, although according to the minutes of London Headquarters, C Company had been enrolled on 30 May 1899. The four Companies had a combined strength of 167 lads and 14 officers in 1901, had achieved official recognition as a Cadet Corps by the Militia Department in Canada and ambitious plans were made to start units in Ottawa, Toronto, Winnipeg and Vancouver. According to the 1903 Annual Report, Montreal was making 'excellent' progress. Nevertheless, the Canadian outpost of the JLB disappears without trace from the subsequent record.

In October 1898 a public meeting, presided over by Dr J.H. Hertz, Rabbi of the Witwatersrand Old Hebrew Congregation and future Chief Rabbi of the British Empire, was held at the Jewish Schoolrooms in De Villiers Street, Johannesburg with the purpose of forming the first South African Company of the JLB. Johannesburg was a city which attracted substantial Jewish immigration especially from Lithuania in this period but which already boasted an acculturated 'native' Jewish community which looked to the 'Mother Country' and Anglo-Jewry for inspiration. The Boys' Brigade was established in South Africa from 1889 and no doubt provided the role model for Mr Ben Lazarus who took the initiative in convening the meeting. The perception that Colonel Goldsmid was instrumental in forming the JLB in South Africa is entirely erroneous. He was in Britain at that time and the association probably arose on account of his service subsequently in the Boer War. Over £100 was collected in subscriptions at that first meeting and uniforms and equipment were pledged. Fifty-one boys were enrolled between the ages of 12 and 17.

The first officers were Captain B.P. Marks, H.C. Carter, M. Myers, D.M. Joel and Captain A.M. Brown, an officer in the British Army. In December 1898 the first Synagogue Parade was held. Sixty boys took part 'dressed in blue jerseys and brown belts, the Shield of David emblazoned on their breasts'. By May 1899 the London *Jewish Chronicle* reported that the Johannesburg JLB had 'made surprising progress . . . number[ing] one hundred rank and file, being divided into two companies, and a drum and fife band of twelve'. Their uniform had undergone several refinements by this stage and now consisted of 'blue jerseys, with the shield of David on the left breast, brown leather belt with brass buckles, and blue field-service caps piped with white'.[35] Company and rifle drill was being held regularly, a football and cricket club had been formed as well as an ambulance section and a shorthand class. A.M. Brown was now the Officer Commanding. He was assisted by a staff of eight which included two instructors and a bandmaster.

Nevertheless, it seems that the Johannesburg JLB ran out of steam. In December 1903 Headquarters received a communication from H.C. Carter stating that the Company had been 'restarted' and in the following month the *Jewish Chronicle* reported that the Brigade had been resuscitated by Mr D. Levine with Major B.H. Myers as Commanding Officer. Over five weeks 'some sixty lads' had been enrolled and by the following September the Company was 130 strong. Early in 1904 'application for the attachment of the Brigade under direct military authority' was successful and the lads became Cadets under the aegis of the Transvaal Light Infantry Volunteer Corps.[36] Government equipment, including carbines, was henceforth made available. The progress being made by the South African JLB was, however, disputed. The *Chronicle* was being fed contradictory reports by rival correspondents in Johannesburg. According to one report 'the Brigade in Johannesburg [was] a very great success'. By contrast, another grumbled that the Brigade was failing to reach the 'several hundreds' of potential recruits in the city. 'The reason for non-success,' it continued 'is to be found in the fact that no public meeting has been called, and that the organisation, as at present constituted, is a self-appointed one, resting, as it actually does, with one gentleman only.'

Moreover, in the opinion of this correspondent:

It [was] also undoubtedly a mistake to make this movement a narrow one, as emanating from one particular congregation. Such a course in a community so peculiarly constituted as that of Johannesburg is creating unnecessary bitter feeling, which a powerful section like the Johannesburg Hebrew Congregation should certainly make a point of avoiding.[37]

One has to turn to the pages of the *South African Jewish Chronicle*[38] to find the source of the 'bitter feeling' within the Johannesburg Jewish community in 1904. The Johannesburg Hebrew Congregation – or 'New' Congregation – had recently acquired a new and dynamic spiritual leader in Rabbi Dr J.L. Landau who, in effect, became a rival to Rabbi J.H. Hertz of the Witwatersrand Old Hebrew Congregation, for domination of the religious life of South African Jewry. Landau declared his intention to establish his own *Beth Din*, as a power base of his own without reference to either Rabbi Hertz or the Chief Rabbi's (Adler) Ecclesiastical Court in London. The Jewish Lads' Brigade became only one of a series of communal institutions which suffered as a result of this struggle. Hertz was one of the founders of the Brigade in 1898. In his congregational report for 1904 he complained that it was 'a matter of regret' that the JLB 'should be made to appear, unpremeditatedly I hope, as an annexe to one Congregation', i.e., Rabbi Landau's. Several weeks later the London *Jewish Chronicle* reported that a Cadet Corps attached to the Transvaal Scottish Volunteers had been started at the Marist (Brothers') School in Johannesburg.

> Though the school is . . . an undenominational one, it is significant that the cadet corps is chiefly officered by Jews, and has Mr Max Langermann for its honorary Colonel. This undenominational corps numbers almost as many Jewish boys as the Jewish Lads' Brigade.

Perhaps it was not insignificant either that Rabbi Landau had taken upon himself the teaching of Hebrew at this school as there were 100 Jewish children there.

Despite the attempts of the Landau camp to depict the Johannesburg JLB as 'a dismal failure'[39] it does seem as if Government recognition prevented its complete demise, for the 1903 JLB Annual Report from London had stated that both the Johannesburg and Port Elizabeth Companies (about which nothing else is known) had suspended drill 'since outbreak of hostilities'. The JLB in South

Africa reemerged after the Boer War, but disappears from our story sometime after 1904.

The JLB Executive Committee in London had to turn to the Boys' Brigade and Church Lads' Brigade for advice on how to handle the formation of Companies overseas. The Boys' Brigade had branches in the USA from 1887, and in Canada and South Africa from 1889. The JLB decided to register Companies abroad as legitimate members of the movement but without taking on any financial responsibility for their upkeep. In 1902 a certain Nissim Behar wrote from New York asking for advice about setting up an American Brigade. His Manhattan Rifles were apparently modelled on the JLB.

The rapid expansion of the JLB and its obvious popularity led to its formal separation from the Maccabaeans after two years of close co-operation. Many years later, Algernon Lesser claimed the credit for initiating this move:

> Soon after the first Camp I came to the conclusion that the movement would never grow so long as it was run as a branch of the Maccabaeans. I got that Society to agree with my views, and accordingly steps were taken to restart the Brigade as a distinct communal institution.[40]

On 14 February 1897, a public meeting at the Central Synagogue Chambers resolved that the JLB should form an independent Executive Committee and go it alone. Nevertheless, the role of the Maccabaeans, in terms of both the provision of personnel and financial underpinning, was clearly crucial in the establishment of the JLB. Vice-President Colonel Goldsmid gave up his army career to devote himself entirely to the Brigade's development and served as Commandant until his death in 1904. While he was away on active service during the Boer War, Lieutenant-Colonel Emanuel Montefiore, a fellow professional soldier who had been in India, stood in as Acting Brigade Commandant. Other leading Macca-baeans, Major H.B. Lewis-Barned (another professional soldier) and Cecil Sebag-Montefiore became Assistant Brigade Commandant and Chief Staff Officer respectively. Revd Francis L. Cohen, who had first mooted the idea of such an organisation, became Staff Chaplain until his emigration to Australia in 1905 and Dr Bertram Abrahams, a high-flying young physician at Westminster Hospital and son of the headmaster of the Jews' Free School, became Staff

Surgeon. Both Cohen and Abrahams had been members of the Maccabaeans Physical Education Sub-committee along with Gold-smid. Another Maccabaean, the solicitor Algernon Lesser, who was also involved with the Brady Street Club, became Brigade Officer responsible for Supply and Transport (subsequently termed Quarter-master) and Herman Cohen joined the newly formed Executive Committee.

Despite the formal separation, the Maccabaeans continued to vote annual subventions to the Brigade. This funding was essential as, from the outset, it was anticipated that the movement would not pay for itself. Each recruit was charged 1d per week for membership and 5/- for the week-long summer camp. This was increased to 6/6d in 1902, a 'totally inadequate' contribution which did not even cover the train fare. Needy cases were taken for nothing at the discretion of HQ and a special fund was set up for this purpose. After satis-factory attendance at six successive drills, each recruit was issued with his uniform free of charge. Especially in the initial stages, the sums so raised could not possibly cover the outlay required to hire or purchase equipment: the uniform such as it was, dummy rifles for drill, tents, cooking utensils and other camping and sports equip-ment. Indeed, the Brigade's first financial statement in 1898 reported 'a considerable deficit'. Local Companies, despite securing the use of school playgrounds and drill halls free of charge, found them-selves strapped for cash. Captain Yates in Liverpool complained that

> Funds [are] the weak point of the Company. The Liverpool Jewish Community, with the exception of a few gentlemen, whose assistance has been most valuable . . . has abstained as yet from giving any support to, or taking any real interest in, the Company.[41]

Indeed his Company was 'treated by the members of the Jewish community of Liverpool' in a generally 'apathetic and neglectful manner'. So disheartened was he that he wrote a letter to the Jewish press in similar vein.

The solution, at least for the capital, was the creation of a central fund at Headquarters from where monies could be distributed on an efficient, capitation grant basis. But it was the assistance of these 'few gentlemen', many of whom were connected with the most aristocratic families in Anglo-Jewry, if not with the Maccabaeans, which kept the JLB in business in the early years and for a long time thereafter. The subscriptions list of 1898 reads like a roll call of the great and the good: *inter alia*, Beddington, Cohen, D'Avigdor, Franklin, Goldsmid, Henriques, Jessel, Montefiore, Mocatta, Montagu, Samuel, Sassoon and Tuck. Some ladies too were prominent benefactors, including Louisa, Lady Goldsmid and Mrs Nathaniel Montefiore. The Anglo-Jewish press assisted by giving the Brigade advertising space free of charge, not to mention glowing accounts of the Summer Camp and laudatory editorials. Even so, funding remained a constant problem. Although the Brigade opened a deposit account in 1900 and began to invest donations in stock, it again went into the red for a couple of years (1901–2) and was only rescued by a major appeal for funds in 1902. Indeed, special appeals, fundraising parades, concerts and dinners very quickly became a feature of the Brigade's activities. In 1905 JLB funds were at last stabilised, owing to a very successful appeal launched with the help of Rufus Isaacs, later Lord Reading, and a member of the Government. The appeal netted over £4,000 and Isaacs was thereafter recruited to the Brigade Council. The following year the JLB became a beneficiary under the will of Mrs Ada Lewis-Hill, the wife of Samuel Lewis, the phenomenally wealthy Victorian Jewish moneylender. Brigade funds were enhanced by the unprecedented sum of £1,000 through her generosity.[42]

But by 1909 the current account was registering a deficit once again and a fresh appeal for £5,000 was launched. Two large public displays were held in 1910, one at the Queen's Hall for the 'wealthier members of the community' and the other at the People's Palace in the East End. The latter was clearly aimed to impress poor parents with the work of the Brigade.

By 1914 the JLB boasted 48 Companies on paper with a combined strength of 3,500–4,000. In London the headmaster of the Jews' Free School, Louis B. Abrahams, encouraged his pupils to drill on school premises with a view to their joining the Brigade. In 1901 he was appointed Recruiting Staff Officer to the London Regiment. His efforts paid off. The number of London Companies rose steadily (excluding the Bearers' Company, May 1897 and Bands), especially in the East End (Bow and Hackney, December 1901, amalgamated

December 1902; East Ham, March 1906; Myrdle Street Schools, April 1906; Commercial Street Schools, December 1906, amalgamated with Chicksand Street 1908; St George's, successor to Brady Street, 1910). By 1909 JFS itself had three Companies and Deal Street, two. There were three Companies in the West End (Bayswater, Hammersmith, June 1902–February 1903, revived January 1914, and West Central, December 1903) and two in north London (Brondesbury, February 1907, Stamford Hill Scouts, 1913). A special Company was formed at the Jews' Hospital and Orphan Asylum at Norwood probably in 1898 and, through the generosity of Daniel Marks, a band was established. Every summer, from 1898 onwards, it became a tradition for the Norwood Band to lead the march from Deal station into camp on the Sandhills. Additional JLB Companies were formed at South Essex, 1906–8, and Southend and Westcliff in 1912 (to November 1914).

After Liverpool, the senior provincial Company, came Manchester. The Manchester JLB was formed in February 1899 under the command of Captain Henry J. Dreschfield, who served in the local Volunteers. As Anglo-Jewry's second city, Manchester very soon predominated as the foremost JLB centre outside of London. Numbers grew from 80 to 278 within the space of three months. Headquarters were initially at the Jewish Schools in Derby Street. Manchester formed its own Battalion, consisting of five Companies: the Jews' School, Southall Street School, Waterloo Road School, Working Lads' and the Bugle Band. As in London, local headmasters, especially William Shaer of the Southall Street Board School, took a keen interest in the Brigade. Manchester set up its own Drum and Fife, and Bugle bands, a gymnastics class and ambulance and cycling section. Manchester JLB organised its own Summer Camp by the sea at Lytham in August 1899. Some 240 boys attended, housed in 50 tents – a large turnout, given that Liverpool did not join them, preferring to camp with London at Deal. In subsequent years, the Manchester contingent was joined at the Northern Camp by other provincial Companies.

Yet even Manchester had its problems. In 1902 Camp did not take place due to lack of funds. As was the case in London, camp charges were heavily subsidised: lads were charged an average of 7/6d per head (except in needy cases), but the real cost was about £1 to house and feed them. Dreschfield reported that there were 192 lads on the roll of the Battn. of which number, however, 100 had not attended for a considerable time, the average attendance of the remaining number was about 25 at each drill, the attendance on some occasions being as low as 12.[43]

Dreschfield blamed the 'apathy' of officers and shortage of funds. Manchester needed an annual budget of £150 in 1903; in 1908 'six of its subscribers . . . gave one third of its income and this was under half of what was needed'.[44] The strict regime which the Manchester JLB imposed on its officers who, after all, were all volunteers, no doubt played some part in putting off potential recruits. Officers were charged a hefty 10/6d on gaining a commission and a further £1 10 6d on each subsequent promotion. In addition, officers were subject to an arbitrary levy of up to two guineas per annum for Brigade funds, as well as to a system of fines for unauthorised absence from duty. Moreover, they were expected to provide their own uniforms at their own expense. This consisted of a

Serge suit, with black neck tie, field service cap, cross belt, brown gloves, brown boots, and . . . (in lieu of sword) a black swagger cane. Brown leggings must also be worn when ordered. Mess Dress shall consist of ordinary dining coat, with 2 inches wide mohair stripe down trouser seams, patent leather boots and small black tie. Cross belt will be worn over the jacket. All rank badges will be worn on the cap.[45]

Such regulations implied that only young gentlemen of means could apply for commissions. The social implications of this situation will be studied presently.

In 1899, the *Jewish Chronicle* had another explanation for the failure of the Manchester Battalion to recruit satisfactorily:

some of the foreign Jews in Manchester seemed to view the movement with suspicion, evidently finding it difficult to realise that an organisation which practises military drill, carries arms and bears a military title, can yet be an entirely private and self-directed affair.[46]

To counteract this impression, letters of endorsement from Chief Rabbi Hermann Adler and Haham Moses Gaster were featured prominently in the Manchester Battalion's First Annual Report in 1903. Gaster professed his great surprise to hear 'that the military training of the young encounters opposition on the part of some

25

parents and teachers. Surely there must be some misunderstanding somewhere.'

Commending the work of the Brigade to the Jewish public he added, 'I have no doubt that every precaution is taken that the training should not in any way clash with our religious precepts and commands'. Nevertheless, Manchester's problems proved so acute that the Company was obliged to surrender the instruments of its defunct brass band to HQ in London in order to pay off its debts.

Manchester's fortunes revived after the retirement of Dreschfield in January 1905 and the rapid rise to prominence of Edward C.Q. Henriques who had taken command of the Lytham Camp in 1904. Henriques had joined the Brigade almost upon its inception in April 1899, and in 1907 became Commanding Officer of the Manchester Companies, which position he retained for another 40 years. It was Henriques who was responsible for moulding the character of the JLB in Manchester. Like Ellis Yates in Liverpool, Henriques sprang from the old Anglo-Jewish 'aristocracy'. His father, also Edward, was a pillar of Manchester Jewry, a merchant and Justice of the Peace. Edward the younger followed in his father's footsteps. He was Manchester-born and bred, educated at the grammar school and trained as a civil engineer, becoming owner of a local gear engineering firm. In the 1914–18 war he served as a major in the Royal Engineers and subsequently went on to serve in many civic and communal capacities: as a JP, vice-president of the North Salford Conservative Association and on various committees concerned with youth and juvenile offenders. He became president of the Council of Manchester and Salford Jews and president of the local Jewish Board of Guardians.

Under Henriques' capable guidance, the fortunes of the Manchester Battalion began to revive. By 1908 it comprised some 280 lads in five Companies, representing 'practically half the strength of the Provincial Regiment'.[47] The Manchester Officers' Minute Book records accurate statistics on Brigade membership between 1908 and 1912. In August 1909 there was a total of 274 all ranks, exactly 50 per cent of the strength of the Provincial Regiment. Numbers dropped back to 176 lads in August 1911, with between 20 and 40 in each Company. An estimated 1,200 boys had passed through its ranks. Manchester too, almost from its inception, had its own social club for the boys when they were not on parade. Designed 'for the social and intellectual intercourse of its members', it organised debates, concerts, indoor and board games and the occasional outing. In 1903 there were 50 members with an average attendance of 40 every weekday evening, except Friday, and on Sunday afternoon. They paid a weekly subscription of 1d in addition to their Brigade membership for the privilege. The club was initially housed at the Jews' School, but permission was withdrawn to use the classrooms in 1905 and the club lapsed. In 1906 the club was restarted and a benefactor stepped in to provide it with its own premises in a converted private house in Cheetham. The generous patron was Isidore Frankenberg, later Mayor of Salford. The Grove House Lads' Club opened its doors in 1907 and became the hub of Brigade social life in Manchester, acting as an 'inducement'[48] for boys to join. Schoolboys were charged ½d a week and working boys 1d subscription. The concept of combining Brigade membership with membership of a youth club was thus pioneered in Manchester.

Further JLB Companies were formed at Hull (May 1899); Cardiff (March 1899–September 1900) at Cathedral Road Synagogue; Birmingham (July 1899) at Singers Hill Synagogue (B Company November 1913); Leeds (March 1900) at Brunswick Place, with 27 boys and three officers in 1905; Sheffield (March 1900–5); Newcastle (December 1897) at the synagogue, apparently on the initiative of Revd M. Rosenbloom, the minister (restarted May 1901); and Bradford (August 1901–5), 23 all ranks, on the initiative of Edwin J. Strauss at the synagogue under Harry Kramvisch, who had been a captain in the Austrian Army;[49] a total of ten in the Provinces. Companies were set up independently of London at Belfast (c. January 1902) and Glasgow (1904).

The idea of setting up a Jewish Boys' Brigade in the home town of William Smith was first mooted at the Annual General Meeting of the Garnethill Synagogue, the 'cathedral' of the established Jewish community in Scotland, in May 1902.[50] In practice, however, the moving forces hailed from the Gorbals, the immigrant, working-class district of Glasgow Jewry. This is not to say that the initiators were themselves from the poorest classes. In December 1904 the Glasgow correspondent of the *Jewish Chronicle* reported that 'The

Brigade was founded in May last by a few private gentlemen on the South Side, practically unassisted and unaided by any of the West End members'.[51]

John Hershfield (or Hirshfield) may be credited with founding the Brigade in Scotland, known at this stage as the 5th Company of the Scottish Boys' Brigade. It was staffed by Gorbals Jews: Captain L. Cohen and Lieutenant Harry Ognall, with Revd Jacob Bogdansky of the Oxford Street Synagogue as the first Chaplain. The boys, 120 in all, wore the cap, belt and haversack of the Boys' Brigade with a distinguishing 'J' for 'Jewish' after the Company number on their hats. After two years it was decided that 'the "J" was not the correct thing'[52] and it was replaced by 'two yellow bands'. In November 1908 the Glasgow JLB sought and gained official recognition as a branch of the movement emanating from London. Although never achieving the status of a regiment, Glasgow formed two Companies, the 40th and 41st, with a bugle band before 1914.

Almost from the beginning, the Glasgow JLB was closely identified with the Strump family. In 1904 Benjamin Strump (1872–1949) was a member of the Garnethill Synagogue council and a treasurer of the local Jewish Board of Guardians, and later he was to become president of the Glasgow Jewish Representative Council and a Justice of the Peace. In 1908 he was made Commanding Officer of the Glasgow JLB, an association which was to last half a century. Nevertheless, it was his younger brother Nathan Strump, a gentleman's outfitter in the Glasgow Saltmarket, who 'was the first of that family connected with [the] JLB'.[53] He joined the ranks as a lad and was a captain by January 1906. Both Nathan and Ben served in the 1st Lanarkshire (Rifles) Volunteer Defence Corps. Indeed, between 1889 and 1908 Ben served under William Smith himself. Nathan's son Gerald recalled in about 1980 that 'my late Father had been a member of the B[oys'] B[rigade] in the 1890's [sic] and, in fact, had served with the founder of the B.B. . . . namely Sir William Smith, and there is no doubt that my Father was greatly inspired by this man'.[54]

When Smith died in 1914, 50 members of the JLB attended the public memorial service. In 1910 the Glasgow JLB had 86 members recruited in the main from the immigrant community in the Gorbals. In 1912 drill was being held at the Beth Hamedrash Hall at 42 Govan Street.

28

In July 1907 London Headquarters received 'An application . . . from Mr S[am] Weinstock of 79 Harcourt Street Dublin, for a Commission in the Jewish Lads' Brigade and for the enrolment of a number of lads at present drilling in Dublin, as a Company'.[55]

Permission was granted. Dublin became the 39th Company and drill took place at the Adelaide Road Synagogue, whose minister Revd A. Gudansky, acted as Chaplain. Sol Greenburgh (Greenberg) and brothers Harry and Louis Wigoder were early recruits, the former becoming CO by 1912 and the latter sergeant-major, before the family moved to Leeds at the beginning of 1914. Years later, Louis recalled

> My round hat, red sash and three stripes with crown above, on my left arm, were envied by all my subordinates . . . Our brigade manoeuvres were conducted with military precision, and, as a Sergeant-Major, I was instructed to give my commands in a loud officious tone, even if it hurt my throat, and they were really instantly obeyed. This undoubtedly contrasted unfavourably when I attempted to form a brigade when I first came to Leeds. I had received my commission then, but when I tried my Dublin strict tactics . . . in Leeds, I was laughed at by the boys, who could not understand the meaning of discipline or esprit de corps.[56]

Widoger also vividly remembered the first time about 20 Dublin boys crossed the Irish Sea 'in a night cattle boat' to join the JLB Summer Camp at Deal in 1908. The Annual Display was held at the Rathmines Town Hall and was always inspected by a high-ranking British Army officer. This was in the days, of course, before Partition (1922). In its heyday, the Dublin Company was some 40 strong, 'had a Bugle Band, 6 Buglers, 2 side Drums and the large Belly Drum'.[57]

A pattern of provincial development was established which was to remain true throughout the history of the Brigade: a Company was started and thrived on account of the personal interest taken by a particular officer or group of officers. Very often a particular family became identified with the Brigade and developed a Brigade 'tradition' which stretched over two or more generations; the Strumps in Glasgow, Solomons in Birmingham, Henriques in Manchester, following, of course, the example set by the Goldsmids and Swaythlings in London. The personal commitment of such individuals and families is a theme running through the history of the Brigade and will be returned to again in this narrative.

Nevertheless, where such leadership was lacking, provincial Companies had a chequered history. Cecil Sebag-Montefiore, who was appointed Commandant of the Provincial Regiment (1905), had a hard time gathering returns on the strength of the Companies under his authority. In January 1907 he gave up and resigned; Leeds, Newcastle, Hull, Bradford and Sheffield were formally disbanded and the separate Northern Camp was abandoned that year. Indeed by 1909 only Manchester (by then with six Companies), Liverpool, Birmingham, Dublin and Glasgow survived. The Manchester Officers' Minute Book for 1908–12 gives a breakdown of the relative strengths of the provincial Companies in the middle of 1911 as shown in Table 2:

TABLE 2   STRENGTH OF THE PROVINCIAL COMPANIES OF THE JLB,
AUGUST 1911 (ALL RANKS)

Manchester
A Company	22	[Band]	
B	40	[Southall Street]	
C	34	[Working Lads']	
D	34	[Waterloo Road]	
E	26	[Jews' School]	
F	20	[Scouts]	
	176	[plus 190 new recruits]	
Liverpool	44		
Birmingham	99		
Dublin	45		
Glasgow			
40th Company	42		
41st	29		
	71		
TOTAL	435		

Source: Manchester JLB, Officers' Minutes Meetings Book 1908–12, M130 Manchester Central Reference Library.

Often, but not always, this instability was due to lack of money and suitable officer material. The high turnover rate of officers was noticeable; very many, both in London and the provinces giving up their commissions on marriage. In 1903 it was reported 'that several of the [provincial] Companies are in an unsatisfactory condition, as they labour under the disadvantage of opposition upon the part of some of the members of the respective congregations'.[58]

In Leeds there was tangible 'local prejudice' and in Hull this opposition was put down to 'fear amongst the foreign element that the lads are being trained to become soldiers'. This fear can be understood against the background of the Boer War. Numbers of Jewish lads, like their counterparts in the general Brigades, volunteered for service in South Africa. Two JLB officers, F.M. Raphael and George Edward Halford, were killed. A prize was instituted in Halford's memory.[59]

From 1899 to 1906 inclusive (with the exception of 1902) two separate Summer Camps were held: at Sandhills, Deal for the London units and at Lytham for 'my [i.e., Goldsmid's] Northern boys'.[60] The combined London and Liverpool Camp in 1902 attracted some 600 participants, all ranks, and despite 'heavy rain and a gale which carried away the large marquee' was the largest to that date, 564 all ranks.[61] Numbers at both camps grew steadily in these years and from 1906 the Deal Camp was extended from seven to 10 days in length. From 1906, too, a contingent of boys several times marched the 80-odd miles from London to Deal for camp, which journey took about three days to complete. In 1908 the Northern Camp was revived at Prestatyn, North Wales and the following year was switched to Heysham near Morecombe. In 1907 the combined Deal Camp attracted some 1,150 boys nationwide, over one quarter of the total enrolment. A similar number attended the combined camp in 1912, accompanied by 54 officers, contingents from both Glasgow and Dublin included. Camp was a massive operation, requiring some 150 sleeping tents and 10 'huge' marquees. In 1908 the *Jewish World* reported that

> no less than 2,200 loaves of bread, weighing 8,000lbs., are consumed during the week; as well as 300 gallons of milk, 1,000 kippers, 1,000 haddocks, 2,000 pieces of fried fish, 2 tons of meat, over half a ton of flour, nearly half a ton of jam, and the same quantity of sugar.[62]

The boys were certainly well fed, no doubt in many cases far better than at home.

In 1909 membership reached its peak, an estimated 4,000. Six years earlier the *Royal Commission on Alien Immigration* had been informed that there were 'over 1,000' members in London alone.[63] By this time, too, a special Bearers' (first aid, May 1897) and a

Signallers' Company and no fewer than three bands had been formed, the largest of which, the London Regimental Brass Band (1901), made 'such good progress [under bandmaster T. Jarvis] . . . that it ha[d] already been passed by the Band Inspector of the London County Council as qualified to perform in the Council's Parks'.[64]

Since the Regimental Brass Band would be paid a fee for its public performances, it had to look as well as sound professional, so an exception was made in its case to the rule forbidding full uniform. Messrs S. Hess & Son, East End based equipment contractors to the Brigade, duly obliged. The Band's uniform consisted of the following items:

> *Tunic.* Blue serge, red cuffs and collar, with yellow trimming – wings with yellow trimming – Back seams piped yellow, brass buttons, (no shirt buttons),
> *Trousers.* Blue serge with broad red stripe
> *Cap.* J.L.B. Band Sergeant's Pattern
> *Belt, Crossbelt & Pouch.* Pipe clayed leather
> Bands and finishings as for J.L.B. equipment.[65]

The minutes of the Headquarters Committee for April 1906 reported that 'a Tiger skin has been received from Mr Harry H. Lewis, of Nairobi, late Adjutant of the East London Battalion, and would be used as Drummer's Apron. It was resolved that the Gift be accepted with many thanks.'[66]

Nevertheless, the rule that uniform was only to be worn at LCC concerts was strictly enforced.

The growth of the Brigade led to organisational changes. In 1900 the original Executive Committee was replaced by an expanded Brigade Council which subsequently had upwards of 40 members, and a Headquarters Committee ran the Brigade on a day-to-day basis. Meetings were held about once a month and a professional secretary was engaged, Mr Hyam Marks. HQ spawned a number of shifting sub-committees responsible for camp, equipment, canvassing, publishing, pocket book, bands and, later on, rifle shooting and sports respectively. The London Regiment was divided into three Divisions and three depots were established to carry out central training of recruits before their admission to individual

Companies. Sporting activities themselves received a boost both on account of affiliation to the Jewish Athletics Association (1899) in 1912, another cause taken up by the Maccabaeans, and by the institution of an annual athletics meeting at the Stamford Bridge Sports Ground in the Fulham Road in 1910. Trophies, banners and medals donated by various benefactors were presented to winning lads and teams and the JLB instituted proficiency badges in imitation of the Boy Scouts. The choice of sports on offer became more diverse, including gymnastics, cycling, swimming and lifesaving, and boxing.

The Brigade took on a number of public duties, frequently providing a guard of honour at synagogue openings and other parades. In February 1901 they held a special memorial service to mark the passing of Queen Victoria, and a year later, owing to the generosity of theatrical entrepreneur Beerbohm Tree, the first public JLB Display took place at Her Majesty's Theatre in the West End of London. The Brigade received further recognition when its stand at the Military Exhibition at Earls Court walked away with a silver medal. In 1902, the JLB was invited to participate in a Parade of all the Boys' Brigades inspected by the Prince of Wales in Hyde Park. The Chief Rabbi had to be consulted as the parade was scheduled for a Saturday. He permitted the lads to participate on condition that they did not bear arms (carrying is prohibited on the Sabbath). In the event, the JLB did not take part.

The growth of the Brigade made the quest for space more urgent. The original JLB offices were at 63 Finsbury Pavement in the City. In November 1904 they had moved to 20/21 Bucklesbury, a short distance away. The premises were shared with the Russo-Jewish Committee and the Jewish Athletics Association. Eventually, in 1913, the purpose-built JLB centre named Camperdown House was opened. Camperdown House was designed by Ernest Joseph who was the youngest son of Nathan S. Joseph, the architect. Brother-in-law of Chief Rabbi Hermann Adler, Nathan had established himself as *the* architect of the United Synagogue and was largely responsible for the development of the 'Cathedral Synagogue' style which became the hallmark of that organisation. Two of Nathan's sons, Charles and Ernest, joined the practice, as did his nephew Delissa Joseph. Undoubtedly Ernest's best known building is Shell-Mex

House on London's Strand. But he also designed residential buildings, of the exclusive and not-so-exclusive variety. His father had been responsible for the forbidding mass of Rothschild Buildings commissioned by the Four Percent Industrial Dwellings Company in the 1880s. This development was regarded as highly progressive in its day, a vast improvement on the slums of the East End with their outside toilets and standpipes. After the Second World War Ernest, in his turn, was responsible for planning council housing estates. Camperdown House belonged to this same social side of his architectural work. Here again, Rothschild involvement was central to the success of the scheme; Lionel de Rothschild MP was chairman of both the Building Committee and of the Trustees.

Max J. Bonn, a great patron of youth work in the 1900s, and a character to whom we will return presently, conceived of the idea of a Jewish youth centre – 'a building on the lines of the YMCA but, of course, less ambitious' – and instructed Joseph to search for a suitable site in the Aldgate area.[67] Early in 1912 such a site was found at the back of Aldgate High Street.

Camperdown House was situated in Half Moon Passage, Aldgate in the heart of the Jewish East End. The name was

> a relic of the very fine house, about 200 years old, which was standing on the site at the time of its acquisition by the Trustees. Judging by the size of the rooms it must have been occupied at one time by some important personage, possibly in connection with the military training ground adjoining.[68]

Nevertheless, the house was demolished to make way for a spacious three-storey structure, built in the vaguely neo-classical style fashionable for public buildings in Edwardian England. Inside was a large Assembly Hall, seating 1,000 people, two smaller halls and gymnasia, a common room, store rooms, games, billiards and sitting rooms for both officers and lads, a committee room and offices. Special facilities included the rifle range, a band room, library and spacious kitchen and 'a large number' of bathrooms, an essential facility in the East End where the majority of houses did not have private bathrooms until well into the 1920s. The whole was conceived not merely for the benefit of the JLB but as a resource serving the whole community, Jewish and Gentile. The Hutchison House

Club (1905), which had lost its premises in Hutchison Street, became a tenant of the new building, as did the Lads' Employment Committee (formerly at Hutchison House), the Loyal Jewish Lodge (of which more below) and the Invalid Children's Aid Association. When not in use, all the facilities were available for hire for public meetings of a 'non-political' nature, dinners and dances. The kitchen was fitted with service lifts thus connecting it with the common rooms, halls and workers' mess room, where meals were served on a regular basis 'at moderate prices' to members of the Workers' Mess Club, open to the public. Separate men's and women's clubs were established. 'Cheap meals' were instituted for the lads. At a cost of £10,000, Camperdown House was the most up-to-date facility of its day, presaging the Maccabi Centres and Beaumont Settlements of a later generation, and built, if anything, on a far grander scale. The official opening of Camperdown House by Viscount Milner in December 1913 symbolised an optimistic confidence in the future of the Brigade.

2 · 'Ironing out the ghetto bend': the Ethos of the Brigade 1895–1918

ANGLICISATION AND SOCIAL CONTROL

When Captain Sebag-Montefiore and Captain Algernon Lesser came to my home about camp, I acted as interpreter for my father. They were English gentlemen of course and when they had gone my father asked innocently 'They're Jewish ?' To the officers the company roll must have read like a winelist.[1]

So recalled an Old JLB Comrade in 1972. Joe Rose, who joined the Brigade in 1898, remembered 60 years later that the officers

were recruited from that section of the community which was looked up to as the Jewish aristocracy. They nearly all lived at Hampstead, which to us in those days seemed many miles from the East End and which, with all respect to my many friends who live there now, was then considered a very exclusive neighbourhood!

. . . looking back . . . we can [now] appreciate the work those gentlemen took on when they left their homes (one might almost say 'stately homes'), came to the East End to take us in hand, turn us into decent citizens and good Jews.[2]

Certainly, the officers' roll book covering the period 1895–1908 reveals that the vast majority of JLB Company leaders were drawn from the English-born Anglo-Jewish upper and middle classes – the so-called 'West End' Jews. A crude headcount brings us to an overall total of 282 officers. Out of 85 of these for whom a London address is entered, 68, that is more than two-thirds, lived in areas of secondary or even tertiary Jewish settlement. Addresses in Kensington, Bayswater and Hyde Park proliferate amongst the more senior personnel. Others hail from St John's Wood, Maida Vale and Belsize Park. Southgate, Cricklewood and Dalston are also represented. This pattern is not confined to the capital: in Manchester, Higher Broughton dominates over Cheetham; in Birmingham Edgbaston is an exclusive and recurring address.

As for officer's occupations, the example of Hull may be regarded as typical. In 1899 the officers were:

S.J. Feldman, 25 Park Street, Hull. Solicitor. Captain
E.E. Cohen, 127 Beverley Street [Hull]. Editor. Lieutenant
J. Kanter, 43 Lister Street [Hull]. Commission Agent. 2nd Lieut.
M. Goltman, 65 Freehold Street [Hull]. Clerk. Lieutenant
L.G. Harris , 39 Linnaeus Street [Hull]. Dental Student. QutrMtr.
Rev E. Pearlson, 10 Percy Street [Hull]. Chaplain.[3]

In 1901 the officers of the Newcastle Company consisted of a 'furniture manager', 'medical student' and a surgeon at the Royal Infirmary, whilst Bradford boasted an auctioneer and a clerk. In 1902 Birmingham had a store manager, and a jewellery manufacturer. All three of the officers in Dublin were apparently dentists. Whilst hardly the 'Cousinhood', officers even in the provinces were solidly middle class.

The majority of the Companies, by contrast, were situated in the immigrant working-class neighbourhoods, above all in the East End of London.

This phenomenon of the educated upper classes 'going down' the East End to assist the poor was by no means unique to the JLB. Indeed, the Brigade may be seen as part of a wider trend in late Victorian Britain.[4] The 1880s and 1890s were the heyday of the university settlements and public school missions, of Fabian Socialism and the birth of the Independent Labour Party. The uniformed youth movements, too, set out to do their bit to alleviate the appalling social conditions of the urban masses and to 'improve' them through education and training.

Nowhere was the need more pressing than in the East End which between 1881 and 1914 became the overcrowded home of some 100,000 Jewish immigrants from eastern Europe. They were part of the great westward migration from the Russian Empire, Romania and Galicia, driven by economic hardship and religious persecution to find a better life. The Lower East Side of New York City was a vastly more popular destination than the East End of London. Nevertheless, the numbers of Jews who came to London – and to Cheetham Hill in Manchester, the Gorbals in Glasgow, the Leylands in Leeds and Brownlow Hill in Liverpool – succeeded in doubling the size and transforming the character of British Jewry.

Almost overnight, Jews stood out. The popular image of the Jew was no longer the well-heeled acculturated banker or broker, but the sweatshop worker, talking loudly in Yiddish and practising exotic religious rituals. Neither image of the Jew, 'rich' or 'poor', was entirely accurate, but the fact remains that East End Jewry became, by dint of numbers and geographical concentration, the most high-profile section of Anglo-Jewry. For the older families who had been quietly working for social acceptance ever since the Resettlement in the seventeenth century, the advent of this new community filled them with unease. It should be remembered that British Jewry had achieved full political emancipation only comparatively recently, when Lionel de Rothschild finally took his seat in the House of Commons in 1858 after a struggle which had lasted 30 years. Moreover, the Jews were the most numerous immigrant group of the period, leaving aside the Irish Catholics.

The uniformed youth movements had a double agenda: social work and social control. They provided a medium for working-class youth to escape their squalid surroundings, at least briefly, and to expand their horizons. Drill, sports and camp all promoted physical fitness and, as the saying goes: a healthy body is a healthy mind. The Brigades inculcated self-discipline, leadership, punctuality, obedience and hygiene, morality, thrift, social responsibility, self-help and numerous other such desirable aims. All of which would, it was assumed, protect the young from crime and vice and, perhaps more significantly, protect society from delinquency, class conflict and the spread of 'dangerous' socialist doctrines. In short, the Brigades promoted a code of conduct in the best English public school traditions of fair play and sportsmanship, whilst, at the same time, perpetuating the English class system and deference to authority. The Brigade idea was intended to preserve the social order. Indeed, the

3. The Brothers Lipson, Liverpool Company, *c*.1901

4. Colonel Albert Goldsmid, the founder of the Jewish Lads' Brigade

5. Gladys, Lady Swaythling, Colonel Goldsmid's daughter and Honorary Life President of the Brigade, *c*.1959

6. 'The Raw Material and what the Brigade makes of it', from the *Jewish Chronicle*, 6 November 1903

7. Hackney Company, 1914

8. Dinner time at Summer Camp, Deal, in the 1900s

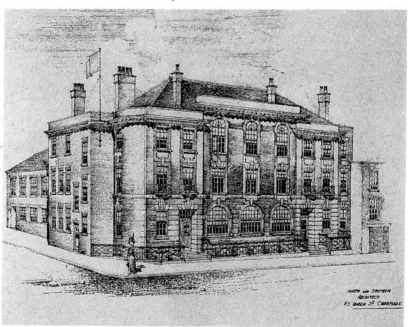

9. Camperdown House, from the brochure prepared for its opening on 16 December 1913. Architect, Ernest Joseph

10. The Hall at Camperdown House

11. The Prince of Wales (later Edward VIII) visiting Camperdown House in 1921

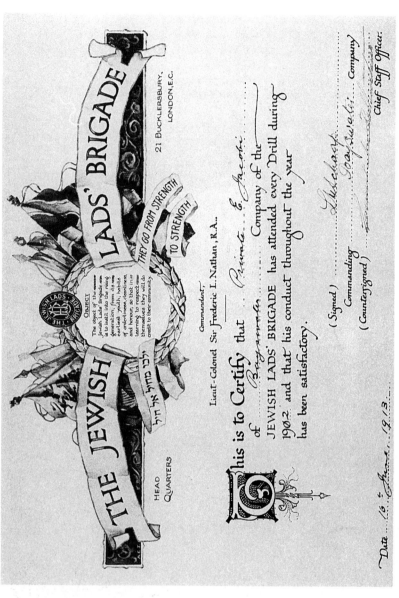

12. Drill certificate presented to Eric Jacobi in 1913

THE JEWISH LADS' BRIGADE.

OFFICERS' MESS.

CAMPERDOWN HOUSE,

HALF MOON PASSAGE,

ALDGATE, E.

[handwritten letter]

24/9/16

13. The last letter to the Brigade from Denzil Myer before he left for Mesopotamia in 1916

14. Denzil Myer, *c*.1916

15. Glasgow Company *en route* to Summer Camp in 1938

16. The Quartermaster's stores at Summer Camp in Deal in the 1930s

17. The Summer Camp, Deal, in 1959

18. Bell tents at the Deal Camp in 1907

19. Physical training at Birchington-on-Sea in 1926

20. The Drum Head service at Camp in the 1930s

21. Ernest Halsted (1873–1951), a portrait by Flora Lion which was the frontispiece of the 1951 Annual Report

22. Sir Louis Gluckstein (1897–1979), Brigade Commandant from 1945 to 1955

23. Lord Swaythling with Field Marshal Viscount Allenby at the George V Silver Jubilee Camp, 1935

24. Liverpool's first women officers – Rita Applebaum, Pearl Malits and Victoria Tenser – in May 1964

25. Lady Swaythling, the former Major-General Mrs Jean Knox, inspecting the lines at Summer Camp, 1965

26. 'Setting about the Seventies', a publicity photograph from the 1968–69
Annual Report

27. Bandmaster Henry Morris, over 90 years old, and the youngest recruit at Summer Camp in the 1960s

attempt to bring public school ideas to the poor was not a disembodied, altruistic exercise, but a thoroughly political act with significant social consequences. Victorian and Edwardian youth organizations – and the Scouts were no exception – clearly saw themselves as agencies of social control, designed to monitor the conduct of their members and shape it into forms acceptable to the middle- and upper-class perspectives of their founders.

For Baden-Powell and other social imperialists, as will become clear presently, the youth movements were a training ground for the army and aimed to produce a fit and patriotic race of Englishmen at home, ready to carry out the Imperial Mission abroad. The Anglo-Jewish gentlemen who established and ran the JLB had much the same aims in mind. Only they had an additional objective, summed up in that celebrated phrase 'to iron out the ghetto bend',[5] that is, to turn working-class and foreign Jewish youth into fit and respectable 'Englishmen of the Mosaic persuasion'.

In welcoming the establishment of the Brigade in 1895 the *Jewish Chronicle* editorialised:

> It aims at cultivating the physique and spirit of the sons of our working classes . . . so giving them the English tone and bearing in certain directions in which . . . those sections of the Jewish public have hitherto lagged behind their more fortunately situated brethren.[6]

These latter, 'young men belonging to the upper and middle classes', were exhorted by the press to become officers in the Brigade. The class distinction between officers and men was real and rigidly maintained. The principal means was through use of military rank and etiquette. The 'Rules for Members' of the Manchester JLB in 1903 gave the following instructions: 'Members must always salute their Officers when they meet them and must always address them as "Sir". If sitting when an Officer passes, they must immediately rise, stand to attention, and salute.'[7]

Naturally, such a strict regime required practice. The Camp Order Book (Deal) for 1902 noted 'Many lads salute with the wrong hand'![8] Such unforgivable defects, the Brigade set out to rectify. There was no uncertainty about the aims of the movement: 'The narrow-chested, round-shouldered, slouching son of the Ghetto becomes converted with extraordinary rapidity into an erect and self-respecting man, a living negation of the physical stigma which has long disfigured our race.'[9]

Not only would the Brigade serve to improve the 'image' of the Jew but it would have the benefit of channelling the energies of the 'hooligan' element which was apt to assimilate the less desirable aspects of English 'culture' – in its working-class guise at least: gambling, horse-racing and hanging out at dance halls. Reporting on a parade at a smart West End synagogue in 1898, the *Jewish Chronicle* remarked: 'No one, indeed, could have believed that many of these bright and erect lads belonged to the class from which are also recruited the slouchy guttersnipes who loaf about the lanes and alleys of the East End.'[10]

The underlying assumption, of course, was that the young were malleable material, easily influenced and amenable to strict discipline and the 'stiffening of the Jewish muscle'.[11] The 12- or 13-year-old boy, wrote the editor:

> is poured forth into the world like molten metals, only too ready to take the form of a mould into which he may run. The only impress which his plastic nature has received is that of the stern discipline of school life, and any movement which is intended to conserve the good which he has acquired must, of necessity, have a disciplinarian basis.[12]

The 1890s saw the emergence of 'adolescence' as a distinct social 'problem' demanding a solution. Working lads in their early teens, with a few pennies in their pockets to spend on 'undesirable' commercial entertainments were regarded by social reformers and church missions alike as juvenile delinquents in the making. Thus it was that the JLB was early represented on the Mansion House Committee for the Suppression of Street Ruffianism, known as the Twentieth Century League. In 1900 the Brigade gave its fullest support to the campaign being waged in the Board Schools and spearheaded by the Boys' Brigade to counteract 'the prevalence of smoking amongst boys . . . [which was] a serious and growing evil in London'.[13] Brigade officers were vetted to ensure that they were suitable candidates who would set a good example to the boys in their charge. In 1898 one Alfred Solomon was rejected as Captain of the North London Company on the grounds that he 'carried on the business of a bookmaker'. In 1899 a Leicester 'Bill Discounter' received similar treatment.[14] The Manchester JLB Social Club Rules baldly stated that 'all games of chance, cards, dice, etc. etc., are forbidden, and any member introducing such games will immediately be expelled from the Club and the Battalion'.[15]

In 1909 a proposal to hold a fundraising draw with 1d tickets and prizes was criticised at the regular Manchester Officers' meeting in the following vein:

> Mr Shaer [headmaster of Southall Street School] expressed an unfavourable opinion on the scheme, saying that the morality of the thing was wrong and that it was against Brigade Principles. The 'Draw' itself was an evasion of the Lottery Act and it was putting a temptation to dishonesty before the lads.

The officers decided to go ahead with the draw with the proviso that 'the sale of tickets be limited to adults'.[16] Smoking and gambling were frowned upon. Alcoholism, the vice of English society which so exercised the Victorian Temperance Lobby, did not even qualify for the attention of the JLB. This was one scourge which did not afflict the Jewish community.

Nevertheless, Anglo-Jewry had an even greater incentive than other sections of the population to keep its 'lower orders' in tow: the fear of anti-Semitism. Unchecked immigration of foreigners into England, not entirely unpredictably, provoked 'anti-alien' sentiment. Some elements of organised labour, anxious to protect their members from unfair competition for housing and jobs, were just as susceptible as sections of the Conservative Party. Growing agitation to end Britain's 'open door' policy on immigration bore fruit in the 1905 Aliens Act. The Aliens Act was, in practice, largely targeted at east European Jewish refugees, given that, as we have already pointed out, they were the only significant immigrant group of the period. The distinction between anti-alienism and anti-Semitism was a fine one. It is therefore understandable that the established Jewish community should have sought to absorb the newcomers with as little fuss as possible. Encouraging adaptation to English ways would help ensure the 'good name' of British Jewry in the eyes of society at large.

A number of institutions and strategies were developed in the years after 1881 to achieve this end. The United Synagogue (1870), dominated by Chief Rabbi Dr Hermann Adler and his *Minhag Anglia*, expanded its activities into the East End. In 1887 the Federation of Synagogues was created under the patronage of Samuel Montagu, the first Lord Swaythling, to bring the independent *chevrot* proliferating in the immigrant neighbourhoods under established Jewish control. Naturally, the English-born children of the immigrants became the chief focus for anglicising efforts, through the medium of the Jews' Free School – which banned the speaking of Yiddish on school premises; the more subtle tactics adopted by the Federation's Talmud Torah Council, designed to replace the traditional *cheder* system by more efficient, and sanitary, classes still based upon traditional values and teaching methods; and by the explosion of Jewish youth clubs: Brady Street (1896), West Central Girls (1896) and Boys (1898), Victoria (1901), Stepney (1901), Hutchison House (1905) and Basil Henriques' Oxford & St George's (1914). The Jewish Lads' Brigade fitted this pattern very well.

That the JLB had consciously taken on the task of anglicising the immigrant is borne out by their determination to give evidence before the Royal Commission on Alien Immigration in 1902. Jack Myers, who was a manager of the Brady Street Boys' Club as well as an officer in the Brigade, told the commissioners that:

> I have found boys coming up in my company . . . who cannot speak English well, but who take up the work in a most enthusiastic spirit. Last year, in Deal, where we had 500 boys down in camp, we took a census, and we found over 75 per cent of the boys there were of foreign parents, and that a very considerable number were boys born abroad.[17]

Hermann Landau of the Jews' Temporary Shelter, Joseph Rawden, headmaster of the Deal Street board school, and Captain E. Warden Denniss, the only non-Jewish officer in the Brigade, who worked as a curator at the Bethnal Green museum, all attested to the effectiveness of JLB training on immigrant youth. A display was organised to impress upon the panel 'the work the Brigade [was] doing amongst the younger portion of the Jewish foreign element'.[18] At the glittering public display mounted at Her Majesty's Theatre in January 1902, Colonel Goldsmid himself got up on the stage and said:

We are working on the same lines as the Church and other Boys' Brigades, but our task is a more difficult one . . . You have all read the Ghetto stories by Mr Zangwill, imagine the old Ghetto Jew coming here and seeing these splendid specimens. What a revelation the spectacle would have been to him. – (Cheers) . . .

Seventy-five per cent of [the lads] are children of people of foreign birth. Instead of wringing our hands and sitting still and doing nothing, or joining the outcry to keep foreign Jews out of this country, we say that we shall make them a credit to the country. This is the true policy for dealing with the so-called Alien Question. (Hear-hear)[19]

In 1906 it was estimated that '80 per cent of the lads were children of Aliens'.[20]

In 1910 Dayan Moses Hyamson, a member of Chief Rabbi Adler's *Beth Din*, addressed a JLB parade at the Queen's Hall in the following vein, according to a report in the *Jewish World*: 'He exhorted the lads at all times to be quiet in dress, manner, and tone, and concluded by pointing out how one could at the same time be a good Jew and a good Englishman.'[21]

This was the essence of respectability. And the desired effect was being achieved, if the opinions of outside observers are to be believed. The conservative newspaper, the *Daily Telegraph* (incidentally, founded by the 'Levy-calling-themselves-Lawson' family), certainly approved of the Brigade:

By regular attention to physical exercise, by the inculcation of habits tending to mental and moral improvement, by the fostering of a spirit of loyalty to the highest objects, it has succeeded, in no small degree, in combating the inherent difficulties besetting the path of young Orientals planted in Occidental surroundings. The result has been a marked improvement in the physique and morale of Jewish lads throughout the land.[22]

The racist overtones of this description, whilst not hostile, were typical of the era. 'Orientals' of whatever ilk were presumed to be inferior to Westerners in general and to Englishmen in particular. The arrogance of Empire took this fact for granted. English Jews felt the need to prove themselves according to the scale of values of the host society. The *Jewish World* opined:

It does one good to look at the sturdy youngsters [at the JLB camp in 1910] who are being inculcated with the most valuable ethics of duty and obedience, towards command, and to the ripe development of the human body. Lithe and with the grace of trained athletes the boys indeed gave the lie to the reproach so often levelled against us, of being undersized, underdeveloped and weakly.[23]

Upper- and middle-class Anglo-Jews who had absorbed English values through a public school or university education and/or via the officers' mess, sought to transmit these same values to the sons of the immigrant working classes, through the medium of the Brigade. The Brigade could indeed 'rightly claim to be the material and moral nexus between the upper and lower strata of our [Jewish] community'.[24] Nor did they doubt the benefits which such values could have upon 'the foreign element', living as they did a 'narrow' life in the 'ghetto'. They saw nothing incongruous in seeking to 'graft' English public school ideals onto a population which came from an entirely different tradition, with a vibrant cultural life of its own, and which lived under economic and social conditions which were not at all comparable.[25]

In our own day, the uniformed youth movements in general have come under hostile scrutiny for being guilty of imposing an alien public school code of conduct upon their working-class members – at best patronising and at worst an instrument of social control. The JLB may be similarly criticised in the light of contemporary theories of cultural pluralism and racial integration born of a multi-cultural society. But the job of the historian is to see personalities, organisations and events as the product of their time and not to superimpose value judgements based on hindsight or current fashion. Presently, we will look at how the lads themselves experienced the Brigade and at the attitudes of their parents towards it. We will also, to some extent, challenge the view that the JLB simply took on board the rigid class stratification which characterised the non-Jewish youth movements. The officers of the JLB aimed to anglicise their members and to make them acceptable and 'representative' British and, in the first instance, working-class citizens. Nevertheless, they had no real long-term interest in perpetuating the English class system within the Jewish community. Jews, after all, are a socially mobile group. An assessment of the impact of the

JLB on its members and their families will no doubt modify the view we have gained of the movement thus far.

Nor, by an analysis of the ideological considerations under-pinning the movement, is it intended to impugn the character of its officers. Undoubtedly, many JLB officers, like their counterparts in the general Brigades, took a genuine interest in the welfare of their lads, and were motivated by a strong sense of social service. Often, they combined their role in the JLB with managing other youth groups. Sometimes they became extremely influential on the boys; they transmitted middle-class values unconsciously to their com-panies, and their desire to help – and their many acts of personal generosity – did not necessarily preclude a desire to control. The Brigade as a whole took an interest in wider issues of education and training with a view to assisting its members in finding employment. Louis Abrahams, the headmaster of JFS, encouraged lads to enrol in technical classes held at the school. In July 1898 Colonel Goldsmid himself made a suggestion which was taken up by the Executive Committee with enthusiasm:

> that Officers Commanding Companies should be requested to note the names of any well conducted smart lads . . . who may be desirous of obtaining employment, so that, in the event of application being made, full particulars as to the character and capabilities of a lad, will be forthcoming. The greatest care should be exercised in recommending lads. Forms of Employment Register Sheets to be printed by Head-quarters for the use of Officers Commanding Companies who should . . . keep a record of all lads obtaining employment and to furnish a return annually for insertion in the Brigade Report.[26]

Ernest Joseph, at this time Lieutenant of the Hanbury and Deal Street Company set up by his father, conceived of the idea that the JLB should liaise with the Jewish Board of Guardians (1859). In January 1899 he suggested that officers take on the responsibilities of Visiting Guardians to boys in their Companies who were learning a trade under the Board's Apprenticeship Scheme (estimated at some 600 in 1898). The Jewish Board of Guardians welcomed the initiative and its Apprenticing Committee, in its turn, began to send along prospective recruits to the JLB. An agreement was reached between the two organisations whereby boys who were found

45

apprenticeships through the intervention of the JLB were, wherever possible, placed under the guardianship of their Company Officer, who, for his part, undertook to see him once a week. The officer would thus be able to keep an eye on his lad's progress and, if necessary, take up any problems or complaints about pay and conditions with his employer.

The idea of creating a Lads' Employment Committee was first mooted by Max J. Bonn (1877–1938), the American-born millionaire merchant banker who had been instrumental in the establishment of the Hutchison House Club. Bonn took a great interest in youth work and was later appointed chairman of the National Advisory Council for Juvenile Employment which grew out of the Juvenile Organisations Committee (1916), and president of the Association for Jewish Youth. In 1960 Ernest Joseph recalled:

> It was not long before Max Bonn, who was always the leader of the team, was agitated by the very large measure of unemployment that was prevalent amongst members of [Hutchison House] and in conference with Lionel de Rothschild he decided to establish a 'Lads Employment Committee', the cost of which experiment these two gentlemen agreed to share.

The idea was floated in the councils of the JLB and Hutchison House in 1905 but the committee was set up independently of both. Max Bonn himself attended its meetings at which prospective employees were interviewed. During one of these interviews Bonn enquired of Mr Sheen, the clerk to the committee:

> 'Why do some of the boys slouch into the room, with their caps on, dirty in appearance and, when questioned, hang their heads, mumble their answers and generally have a hangdog manner, while others come to the table, hold themselves erect, look clean and tidy and answer clearly and always add the word "Sir"'.

> The Clerk explained that these latter boys were invariably members of the Jewish Lads Brigade.

> 'That is interesting' said Max Bonn, . . . [and] he sent a cheque to the officers of the Brigade for 100 Guineas . . . Thus began his interest in the JLB.[27]

Other Jewish boys' clubs were invited to participate in the Employment Scheme. Lads seeking work could apply to the Brigade Office with a letter of recommendation from their Company Officer, headmaster or club manager. An interview followed at the office, attended by the boy's parents, and the suitability of the candidate was assessed. A Brigade official was paid to look for vacancies and endeavoured to find jobs where the Jewish Sabbath could be observed. Each applicant was charged a fee of one shilling for the services of this 'agent', the money being refunded if no employment was found within one month. In 1908 the *Daily Telegraph* reported that in the previous 18 months 346 jobs had been found by the JLB for lads from various clubs.[28] 'Overcrowded, underpaid, and otherwise undesirable' occupations such as 'tailoring, bootmaking [and] capmaking' were avoided. Skilled jobs such as electrical engineering, metalwork and bookbinding were encouraged, as was small-scale business experience in jewellery or confectionery. Diversification was the aim. The total and range of employment found was an achievement, considering the shortage of places for school-leavers and the additional handicaps faced by Jewish boys in the way of discrimination and who, in any case, could not work on Saturdays. Given the social circumstances under which it operated, the criticism that the Lads' Employment Committee did not encourage the entry of East End boys into 'middle-class' professions would perhaps be too harsh. The educational opportunities open to immigrant Jews, and their sons, before the First World War were, with few exceptions, still very limited. The Lads' Employment Committee, and its counterpart set up in Manchester, was indeed progressive by the standards of its day, anticipating the establishment of employment bureaux by the Board of Trade under the 1906 Liberal Government. In fact, the Lads' Committee was consulted about the proposed reform.

In a similar spirit, the Brady Street Company was the first to set up its own Savings Bank. From 1897 lads were invited to invest 3d a week. This was clearly a strategy to encourage thrift, self-help and adult responsibility. In 1901 Ernest Joseph attended a conference sponsored by the Charity Organisation Society which brought together representatives of the Brigades and friendly societies to discuss the formation of provident funds for young people. In 1912 the JLB co-operated with other Jewish and general boys' clubs in London in the formation of a special Lodge of the Manchester Unity of Oddfellows, to be called the Loyal Jewish Lodge. The aim was to help the young take the fullest possible advantage of the benefits obtainable under the 1911 National Insurance Act. On the eve of the First World War the JLB established a central Penny Bank. Clearly, Jewish youth organisations, and the Brigade in particular, were leading the field in youth work nationally.

MILITARISM

With the death of Colonel Goldsmid in March 1904, the JLB entered a new phase in its development. Between 1904 and 1906 Emanuel Montefiore (1842–1933) was official Brigade Commandant. Monte-fiore, like Goldsmid, had been in the Indian Army, entering the Bombay Artillery in 1860. He served for 21 years in India, Nova Scotia and the West Indies and was invited to head the Brigade, by Goldsmid himself, having already stood in as acting commandant whilst Goldsmid was away fighting in the Boer War. Montefiore, nevertheless, resigned at the beginning of 1906 'owing to his increasing age'.[29] Colonel Sir Frederic Nathan replaced him and occupied the post of Commandant for the following two decades. His period in office thus spanned the crucial period before and throughout the First World War. Nathan, too, was a career soldier, trained at the Royal Military Academy at Woolwich, and in charge of explosives at the Ordnance Department – the Royal Gunpowder Factory at Waltham. Like Goldsmid, he came from a very dis-tinguished family, with three brothers who had gained knighthoods: Sir Nathaniel Nathan, a former Attorney-General of Trinidad; Sir Matthew Nathan, Governor of the Gold Coast, Hong Kong, Natal and Queensland and the first Jew to receive a Colonial Governership in 1904; another brother in the Indian Public Works Department; another, Mr Robert Nathan, in the Indian Civil Service and Viceroy Lord Curzon's private secretary; and yet another, a major in the Engineers. Like Goldsmid, Nathan too served in the Indian Army at Benares early in his career. In 1909 he resigned his commission in the Royal Artillery, and went into industry. During the First World

War he became adviser to the Admiralty on cordite supply (in which capacity he may well have come into contact with Dr Chaim Weizmann, who was working on acetone. Weizmann was made an honorary vice-president of the Brigade in the 1920s). Nathan was president of the Institute of Chemical Engineers from 1925–27.[30]

Brigade Headquarters staff, in many cases, had some military training; Ernest Hallenstein, Algernon Lesser, David de Lara Cohen and Cecil Sebag-Montefiore all served in the Volunteers.

Clearly, the presence of so many military men in the early history of the Brigade had a decisive influence on its character, as it did on the general uniformed youth movements in Britain. Both William Smith and Walter Gee had joined the Volunteers before embarking on their respective careers in youth work. But the prime example is, of course, Robert Baden-Powell who founded the Boy Scouts in 1907. Like Goldsmid, Baden-Powell was a professional soldier, although not formally trained, who had seen active service in South Africa and India. During the Boer War, he became a household name as the 'Hero of Mafeking'. The Scouts differed from the Brigades in that less emphasis was placed on drill and discipline and that, although conceived of as a Christian movement, their activities did not include an act of worship or religious instruction. In this way, Baden-Powell avoided the thorny issue of denominationalism which plagued the Brigades. This more relaxed approach proved very popular as the rapid expansion of the movement testified, embracing some 130,000 members nationwide by 1909. Nevertheless, the Scouts exhibited much the same preoccupation with physical fitness, self-discipline, character training and patriotic service to the state. Baden-Powell had hit upon a successful formula which embraced military, educational and ethical concepts which were undoubtedly capable of broad appeal.[31]

In March 1909 the *Jewish Chronicle* reported that 'a large number of Jewish lads' had joined the Scouts. George S. Ellis, the meticulous 'printer' of the handwritten *Hackney Review* put out by the Hackney Company, was also a Scoutmaster as early as 1908. Inevitably, the JLB found itself in competition with the Scouts. It responded by introducing scouting sections and badges and by adopting a policy of exclusivity. Boys were not permitted to hold dual membership of the Brigade and Scouts. Nevertheless, whole Scout companies were enrolled in the Brigade, in Glasgow in November 1908 under Scout-masters Nathan Strump and M. Harris, in Manchester in 1909 (Manchester F Company) associated with the name of Alex Jacobs, and at Stamford Hill in London in 1913. They were permitted to wear a distinctive dark grey uniform with 'slouch hat . . . with one side of brim turned up' along with the usual JLB insignia, cost borne by themselves.[32] In common with the other Brigade organisations, the JLB came to a *modus vivendi* with the Boy Scouts not to poach each other's members.

Baden-Powell himself was guest of honour at the grand JLB military display at the Queen's Hall in 1910. He was full of praise: 'The Jewish lads had the right spirit. Among his Boy Scouts were a number of Jewish lads, and he knew how well they worked . . . good on parade, and underneath real grit.' The General and other top brass were treated to an entertainment which included drill, pyramids, signalling, gymnastics and ambulance work in which some 500 members of the Brigade participated. It was at this event that Baden-Powell's retirement from the army was announced. He intended to devote all of his time to the development of the Scout movement.[33]

Whilst Baden-Powell was developing his alternative formula, the JLB instituted facilities for shooting practice, an activity made fashionable through the advocacy of Lord Roberts, Baden-Powell's Commander-in-Chief during the Boer War and president of the National Service League from 1906. The League had been founded in 1901 to campaign for the introduction of military conscription in peacetime. In 1906 too, Roberts, as Commander-in-Chief, estab-lished a miniature shooting club movement for young people, known as 'Lord Roberts' Boys'. Both 'Lord Roberts' Boys' and Lord Meath's Lads' Drill Association (1899) – the youth arm of the Volunteer Forces which advocated the formation of Cadet Corps in elementary schools to supplement those in the public schools – were incorporated into the National Service League.[34] The JLB Rifle Range was officially opened in January 1908 by the Liberal Secretary of State for War, R.B. Haldane. The range was situated in the cellar of the Jews' Free School and was fitted out with fixed, moving and disappearing targets. A similar range soon followed in Manchester, at the recently opened (1907) Grove House Lads' Club and Drill Hall

(282 Bury New Road) built by the Jewish Mayor of Salford, Alderman Isidore Frankenberg. Target practice quickly established itself as an activity widespread in the JLB, as it did in the other uniformed youth movements. In 1909–10 some 30,000 rounds were fired at the London range alone.

In fact, target practice had become a Brigade activity even before the opening of the rifle range. Facilities were provided at the Deal camp from 1901, at Lytham from 1899. The Brigade took up an offer by the Society of Working Men's Rifle Clubs, at which the JLB was represented, to try out one of their shooting ranges late in 1901. In 1903 the Brigade reached an agreement with the Brady Street Rifle Club to share its range, guns and cost of ammunition. Secretary Hyam Marks was something of an expert on the subject and had taken up the issue of forming a rifle club at the JFS with Mr Abrahams, the headmaster. Nevertheless, the idea of introducing lads to the art of musketry had originated with Colonel Goldsmid himself, and was borne of practical experience of combat during the Boer War. This campaign had seen the introduction of smokeless powder and quick-firing magazine rifles suitable for use by soldiers in a defensive position, such as would be the case in a national emergency in the mother country. Mobility would thereby be increased. In a letter written from the South African front to his JLB deputy in London, Colonel Montefiore, Goldsmid insisted that the Brigade should do its bit 'in lending a hand towards the defence of the Country' by training its members to shoot, and should set up shooting galleries and acquire arms and ammunition for this purpose. He spelt out the practical arrangements even down to the distribution of decorations to the best shots in competition and concluded:

> I think no better memorial of the part the members of the Brigade have taken in this war can be erected than in the establishment of such shooting galleries . . . and trust the JLB will be in the van and not in the rear of the movement to set in order our national defence.

In the course of this communication, Goldsmid further suggested that all lads be taught to cycle because: 'In a close country like England, with good roads, the cycle will give the mobility to a force in the field, that the Boer ponies give to their masters.'[35]

From the turn of the century, the JLB, in common with the other

Brigades, saw itself as a training ground wherein 'the rising generation . . . would form an inexhaustable source of supply for defensive
purposes, in an emergency'. It is not irrelevant that Goldsmid had
also mooted (in 1898) the notion of setting up Cadet Companies at
Jewish schools, equivalent to the 'Gentlemen Cadets' of Sandhurst
and the English public schools (from 1859). It is not known whether
his suggestion was in fact acted upon.[36]

The addition of rifle shooting, on top of drill, discipline, uniform
and the leadership role played by career soldiers, was certainly
indicative of an increasingly military spirit amongst the youth
movements in the years leading up to the First World War. Indeed,
the very emergence of uniformed youth movements from the 1890s
onwards has been interpreted as symptomatic of a preoccupation
with national efficiency, race deterioration and imperial defence.
Revelations about the poor physical shape of the British Army were
made during the Boer War (1899–1902), especially through the
report produced by the Inter-Departmental Committee on Physical
Deterioration, and General Frederick Maurice's alarmist articles
in the *Contemporary Review*. Confidence was further eroded by
increasing tension in Europe, dominated for Britain by commercial
and naval rivalry with Germany and the race to rearm. The security
of the British Empire, and of the Imperial Mission itself, was under
threat and the mother country was succumbing to social unrest,
decadence and degeneracy, or so it was thought. The solution
advocated by Baden-Powell and others was an appeal to patriotism
and national unity underpinned by a strong infusion of Social
Darwinist theory; the need to build up the British 'race' in order to
survive in an increasingly hostile world.[37] Organisations such as the
National Service League advocated universal military training for
men and preparation for this by means of organised drill, discipline
and rifle shooting for boys.

In 1910 Haldane issued new Army Council Cadet Regulations.
The proposal was to incorporate all of the quasi-military youth
movements into a national cadet force to be administered by the
Territorial Army. Haldane's Imperial Cadet Federation, as it came
to be called, was to embrace an estimated 319,000 youths already
enrolled in the Scouts and the various Brigades – a larger number
than in the Territorial Army itself. Evidently, the youth groups

were looked upon as a pool of potential recruits for the armed forces in the event of war in Europe. In effect, the War Office was presenting an ultimatum to the Brigades: either they applied to their local Territorials for 'official' recognition as Cadets or they forfeited the military equipment and financial assistance which they had become accustomed to receiving from army sources. Thus the Cadet Regulations were a test of the military resolve of the youth organisations: were they simply playing at soldiers or were they prepared to train their members to do it for real? Not surprisingly, the new measures provoked heartsearching and conflict amongst the leadership. There were those who maintained that acceptance of the regulations would compromise the ethos of the Brigades which was essentially religious and social. Right wing and left wing factions emerged; pacifists, socialists and 'Little Englanders' were ranged against militarists, conservatives and imperialists. The Church Lads' Brigade, arguably, as the Anglican Brigade, the one most closely identified with the Establishment, joined the Cadet scheme in 1911. But the nondenominational Boys' Brigade, B-P's Scouts and the Jewish Lads' Brigade were considerably more ambivalent.[38]

In March 1910 the JLB's CSO Ernest M. Hallenstein discussed the Cadet scheme with Lieutenant-Colonel Hyslop, secretary of the City of London Territorial Force. He suggested that the JLB lay down a standard of proficiency and that all boys who met this standard be eligible for the benefits offered by the Cadet scheme. These included 'employment, emigration and apprenticeship'. But the real aim was eventual conscription via the Territorials into the army proper. The JLB response was non-committal. By the summer, however, its officers had decided that the conditions being imposed were unacceptable. The JLB stated that it 'strongly objected to becoming a military organisation' and would therefore not apply for recognition under the War Office scheme. For, such a step would 'fundamentally alter the constitution of the Brigade and the objects of its founders'. Hallenstein enlarged upon this: 'Our sole object is social and the military drill is but a means to an end. We seek to make good and efficient citizens and good and loyal Jews.'[39]

The JLB held out against change until after the start of the First World War. In March 1915 the Brigade Council reversed its 1911 decision on the Cadet scheme. What were the reasons for this change

53

of heart? Was it merely a response to the pressures of war and the call for volunteers? Or does it cast doubt on the earlier sincerity of JLB opposition to 'militarisation'? As in the case of the other Brigades, mixed signals had emanated from the higher ranks of the JLB throughout the 1900s. On the one hand, Goldsmid had declared from the outset that 'if, in the course of time, the Boys of the Brigade should wish to enter the army or navy in defence of their country, the Jewish Lads' Brigade would be found a splendid stepping-stone by which these objects might be achieved'.[40]

In 1912, Lord Rothschild declared that he and his family 'felt very strongly that Jewish lads, after leaving school, if they had the time, and it did not interfere with their career, should join some branch of the Territorial Army and help England which had done so much to help the Jews'. On the other hand, Captain José R. Landsberg added that 'The Brigade was not formed to train boys for the Army but if a boy did ultimately join the Forces he wished him good luck'.[41]

In the discussion at the Brigade Council in March 1915, it emerged that the underlying motive for resistance to participation in the Cadet scheme before the war had been fear that by so doing the JLB would surrender its autonomy. It was thought that the movement would suffer from interference by the military authorities. This had proved not to be the case for other organisations which had joined the scheme. Moreover, the JLB was worried about its image. Association with 'military' objectives set by the Government might lose it subscribers. Before the war, even Haldane himself had to deny that he was promoting 'militarism' because of the unpopularity of that cause. The JLB did not like to be labelled 'military', but the fact remains that it offered a military-style training and, more importantly, was convinced of the educational value of such a regime. When war broke out, it was natural that all such scruples should have been swept aside. Army assistance and financial help were welcome, not least because conscription was now in the offing (April 1916, in fact); as was the compulsory drafting of under-age lads into Cadet units which would almost certainly accompany it.

The Brigade duly applied for recognition by the Territorial Forces Association and, for the remainder of the war, the London Battalion styled itself '1st London Cadet Battalion, Jewish Lads' Brigade' and

Manchester, the '1st Manchester Cadet Battalion JLB'. Indeed, the Manchester, Birmingham and Glasgow companies sought permission from Brigade HQ to affiliate to their local Territorials. The request was granted but not before enquiries were made as to 'how affilliation [sic] would affect the control of J.L.B. Headquarters over the companies, especially in regard to the appointment and control of officers'. Again, the issue was not one of principle. In the event, all JLB Companies, except Dublin, transformed themselves into Cadet units and adopted uniform of regulation 'service pattern.' Accordingly a 'Khaki scheme' was drawn up for the Brigade as a whole. Arguments about its acceptance revolved around the best methods of financing purchase and distribution of the uniform. The *need* for uniform was not questioned. Eventually, it was decided that each lad should pay 2/6d towards the cost of outfitting and that only boys over 13 years of age and 'not less than 4ft 4in in height' be allowed to wear uniform.[42]

This strong emphasis on duty bore tragic fruit during the First World War. A total of 525 names appear on the JLB Roll of Honour. This figure accounts for almost one-third (27 per cent) of all British Jews who died for their country during the conflict (1,949). It represents 80 per cent of casualties amongst Jewish serving officers. *The British Jewry Book of Honour* notes that 80 out of a total of 90 JLB officers joined up as volunteers in 1914;[43] 38 of them never returned. Amongst their number were some of the longest serving JLB officers: Victor B. Barnett, Ernest M. Green, Victor V. Jacob, Edgar E. Kahn, Nathaniel Marks, Denzil Myer, Ellis J.A. Paiba, Edgar B. Samuel, Leonard Solomon and Arthur Solomon. In all, 19 out of 35 officers of London Companies before the war made the 'supreme sacrifice'. Henry Dreschfield, founder and first Commanding Officer of the Manchester JLB, was also killed in action along with Captain Jack E. Rothband, Ralph Besso, Harry Levi and Ralph Frankenburg. This Company won the highest of battle honours. Private Jack White (Weiss) of the 6th King's Own Royal Lancashire Regiment, and a member of the Manchester JLB, won the Victoria Cross for saving an officer's life under fire in Iraq. Another JLB member, Gordon Hyams, was the first Jew to be awarded the DFC on the creation of the RAF in 1918 for his piloting of early bomber aircraft over the North Sea and Egypt during the Great War.[44]

In 1913, at the last full Summer Camp before the outbreak of war,

The NCOs of the 'C' Company of the Brigade, to the number of 40, were taken in a brake by Capt. Denzil Myer to Ramsgate, where they partook of a substantial tea. It may be added that Mr Myer is known throughout the Brigade as the man with a large heart. He is certainly the beloved one of the lads.[45]

On the Saturday night he provided a firework display for their entertainment. On 24 September 1916 he penned a poignant message to the Brigade: 'Goodbye to all the JLB officers & boys – Under orders for Mesopotamia & hope to return & find the JLB still going strong.'

Second Lieutenant Myer was killed in action on 25 February 1917. His last letter, together with a portrait photograph in army uniform, survives in the Brigade archives.

Ten former 'lads' were killed in action as members of the 38th or 40th Royal Fusiliers in 1918 and the beginning of 1919. Their sacrifice was of especial significance, as members of the Jewish units or 'Judaeans', set up in 1917 on the initiative of the Russian Zionist Vladimir (Ze'ev) Jabotinsky. Most of these casualties were, it may be deduced, sustained in the Holy Land where fighting against the Turks continued throughout the summer and autumn of 1918. Those who did not die in actual combat doubtless succumbed to the malaria rife in the Jordan Valley.[46]

More fortunate was Ben Levinson, a veteran of the Allenby campaign. He was one of the first boys to join the Manchester JLB in 1902 and remained in the Brigade until he reached 19. In 1910 he joined the Territorials and served in both world wars. In 1917 he elected for tranfer to the Jewish Regiment where he 'worked with Zev Jabotinsky'. After training at Plymouth, the Regiment travelled overland through France and sailed from Italy to Alexandria 'in spite of the subs [German U-Boats] chasing in the Med'. On eventually reaching the Palestine front, Levinson recalled, at the age of 97 in 1985, that he 'was wounded in a Night Patrol and taken prisoner. After moving from Hospital at Amman, Nazareth, Damascus and Aleppo where I was recaptured [by the Cavalry] as the Turks retreat[ed] before Gen. Allenbys [sic] victorious Army'.[47]

Major Max Karo, later founder of the Stock Exchange Cadet

Corps and an officer in the Brigade, served in the 38th Royal Fusiliers. In 1925 he 'took the King's Colours of the Jewish Regiment to Jerusalem, where they were deposited in the Churvah Synagogue, destroyed in the Israeli-Arab War [1948]'.[48]

Julius Jacobs, a son of JLB Scoutmaster Alex Jacobs of Manchester, also served as an adjutant with the Judeans, as did Nathan Strump of the Glasgow JLB who was in the 39th Royal Fusiliers. Jacobs survived the Great War, entered the British Mandatory Administration in Palestine and was blown up in the King David Hotel bombing in Jerusalem in 1946.[49]

The image of the Jew as soldier jarred in the eyes of both Jews and non-Jews, certainly until the creation of the State of Israel in 1948. Viewed from the dominant Ashkenazi religious and cultural perspective of eastern Europe, the army was a decidedly un-Jewish vocation. In Tsarist Russia, home to the vast majority of world Jewry in the nineteenth century, military service meant forcible conscription, brutal repression and often conversion to Orthodox Christianity. Under Tsar Nicholas I (1825–55) Jewish boys were press-ganged into the army at the age of 12 – the notorious system of Cantonment. Even so, Jews were barred from gaining commissions in the Imperial Army. Preferment in the army was regarded as a privilege open only to those who were true citizens of the state, not Jews who were merely the stepchildren of Mother Russia. Not surprisingly, Russian Jews sought to evade conscription as much as possible.

It is against this background that the aspiration of acculturated Jews in central and western Europe for military careers must be understood. The struggle for civil and political emancipation meant that western Jews sought, and felt the need to be seen seeking, both the privileges and the duties of citizenship. In France, Germany, Austria-Hungary, Italy and Holland, upper-class Jews viewed a military career as a measure of social acceptance, and won, with varying degrees of success, the right to promotion from the ranks during the course of the nineteenth century. Even in England, where Jews had never been confined to a ghetto, they were barred from holding commissions until the Repeal of the 1673 [religious] Test and Corporation Acts in 1828, which primarily affected Dissenters (i.e., Christians not conforming to the established Church of

England). The whole was tied up with the campaign for Catholic Emancipation which succeeded the following year. Unlike the case of public office holders, however, commissioned officers below the rank of Rear Admiral and Major-General, were not obliged to swear the oath 'on the true faith of a Christian' after the Repeal. Thus Jews achieved equality in the armed services a generation before they gained full political emancipation.

Prior to 1828, Jews had seen active service in the ranks of both army and navy (where the restriction, in fact, never really applied) and well-to-do Jews had joined the Militia, Yeomanry and Volunteers especially in London during the Napoleonic Wars. A small number, mostly of Sephardi origin, achieved officer status, but in all cases either hid their religion or converted to Christianity. By the mid-century, an army career became acceptable amongst the privileged classes of Anglo-Jewry; Rothschilds, Montefiores and Sassoons were commissioned. In the Colonies of North America, the West Indies and South Africa, Jews were more readily accepted in the army. Evidently, English Jews identified with and took the 'Imperial Mission' seriously. The Indian Army was a particular favourite. The Goldsmid family contributed several members to the British Imperial Forces overseas, including Colonel Goldsmid's grandfather Lionel Prager Goldsmid (1797–1866) who held a commission in the 19th Dragoons, and his uncle Major-General Sir John Frederick Goldsmid (1818–1908). A great-uncle and namesake Albert Goldsmid (1793–1861) had also risen to the rank of Major-General and fought at Waterloo. The founder of the JLB thus came from an assimilated Anglo-Jewish family which had developed a strong military tradition. Colonel Goldsmid, moreover, on his appointment to Headquarters Staff in 1884, became a prime mover in securing recognition for Judaism as a separate 'denomination' in the army. For, whilst Jews could join the army as private soldiers, they were denied any corporate identity as Jews owing to the fact that no religion other than Christianity was recognised in the services, for the purposes of public worship. In the revised edition of the Queen's Regulations published in 1886, Judaism was at last recognised, and the way was open for the appointment of the first Jewish Army Chaplain, Revd Francis Cohen, as we have already seen. His successor, both as Jewish Chaplain to the British Forces and as Chaplain to the Jewish Lads' Brigade, was the Revd Michael Adler. Adler had the distinction of becoming the first Jewish Chaplain to see active service – on the Western Front during the First World War.[50]

Some 2,000 British Jews saw active service in the Boer War. Colonel Goldsmid himself and ten officers of the JLB were amongst their number: Captain J. Waley Cohen, Arthur S. Joseph, Jose Landsberg, Percy R. Josephs, J. Hoffman, E.R. Harris, H.H. Lewis and three lieutenants, all members of the Halford family, George Edward, John M. and Edgar. A few lads also served; four from the Brady Street Company including Staff Sergeant Mark Moses Sonnenfeld who was a hospital orderly in the Royal Army Medical Corps. Many lads, of course, were under age. A total of 114 British Jews were killed in South Africa including, as mentioned above, George Halford and F.M. Raphael.

Thus, the formal granting of political emancipation in 1858 had reinforced the Jews' anxiety to uphold their end of the bargain, the unspoken 'Emancipation Contract' under which they were required to express their gratitude for the gift of emancipation by demonstrating their loyalty to England. Henceforth, Jews in Britain, as elsewhere in western Europe, were committed to liberal values and identified themselves completely with the interests of the host nation. This burden native British Jews took on with enthusiasm.

Some would argue that they did so with too much enthusiasm. The disproportionate contribution of Jews to the British effort in South Africa and to the 'Imperial Mission' in general was hardly rewarded. The Boer War was accompanied by a virulent press campaign alleging that it was being fought for the benefit of 'German Jewish capitalists', such as Alfred Beit and Barney Barnato, who were exploiting the mineral resources of the Rand for their own gain. Influential thinkers, the liberal J.A. Hobson and the socialist H.M. Hyndman, propagated such views. At home, fears about 'degeneracy' were linked with the Aliens Question. The government-appointed enquiry into 'Physical Deterioration' sat side by side with the Royal Commission on Alien Immigration. The unhealthiness of the nation was perceived as an essentially urban problem – and the cities were being 'swamped' with the 'refuse' of east European ghettos.[51]

The proportion of adult Jewish males who served in the British Army during the First World War was greater than that of the general population. *The British Jewry Book of Honour* published in 1922 assembles the relevant statistics. Ironically, however, the facts did not entirely erase the persistent image of the Jew as a poor soldier who wanted to 'shirk' his duty. This image was reinforced by the well-publicised resistance to conscription on the part of Russian Jewish immigrants, especially in the East End of London during the First World War. Many young men had come as deserters from the Tsarist Army and did not see why they should be forced to serve in another army fighting on the same side as their erstwhile anti-Semitic overlord. The question of Jews and military service, perhaps more than any other single factor, fostered anti-alien and, ultimately, anti-Semitic sentiment in Britain during the war. This fact, especially when translated into a virulent newspaper campaign, and anti-alien riots – the most well-known incident being the so-called 'Lusitania Riots' in the East End in 1915 when property and shops owned by 'foreigners' were smashed – acted as an even greater incentive for British-born Jews to demonstrate their patriotism to the cause. In 1917 there were outbreaks of rioting in Leeds and Bethnal Green. In August 1914 the *Jewish Chronicle* buried any scruples it may have entertained about Allied Jew being pitted against German or Austrian Jew and ran the banner headline: 'England has been all she could be to Jews, Jews will be all they can to England'.[52]

The pressures of war took their toll on the JLB – and not only in terms of the large number of casualties referred to above. Since such a high proportion of officers volunteered for army service in 1914, the organisation was depleted of leaders. Indeed, the Brigade was at the forefront of the recruitment drive at the beginning of the war. In September 1914 a recruiting meeting at Camperdown House, attended by a representative of the War Office, the Mayor of Stepney and Stuart Samuel MP, netted 150 Jewish volunteers for the British Army. The JLB was represented, through chairman Max Bonn, on the Juvenile Organisations Committee, set up by the Home Office to encourage voluntary war work amongst young people. Ernest Woolf, who joined Hackney Company in 1914 and was later chairman of the Old Comrades' Association, remembered 'marching round the streets of Hackney with band playing, finishing up on the steps of the Town Hall. I was a bugler at the time and we were all blowing away like mad to attract the people to come and listen to an Army Officer making his speech calling for recruits.'[53]

Less publicity was given to the fact that Captain L. Mendl, commander of the largest JLB Company at JFS and 'one of our most popular officers', was 'summoned to the colours in the Austrian Army'. He reportedly 'sent a cheerful telegram on his way out from Nuremberg'.[54] In March 1917 Camperdown House was used as the venue for a public meeting called by the militantly anti-conscriptionist Foreign Jews Protection Committee 'to protect the Right of Asylum and Cheer the Russian Revolution'. Day-to-day Brigade activities were inevitably run down, many Companies collapsed, and the 1914 Summer Camps were hastily curtailed on the outbreak of hostilities. Full camp was not resumed until 1918 (for London at Wallingford and for the provinces at Penrhynside, Llandudno; Birmingham Company held a separate camp at Stone-leigh Park). The Sandhills site at Deal was appropriated by the War Office. However, small camps were held in August 1917 for about 60 lads at Goring and for 150 lads from Manchester at Kettleshulme in Derbyshire. The Manchester JLB Scout Company also held week-end camps at Marple during the war and the Glasgow Company held two camps of its own.[55] During this fallow period, the JLB was kept going largely owing to the dedication of older officers and those ineligible for army service, especially 'the two Ernests', Joseph and Hallenstein, who were 'best friends', and the acting paymaster, Max Bonn. Hallenstein (1873–1951) was the son of a German-Jewish leather merchant who had emigrated to Melbourne, Australia as a young man. Ernest was brought to England at the age of six months, as an adult went into the family business, married into an old Anglo-Jewish family, the Jacob family of Falmouth, and pursued a part-time career in the Volunteers. Like so many Jews with 'German' sounding names, Hallenstein anglicised his name in response to rising xenophobia at the start of the Great War, during which he saw service as a Special Constable. Ernest Halsted, as he was hence-forth known, was to play a central part in the subsequent history of the JLB.[56]

3 · 'The Two Ernests': 1918–1945

In 1919, the JLB, like the country as a whole, applied itself in earnest to the task of post-war reconstruction. The Annual Report for that year noted that the Brigade was 'faced . . . with the task of creating itself afresh'. Commandant Sir Frederic Nathan returned from war service to find the organisation badly depleted of both officers and funds. Companies had lost a large number of members and some had disappeared altogether. Dublin collapsed 'just before' the war and 'only a couple' of those who volunteered returned in 1919.[1] The Company was disbanded in January 1921. In any case, the Troubles in Ireland, resulting in Partition in 1922, precluded any subsequent chance of revival.

Morale was revived by a visit from Lieutenant-General Sir John Monash, the Jewish Commander of the Australia Corps, to Camperdown House in the summer of 1919. He praised the war record of the Brigade in glowing terms and expressed his pride in 'what the Jews of the British Race had done in the great fight for justice and liberty'.[2] Nevertheless, there is evidence that the JLB, in common with the Christian Brigades, suffered from the public revulsion against militarism which swept the nation after the Great War. The retention of khaki uniform in particular 'adversely affected the membership of the Brigade and proved a great obstacle to recruiting'. This was apart from the financial burden which it imposed upon the Brigade's resources; provision of regulation equipment cost some £1,000 in 1919. Many lads were thrown out of work during the post-war trade depression and could not afford to contribute towards their uniform. By the end of that year, officers in the London Battalion were 'almost solid against the retention of uniform', and Halsted attested to 'its unpopularity amongst a large number of parents'. Propaganda was needed 'to dispel the prejudice of parents who regarded the Brigade as a military organisation'. The press concurred: 'No doubt the khaki uniform is the real bogey' the *Jewish World* commented, whilst an ex-Brigader complained that the Cadet Grant had 'altered . . . the whole atmosphere' of the Brigade with the consequence that 'thousands of old Brigade boys who are in a position to render assistance are today standing aloof from the Movement'. Goldsmid's 'social movement' had been converted into an organisation dedicated 'to carry[ing] on the work of the War Office'. This criticism notwithstanding, Nathan maintained that 'the uniform [was] a great attraction to the lads'.[3] Whilst individual London Companies elected to abolish khaki, this step was not taken throughout the London Brigade until late in 1921. A new form of equipment was henceforth adopted as set out below:

Form of equipment

Cadets and NCOs
    Leather JLB waistband
    White haversack
    Service cap in blue melton cloth, with blue band, cloth peak,
        polished chin strap and cloth buttons
    Cap badge as worn with khaki uniform.

Sergeants
    Equipment as for cadets with the addition of
    Leather cross belt and
    White cotton gloves.

Warrant Officers
    Special pattern hat with shiny peak with an edging of gold braid
    Cadet's waistbelt
    Red sash
    White cotton gloves.

NCOs Chevrons
    to be of gold braid and worn in the usual position on the left arm
    In the case of WOs Crown, to be worn on the right forearm.

'A Good Jew and a Good Englishman'

Officers
Equipment to be of same pattern as originally worn in the days
of the pill-box equipment, viz.,
Forage Hat, with old pattern JLB badge
Crossbelt
Brown Kid gloves
Dark Blue suit
White stiff collar and black tie
Black boots or shoes
Plain malacca crook cane 3ft.

Battalion Staff
To have red inset to the cap and wear
Whistle and lanyard.

Brigade HQ Staff
To have red inset to the cap and wear
Whistle and chain on crossbelt.

Junior Companies
The pill-box equipment be retained for the junior companies.[4]

A Junior Company, ages 10–12, had been established at Camperdown House just before the war. These boys were to be charged
2/– for the issue of the old pillbox equipment, whilst their senior
counterparts had to pay 3/– for hire of the new clothing.

The provincial Companies, however, remained in khaki during
the whole of the inter-war period. Commanding Officers even continued to appear at official events sporting First World War puttees
and the lads often marched with dummy rifles. In Manchester,
Henriques and his staff insisted on khaki, despite the fact that it cost
more than double to kit out the lads in army surplus than in cap, belt
and haversack. The Glasgow Company wore tartan kilts on parade
and boasted what was claimed to be the only Jewish bagpipe band
in the world! According to a Scottish local newspaper in 1930, the
Pipe Band presented a fine picture on display:

> They wore kilt and sporran, plaid socks, Border tunic, glengarry, and a
> general air of 'wha'hae' – and played the bagpipes with an effect not
> noticeably worse than one has heard elsewhere. They also danced the

strathspey and the reel to good Highland tunes, and danced them well
. . . any double-distilled Caledonian might have applauded . . . [Then]
the claymore sheathed, the pipers had a grand finale and skirled – the
Hebrew anthem![5]

The JLB continued to enjoy War Office recognition during the
1920s, and the benefits of the Government grant and supplies of
free equipment which went with it. Nevertheless, the Brigade
eschewed closer affiliation with the Territorial Army (TA). In 1924,
the War Office issued new regulations which were more restrictive
than those originally drawn up by Haldane. Henceforth, every
Cadet unit was required to affiliate to the TA and to carry out an
approved syllabus of elementary military training. This development found the various Brigades badly divided. The Boys' Brigade
severed its link with officialdom, whereas the Church Lads' Brigade
decided to co-operate. The JLB followed the lead of the latter. The
historian of the Brigade movements draws a contrast between the
expansion of the Boys' Brigade and especially of the Scout movement in the inter-war period, as compared with the other Brigades
which, he claims, went into permanent decline. He attributes this
trend to the key decision to co-operate with the military – a calling
which went out of fashion during this period.[6]

It seems that the JLB, too, suffered in popularity from association
with 'militarism'. Throughout the 1920s the Brigade leadership
made a point of disavowing 'militarism' at almost every public
opportunity. It was purely 'a social movement' dedicated to pro-
ducing upright British citizens. As E.Royalton Kisch, Commandant
of the 1928 Camp at Birchington-on-Sea put it:

> What is so often lacking is the spirit of sportsmanship, which teaches us
> to play the game for the sake of the game, to play for our side and not for
> ourselves, and to offer a handshake to the man who has beaten us . . .
> Play for the good there can be in the very serious game of life; play for
> the honour of your people.

So important were these sentiments deemed to be that Kisch's lecture was printed and distributed throughout the JLB under the title
'The Camp of God'.[7]

Certainly, the ethos had changed little since before 1914. The
1934 Annual Report stated:

The aim of the Brigade training is to ensure the health of the boy in mind, body and character; to develop in him self-respect, good manners and a cheerful disposition; to bring him to manhood possessing a sense of loyalty and responsibility to his home, his faith and his fellow-citizens. In short, it guides him in his youth, it prepares him for manhood, and it guards him against the many temptations provided by cheap and undesirable amusements which abound in all large cities.[8]

According to a loyal rank and file member of Bayswater Company in 1922:

members of the J.L.B. . . . pride themselves . . . on being 'better than other men.' They are distinct from their school fellows in clean boots, well-brushed hair and clothes . . . they are assiduous, punctual, and tidy, never walk about with their hands in their pockets, or in other people's, and are always smart in appearance. They are sportsmen in the best sense of the word, and have a strong sense of discipline.[9]

Manchester lads were evidently not as well ordered as their London counterparts. In 1924 'the CO commented on the amount of expectorating and urinating which goes on about the [Northern] camp particularly after dark. He stated that he intended taking serious measures to put a stop to this practice.' Nor were they as well scrubbed as the Londoners claimed to be. In 1932 it was recommended to Manchester officers that 'Every boy should be made to have a wash all over within 3 days of going to camp'.[10]

Parental resistance in the original immigrant neighbourhoods remained a problem. One veteran remembers clearly:

In the 1920s I lived in the very heart of the East End of London and I recall very well the feelings of our parents and grandparents that we were to be discouraged from joining uniformed groups including the JLB and the Scouts . . . [There was] a very great feeling against it . . . We don't want our children to grow up as soldiers . . . and hold a gun . . . not to be taught to hold a gun.

Whilst some parents begrudgingly accepted the fact of their child's involvement in the Brigade: – 'At least they knew where I was'[11] – others eventually learned to take pride in it, and even turned out with enthusiasm to watch parades and to see the Company off to Summer Camp. The editor of the Yiddish daily *Di Tsait* was prevailed upon to advertise the advantages which membership of the

EQUIPMENT QUERIES

28. 'Equipment Queries', a cartoon by Phineas May which appeared in *The Advance*, November–December 1932

29. Cartoons by Phineas May, dated 1932

Brigade bestowed, but in doing so felt obliged to emphasise that 'Di Yidishe Lads Brigade iz nisht kein a militerishe organizatsia'[12] and that by joining, youngsters would not be turned into soldiers. Phil Glickman from Manchester, for one, was not convinced. In 1927 he wrote to the *Jewish Chronicle*

> to protest against the existence of the Jewish Lads' Brigade Movement, with its ridiculous mimicry of the British Army. It is really a repetition of the pre-war militarist doctrine that Might is Right; and for Jews to band themselves together for the inculcation of such pernicious teaching into mere children is deplorable in the extreme.

Whilst this onslaught elicited an offical rejoinder from the Brigade, our confirmed pacifist was not to be persuaded:

> All this talk about 'the training of healthy and law-abiding citizens' by means of 'compulsory' drill is so much eye-wash. I have yet to learn that 'lessons of duty before self-interest, willing obedience,' etc., necessitate the wearing of khaki, shouldering rifles, and all the snobbery of difference in rank which are only a few of the 'compulsory features' of the Jewish Lads' Brigade. If this it not militarism I should like to know what is.[13]

In Liverpool, at least, if the local historian of that community is to be believed, a *modus vivendi* was reached. According to David Hudaly:

> In 1929 there was still a discernible demarcation between the 'English' Jews and the 'foreign' Jews in Liverpool. The latter entertained some suspicion about the Brigade, which, they thought, smacked of militarism. That outlook was dispelled in one stroke by a timely and sagacious move. It was the extending of an invitation, which he readily accepted, to the then Rav of Liverpool, Rabbi I.J. Unterman, to consecrate the new premises in Chatham Street [i.e. Harold House, see below]. He was a 'foreign' rabbi, who had then been in England for only six years and whose spiritual jurisdiction was not acknowledged by the Old Hebrew Congregation (Princes Road Synagogue), from which most of the officers and 'managers' were drawn.

> In his consecration address (which was reprinted) Rabbi Unterman warmly praised the aims of the Brigade and in consequence it received the support of all sections of the community.[14]

Sir Frederic Nathan retired, after 21 years as national Brigade Commandant, in 1926. Indeed, it is striking how the Brigade elicited such long-term loyalty from both officers and ranks. Ernest Halsted, who had been in it almost from the beginning, was unanimously elected his successor. He, in turn, remained Commandant until 1946 and continued to work closely with Ernest Joseph who was Quartermaster (a job in which he excelled) and Chief Staff Officer throughout this period. Indeed, for nine months in 1936–37, Joseph stood in as Acting Commandant whilst Halsted was in Australia. Like Halsted, Joseph's own involvement with youth work dated back to his association with both the JLB and the Brady Street Club in 1896. He was a founder of the Old Boys' Club in 1903 and played a key role in the Jewish Athletics Association from 1901. On its merger into the Association for Jewish Youth (AJY) in 1927 he served as treasurer and from 1943 as chairman of the Advisory Committee of the Jewish Youth Fund (1937), which was closely identified with the AJY. As an architect, Joseph was personally responsible, not only for the construction of Camperdown House, but for the headquarters of most of the Jewish youth clubs in the capital, and he was a generous and discreet contributor to their funds.[15]

The JLB connection with the Goldsmid family was maintained through the active involvement of Gladys, Lady Swaythling, for whom the honorary position of President was created in recognition of her assistance, especially on the fundraising side. On 6 June 1937 she made an appeal on the BBC on behalf of the Brigade. Her eldest son, Stuart, who became the third Lord Swaythling upon his father's death in 1927, was also recruited as a Trustee in 1935, whilst his sister Joyce Montagu was prominent on the Ball Committee. Lower down the social scale, plumber Emanuel J. Toff, who had joined the JLB at its very first meeting in 1895, was made a major and attended every single Summer Camp between the first in 1896 and 1939. Sergeant-Major Henry 'Harry' Berly was another long-serving officer who had risen from the ranks, as was Bandmaster H. Morris who served for over 40 years in Birmingham and Manchester. Indeed, sons followed fathers into the Brigade, not only in London but also in Manchester: Cansinos, Laskis, Mandlebergs, Finburghs and Frankenburgs were still active in the interwar period, whilst E.C.Q. Henriques was Commandant of the

Provincial Camp until 1945 with half a century of Brigade experience behind him. The founder of the Birmingham Company, Archie B. Solomon JP, was awarded a long service medal by the Cadet Forces in 1934 and no less than 19 out of the 81 Cadet long-service badges which were awarded in 1935 went to JLB officers. In Glasgow Benjamin Strump JP, managing director of a furnishing company, commanded the JLB from 1908 until the end of the Second World War and brought his two sons up in the Brigade tradition. In 1945 he was awarded the MBE for his services to the Volunteers and Cadet Force. His son Lieutenant-Colonel Reuben Strump went to Sandhurst, was commissioned in the Bengal Lancers and served with distinction in both 1914–18 and 1939–45; his grandson Major Rufus Strump served in the latter war, and a nephew Major Harold Freeman was the first Scottish Jew to win the Military Cross. Strump senior, as we have seen, was prominent in Jewish communal life in Glasgow. He was appointed to the local Aliens Appeals Tribunal which sat during the First World War. The loyalty of such families and their devotion to the welfare of Jewish youth was without question.

We have examined the 'ideology' of the JLB in some detail (Chapter 2) and will return to this theme shortly in Chapter 4. Nevertheless, we must not lose sight of the fact that most members, both officers and lads, unconsciously absorbed the values of the Brigade. Above all, the best officers were motivated by a strong sense of social purpose and a desire to be of service to the community. Moreover, that promotion from the ranks was possible, strongly indicated that the JLB did not blatantly subscribe to the rigid class differentiation so prevalent in the Christian youth movements. As already observed, Jews, as a comparatively socially mobile group outside the rigid structure of the English class system, had no real interest in its perpetuation. In the JLB, the distinction between officers and lads was strictly maintained, in accordance with military tradition, but this did not imply that the latter could not aspire to the status of the former. Boys were taught to obey command, so that they could one day assume command themselves. Young officers quickly learned the responsiblities of leadership. As Phineas May, the founder and Commanding Officer of the Brixton Company, put it after ten years experience in 1936: 'It is impossible to try to pretend to be what you are not with boys. They can rapidly read your character and will stand no humbug. With all the respect in the world, they will tell you exactly what they think of you, which is not always flattering, but invariably true.'[16]

Before the Second World War trained youth workers were unheard of. Officers in the Brigades, both Jewish and Gentile, were volunteers who, in the best English public school tradition, felt keenly the need to serve the community. They had to learn 'on the job'. In 1936 Manchester JLB decided to employ a paid organiser at the Grove House Club. There was a lot of opposition to this decision. Even so, Revd A. de Souza Pimontel, who was appointed Club Warden, may have been a clergyman and Brigade Chaplain, but was not specifically trained for the job.

In common with the other Brigades, the JLB strove to instil English public school values in its members, to mould them into good Englishmen. Anglicisation was the goal. But, it was seen as the key to helping young Jews 'get on' in society – and *not* to 'keeping them down'. By the 1930s, a number of former lads were now 'making good' and not only in the material sense. A market trader, S. Felcher, born in Petticoat Lane (Middlesex Street) in 1887, and who was promoted to the rank of Sergeant-Major in the JLB, was awarded the OBE for public service in 1936. Several Jewish musicians with popular dance bands had made their debut playing on JLB instruments, such as the trumpet player Jack Block, clarinetist Sydney Pyke and flutist Mickey Lewis. Manchester variety artist Joe Stein started out in the JLB, as did Issy Bonn who made a successful stage career for himself in Canada.

Within the ranks of the Brigade itself, by the inter-war period, a growing number of officers had risen through the ranks, in some cases, from humble origins. The master plumber Manny Toff was the prime example. Of course, the 'levelling' of the social classes, the blurring of the distinctions between 'West End' and 'East End', between 'old money' and 'new' in the Brigade, as in other Anglo-Jewish organisations, was a slow process, not to be completed until after the Second World War. Until then, the higher echelons of the Brigade remained the preserve of the Jewish establishment, if not exactly always of the 'aristocracy'.

Despite influential supporters, finance remained a constant

headache for the Brigade. The 1921 camp was curtailed to seven days for lack of money. A more or less permanent deficit – or 'debit balance' as the minute books liked euphemistically to term it – existed in the 1920s and 1930s, which reached nearly £4,000 in 1938. It was deemed prudent to 'interview' the bank manager (rather than vice versa!) on more than one occasion. Fundraising events, especially glittering balls, were notable dates in the social calendar for Anglo-Jewish Society. Often these had an inventive theme, such as the 'SS *Camperdown* Bazaar' in 1935 when the hall at Ernest Joseph's prestigious Shell-Mex House was decked out to look like a 1930s cruise liner. The previous year, a grand concert was held at the Queen's Hall at which the Spanish prima donna Conchita Supervia sang. She was the wife of Ben Rubenstein (having converted through the Liberal Synagogue), a member of the Brigade Council. Her tragic death in childbirth in 1936 was marked by notices in all the papers. In 1938 the Lord Mayor of London invited representatives of the Brigade to a Festival Dinner at the Mansion House 'as a gesture to the Jewish community'[17] where £7,000 was raised. In 1936 the Brigade together with the Association for Jewish Youth was awarded £1,000 by the King George V Silver Jubilee Trust.

The post-war JLB revival was steady. In 1925 there was an estimated national membership of nearly 2,000, some 600 accounted for by London in 1927. In 1919 there were 16 Companies in London; by 1938, 32. Manchester had six Companies in 1933 (Higher Broughton formed 1933), and some 400 lads by 1938. Birmingham and Glasgow remained in being, but Liverpool, as we have seen, had been suspended during the First World War. In June 1924 Ellis Yates took the initiative in reviving the Company and 60 boys were enrolled under the command of Brian M. Green. By the end of the 1920s this city boasted three Companies with a roll of about 100. Leeds was never resuscitated in the inter-war period, although attempts were made. This is surprising given Leeds' position as Anglo-Jewry's third city. Perhaps this state of affairs may simply be attributed to the absence of single-minded officers. However, whilst no direct evidence exists for the demise of the Leeds Company, it may be conjectured that it had something to do with the strong anti-war feeling in that city. Leeds had a strong tradition of radical political activism and was the setting for the June 1917 anti-war Socialist Convention – and for the anti-alien disturbances which accompanied it. Nor was anti-war feeling confined to the secular left. A group of eminent immigrant rabbis challenged a ruling made by the Chief Rabbi in 1916 that there were no specifically Jewish grounds for conscientious objection. Meanwhile, the English-born minister of the Princes Road Synagogue, Liverpool, Revd John Harris, championed the cause of a Jewish conscientious objector before a military tribunal. His stand cost him his job.[18]

Glasgow Company managed to carry on during wartime, despite the call-up of officers including Nathan Strump who, as we have seen, served with the Judeans in Palestine, Arthur M. Cohen and Leon L. Levy (killed in France in 1916). By 1919 the Company was drilling regularly at the Artillery Drill Hall in Butterbiggins Road on the South Side and they remained at this venue until the late 1930s. In 1922 Nathan Strump was instrumental in the formation of the Glasgow JLB pipe band, as mentioned, 'the only Jewish pipe band in the world' and for kitting out its members in the full regalia of kilt (McKenzie or Black Watch Infantry tartan), sporran and glengarry cap. Glasgow held their own weekend and short camps during and after the First World War at Beetlehill in Duntocher, near Ben Strump's country house, and afterwards on Sir Ian Colquhoun's estate at Rossdhu on the banks of Loch Lomond, and at Luss. In 1935 a party of Glasgow lads made the long train journey to London to participate in the King George V Jubilee Camp and, a year later, the grant from the newly created George V Jubilee Trust enabled the Brigade in Glasgow to acquire a Club Room at 81 Nicholson Street, G5.

The Sheffield Company was reformed independently of Headquarters in the summer of 1937 by a tailor, keen footballer and activist in AJEX, Dan Marks, and met at the Wilson Road Synagogue once a week. Joseph Newman JP, chairman of the building committee and subsequently president of the Sheffield Hebrew Congregation, became the Commanding Officer with a roll of about 50 boys. Indeed, the provincial Companies, with a combined membership of over 1,000 in the mid-1930s (Manchester around 500, Birmingham 300, Liverpool 150, Glasgow 100) were run almost entirely independently of London, hardly figuring in the deliberations of Headquarters. Much of their fundraising was done locally, although subsidies were provided from the centre, in particular for the annual Summer Camp.

In London the geographical distribution of JLB Companies began to change, reflecting wider social trends within the Jewish community. At the beginning of the period there were eight Companies in the East End, rising to 13 in 1926 – not the pre-war strength. By 1938, this total had dropped to nine and was matched by north London. Established areas of secondary Jewish settlement, such as Tottenham (1923), Hackney and Stamford Hill (combined 1920), Walthamstow (1921, combined with Leyton 1927), Highbury (1921), Dalston (1922), Stoke Newington (1934) and Finsbury Park (1933) boasted JLB Companies. West London also expanded in this period with Bayswater (restarted 1921), Westminster (restarted 1922), Baker Street (1923), Hammmersmith (1914), Richmond, Ealing (both 1923; Ealing merged with Hammersmith 1927) and Chelsea (1928). In 1928 a Company was also started in Soho, but Fulham (1927) was disbanded in 1935. In the south were Brixton (1926), Southwark (revived 1921), Victoria & Chelsea (1927), Putney (1927), New Cross (1932) and Woolwich (1933); Leytonstone (1937), Forest Gate (1923), South Essex (1924) in the north-east; and Brondesbury, Golders Green (1926), Hendon (1935) and Finchley (1936) in the north-west. Leo Phillips was instrumental in the formation of the latter three Companies. Towns as far flung as Becontree (1936), Portsmouth (1921, at Aria College) and Brighton (1933) had units. In 1922 the London Companies were reorganised into the 1st and 2nd Battalions, the former covering the East End and the latter all other districts. This spread reflected the increasing suburbanisation of the London Jewish community, and its upward social mobility. Although hardly perceptible as yet, the East End had passed its peak as the premier Jewish neighbourhood in the metropolis.

Indeed, by 1923 there was even talk of shutting down Camperdown House due to its underuse. The Brigade was conscious of the necessity of responding to changes in wider society. The 1924 Annual Report observed

> . . . there are still thousands of Jewish boys in London and the other cities of the Kingdom who are untouched by the influence of the Brigade or of any of the Boys' Clubs . . .

[The] problem has changed in many respects since the days before the war. The earnings of young boys are substantially higher than they were then, whilst the multiplication of cinema theatres and other forms of cheap amusement all form counter attractions (sometimes very undesirable ones) to the Brigade and the Clubs.[19]

Whilst attempts to take over the rival troops of Jewish Scouts largely failed,[20] the JLB did succeed in upgrading the youth club side of its activities. Joint membership of the Brigade and Hutchison House Club was encouraged, giving members the free run of Camperdown House. In 1934 the two organisations were finally merged, as was the JLB and the Grove House Lads' Club in Manchester. Indeed, for many years (since 1924) membership of Grove House was only obtainable via the Brigade. Admittance was only gained on presentation of a membership card duly stamped to prove each boy's attendance at the last drill. Such compulsory measures attested to the unpopularity of drill with Grove House members. Membership averaged about 400 throughout the 1930s but was frequently described as 'unstable'; the club experienced a frequent turnover of membership. By the mid-1930s Manchester Jewry was already in the process of northward suburbanisation. Nevertheless, plans to open a branch club at Sedgley, where there was a growing demand for youth activities, came to nothing.

From 1929 the JLB was represented on the Association for Jewish Youth and, in the same year, the link between the Brigade and other youth clubs was strengthened by the acquisition of the premises of the North London Club at 240a Amhurst Road, Stamford Hill on a generous lease. Harold M. Lion initiated the purchase and the vendor was Ben Rubenstein, himself an old JLB staff sergeant. Sir Max Bonn put up a considerable part of the money needed. Amhurst Road became a focus for youth activity in the 1930s, as home not only to the 2nd Battalion of the JLB with 400 members in 1935, but also to the North London Jewish Girls' Club, which had been founded in December 1912 under the presidency of Otto Schiff, and was remodelled in the image of the Brigade in 1929 under the indefatigable leadership of Miss Isobel Aarons. The girls, numbering about 200 in 1935, began annual summer camps at Deal and mixed social events were organised at which the boys and girls could meet. Amhurst Road also boasted its own Brigade Old Boys' Club.

In Manchester, the Grove House Lads' Club was rebuilt on a new site in Hightown in 1924 for a cost of £12,000 and was extended in 1929 and again in 1936 with the addition of the Isaac Cansino wing. This constant building work pushed the Brigade into debt, to the tune of £3,000 throughout the 1930s. A Manchester Old Comrades' Association was formed in 1937 with a membership of about 200. At about the same time (i.e., 1925) in Liverpool a new clubhouse at 248 Upper Parliament Street was provided through the generosity of Harold L. Cohen, the chairman of Lewis's Department Stores of Liverpool.[21] In 1929 Harold Cohen paid for the construction of a purpose-built Headquarters at Chatham Street at a cost of £10,000. Despite the fact that club membership was dependent upon boys joining the JLB, the new Harold House became a focus not only for the 150 members of the JLB but for Jewish youth in Liverpool, with sports facilities and its own cinema. Alan Alfred Isaac succeeded Brian Green as Commanding Officer in September 1928 and remained in this capacity until the outbreak of the Second World War. Like Ellis Yates, Isaac was descended from an old Liverpool Jewish family. He was born in Sefton Park and educated in Liverpool and at Clifton College, Bristol where his uncle, Revd Joseph Polack, a former minister of the Princes Road Synagogue, was his housemaster. However, Isaac left school at 16, saw active service on the Western Front during the First World War and went into the Liverpool cotton market. Through social contact with Brian Green, who had known him at Clifton, and with Edward D. Kamm who was himself a nephew of the Yates brothers, Isaac became an officer on the re-formation of the Brigade in 1924.[22] In 1931 a Liverpool Old Comrades' Association was started.

In 1935 the Birmingham JLB moved from the Thorpe Street Barracks to a purpose-built clubhouse adjoining the Birmingham Jewish Schools in St Luke's Road and shared the premises with the local Jewish Boys' and Girls' Club which had a membership of over 300.

In London, Camperdown House played an increasingly broad social role in the life of East End Jewry. A Junior Company for the 11–13 age group was formed at Headquarters from boys at JFS in 1929, and provision made for the juniors to attend camp. In 1931 a playgroup was instituted for small children under the watchful eye of a band of stalwart women led by Ernest Halsted's wife, Hannah.

Ernest Joseph drew up ambitious plans to turn the roof of Camper-down House into a garden for the children, with the help of a grant from the National Fitness Centre, but this project had to be abandoned on the outbreak of war. Social events were held where officers could meet the – mostly single – manageresses of the playgroup, and of the North London Girls' Club and other clubs for girls. Joseph was also instrumental in finally getting the Old Comrades' Association off the ground in 1929 (started 1927), primarily as an agency for fundraising, given that 'a large number of old Brigade boys had achieved material prosperity'.[23] However, it remained largely inactive until the 1930s. In 1934 it had some 300 members. This Association was distinct from the JLB Old Boys' Club which had been founded on the eve of the First World War, most of whose members had joined the forces. In 1919 it was revived as a separate entity under the title of the *Hagadol* Social Club which continued to meet at the Jewish Institute in Aldgate. Dr E. Bernstein, an ex-officer of the Brigade, was appointed warden of the Institute and headmaster of JFS. In 1939 it was reported that a total of 350 actual members of the JLB plus 50 boys of the 39th Stepney [Jewish] Scout Troop used the facilities of Camperdown House on a regular basis.

In 1932 the *Jewish Chronicle* reported that

> The members of the Camperdown Lodge of Freemasons, mainly composed of ex-members of the Jewish Lads' Brigade, are frequent visitors to Camperdown House, and are actively assisting in all branches of the Brigade work. It is the intention of the members of the Lodge to give a Purim treat to all members of the Play Centre.[24]

The Brigade's house magazine *The Advance* likewise reported that

> His Royal Highness the Duke of Connaught has been graciously pleased to confer upon the Chaplain of the [Camperdown Masonic] Lodge, the Rev. Isaac Goldston, A.K.C., the position of Past Assistant Grand Chaplain of England. This is the first time in the history of English Freemasonry that a Jewish Minister has been promoted to such a position. Members of the Montefiore Lodge, in which the Rev. Goldstone [sic] was first admitted into Freemasonry, and Camperdown Lodge, in which he materially assisted as a Founder, presented the 'Grand Lodge Regalia' as a mark of esteem.[25]

As is the nature of these things, little other information on the Masonic links, which undoubtedly existed and do so today, of Brigade officers and old boys has come to light. I have been informed that the current lodge connected with the Brigade is called the Halcyon Lodge. This lodge was apparently formed in 1910 by Ernest Hallenstein mainly, but not exclusively, for the benefit of Brigade officers. Today, the Halcyon Lodge is still thriving but, apart from the present Commandant, contains only one other Brigade officer.

Whilst both the JLB and the clubs faced challenges from the changing nature of Jewish society in the inter-war period, there is evidence that tension existed amongst the youth organisations on account of their differing approaches to youth work. Relations between the JLB and the umbrella body, the Association for Jewish Youth, were not always cordial. When, in 1936, it was proposed to hold a debate at the Annual Conference of the AJY on the subject 'This House believes that the Club is Better than the Brigade', the idea was rejected by Ernest Joseph who 'felt strongly that it was treading on dangerous ground and raising a contentious matter'. Many senior club managers, it seemed, 'were openly anti-Brigade'. By 1938 the shortage of JLB officers had become acute and those there were were 'overworked': 'It was urgently necessary to obtain a new officer at the rate of one per week for the next year.'[26]

A broader curriculum of sports was introduced, both indoor and outdoor, including gymnastics, badminton, tennis, cross-country running, judo and boxing. The JLB excelled at the latter, walking away with the prestigious Prince of Wales shield 12 times between 1921 and 1939. In 1926, 1927, 1928, 1934, 1936 and 1937 an all-Brigade final was held for this trophy between London and Manchester. In 1921 and again in 1926 and 1934 the London winners were invited to St James' Palace to receive their award from the Prince (the future Edward VIII) in person. The Prince also honoured the Brigade with a visit to Camperdown House in 1921. In 1933 the Manchester champions were presented with the shield by the Duke of Gloucester. Boxing, however, was regarded as strictly for fun. The Brigade refused to associate itself with professionals in the sport, even if some of them were Jews, such as Kid Berg – not a respectable calling for its members. Nevertheless, at least one boy JLB boxing champion, Nat Seller, himself went on to become a prominent trainer for

England. Captain I. Pressman, long-time member and trainer of the winning Manchester team, was a licensed boxing promoter under the Boxing Board of Control, but acted only at charity matches. Harry Lazar, also ex-JLB, was a popular Jewish boxer in East London before and during the Second World War.

The Birmingham Company's forte was table tennis. One of their members, S. Proffit, was ranked second in the national seedings in 1935. Several Manchester JLB members, Cromwell and Laurie and Gus Rich, were also international table tennis players.

After 1929 the Annual Brigade Sports Day was held at Wembley Stadium. The JLB also participated in outside competitions with other Brigades and Cadet units, notably for the trophies presented by the Lucas-Tooth Physical Training Institute in Bermondsey which specialised in the training of PT instructors for the youth organisations. In 1934 the Earl of Athlone Badge, the highest award offered each year by the Institute for best individual work, was won by S. Chernitsky of the JLB and was presented to him by Princess Alice, Countess of Athlone. For three years in succession (1935–37) the 1st Manchester Battalion won the General Nation Cup for the best organised Cadet unit in the country.

The Brigade Employment Bureau was restarted at Camperdown House in 1922 and was to be stretched to the limit during the Great Depression. JLB Headquarters in Manchester and Liverpool also kept registers of boys seeking employment and took steps, not without success, to place them. Grove House Lads' Club ran evening classes for the unemployed 'in tailors' cutting, shorthand, shoe repairing' which 'prosper[ed] exceedingly' although 'courses in English and Hebrew had to be dropped for want of support'. In September 1934 Manchester officers were informed that the JLB Employment Bureau had found work for nine boys. In 1932 *The Times* reported the existence of a physical training centre for the unemployed at Camperdown House – the only one of its kind anywhere in London. Nominally under the Ministry of Labour, the classes were actually funded by an anonymous donor (probably Sir Max Bonn) and used the excellent facilities provided by the JLB. Some 500 unemployed men had attended voluntarily for physical training during the six weeks the centre had been in operation, and were 'provided with a hot midday meal'.[27]

Hardship was not uncommon amongst Brigade boys during the years of the Great Depression. Company Officers were expected to make discreet inquiries about the economic circumstances of lads, to the extent of visiting their homes and interviewing the parents. As late as 1938, '40 per cent of the [Manchester] battalion applied to the assessment committee'[28] for financial assistance towards camp costs.

The JLB also contributed towards the dental scheme set up by the AJY in 1928 to provide free treatment for club members after they left school and before they were eligible for state insurance. A grant of £100 from the Carnegie Trust enabled the Brigade to start a library in 1927. Brigade journals entitled *The Reveille* and *The Advance*, edited by B.M. Woolf and Phineas May, were published between 1922 and 1927 and 1931–35. These succeeded the pre-war monthly (December 1913–July 1914, revived in 1919) *The Brigade Bulletin*, no copies of which have survived in the archives. Brigade magazines and newsletters were published from time to time by individual Companies (e.g., Woolwich's *Pro Bono* 1937) and outside London. The Liverpool Company magazine was entitled *Carry On!* in 1936. Indeed, from the late 1920s a broader programme of cultural activities was introduced. Camperdown House boasted an orchestra, choral society, musical appreciation, literature, art and scientific societies to appeal to the 'brain' as well as the 'brawn' of the lads.

The annual Summer Camp, however, remained the focus of Brigade activity. In 1919 the London Regiment returned to its old camping ground at Deal and the Provincial Companies to Penrhyn, near Llandudno, with a record turnout of 560 all ranks. From 1920 to 1922 however, the London Camp was held at Felpham, near Bognor on the south coast. The 1921 and 1922 Provincial Camps were held at St Annes, near Blackpool. In 1923 the former site at Deal was reverted to. In 1924 London moved to Birchington-on-Sea where they remained until 1933 when they finally settled on Kingsdown, Walmer, near the old ground at Deal, and went back there every summer until the outbreak of the Second World War. The provinces gravitated between Lytham St Annes, Lancashire (1924, 1926, 1929, 1931, 1932, 1934, 1936), Bridlington, Yorkshire (1935, 1937) and North Wales (Deganwy, Llandudno 1923, 1925, 1927, 1928; Rhyl 1933; Penrhyn 1930, 1938, 1939). From 1925 onwards, a Liverpool contingent joined the London campers, rather than their northern counterparts. A group of boys from the Norwood Orphanage with their own band were still frequently to be seen at Walmer. In 1931 the Glasgow Company held a separate camp at Luss, Loch Lomond. In 1927 it was reported that 1,268 all ranks were present at the Birchington camp, exactly twice the number in 1914.[29] A further 400 were encamped at Deganwy. Over 1,000 boys were regularly taken to Walmer each summer during the 1930s and were inspected and entertained by Lord Reading, Lord Warden of the Cinque Ports, at Walmer Castle on several occasions before his death in 1936.

From the late 1920s the JLB entered the market to provide week-end camping, an activity promoted by the AJY and other clubs. Camps were held at Whitsun for NCOs on Charles Joseph's (Ernest's brother) estate at St Mary's Cray and later at Epping, where a permanent campsite was leased in the late 1930s. Discipline at these weekend camps was 'not as rigid' as at the main Summer Camp. Some 500 boys benefited in 1937. Individual Companies, in London and the provinces, began to hold their own weekend camps to cater for boys who now had more leisure time on their hands, staying on at school longer or attending day-release classes rather than having their evenings taken up with after-work further education. From 1931–34 inclusive, the Brigade held two successive Summer Camps at Birchington, 10 days for the seniors and seven days for the juniors. In 1935 an additional special camp was held at Kingston to mark King George V's Silver Jubilee. It was attended by representative boys from all over the country and was inspected by Field Marshal Viscount Allenby, the conquerer of Palestine during the First World War. In 1938 the Glasgow Company organised a semi-permanent camp for the summer and invited the other provincial Companies to avail themselves of its facilities whilst they visited the Empire Exhibition being held in the city. In that year London boys were charged 35/– per head for Summer Camp and 2/6d for week-end camps.

The deteriorating international situation with the rise of Nazism in Europe, and its disturbing implications for Jews in particular, made itself felt on the JLB. In 1935 they were invited by the King George V Jubilee Trust 'to nominate two representatives to join a party of 30 delegates, all representing English Youth, to go to Berlin in July [1936] to witness the Olympic Games as the guests of the German Olympic Committee'.[30]

To accede to this request was 'impossible . . . for obvious reasons'. Instead, in July 1936, the JLB hosted, for the first time, a contingent of 50 German Jewish refugee children at the Walmer camp. The cost was defrayed by an anonymous donor. At the 1938 camp 20 refugees were accommodated at the request of the AJY and in 1939 50 more joined in the Provincial Camp at Penrhyn. Following an approach from Rabbi Dr Solomon Schonfeld, the JLB secretary Jonas May, together with Motel Robins and Jack Wagman, fetched blankets from the campsite at Deal for use by refugees being housed at Avigdor House in Stamford Hill. Others were sheltered temporarily at Camperdown House until private families were found to take them in.[31] In February 1939 the *Daily Express* reported that 54 refugee children from the German–Polish frontier had been rescued through the efforts of Elsley Zeitlyn and George Lansbury MP, and were being equipped with 'warm woollies' for their stay at Camperdown House. Likewise, 15 young refugees were accommodated at the Elizabeth Street JLB Headquarters in Manchester, and about 30 joined in JLB drill on a regular basis. Refugees participated in the popular evening classes at Grove House and special English classes were provided on Sunday mornings.

In the wake of *Kristallnacht*, the 'Night of Broken Glass' when synagogues were burnt throughout Germany (9–10 November 1938), the JLB minutes recorded the Council's 'deep regret at the new tragedy which had befallen their co-religionists in Germany . . .'[32] This sentiment was soon translated into concrete action.

In March 1939 the Anglo-American Council for German Jewry, which had been set up in 1936 to raise funds for the resettlement of refugees, requested the help of the JLB 'in organising, staffing and running of the Kitchener Camp at Richborough'.[33] Ernest Joseph, in fact, was the instigator of this scheme. The plight of the young refugees was brought to his attention through the friendship of his son, Stephen, with Walter H. Marmorek. They had both studied architecture, but Marmorek had had to flee from Vienna, where his brother had been arrested and interned (temporarily as it turned out) at Dachau. On behalf of the Council for German Jewry, EMJ arranged to lease part of the vast site of the disused former First

World War army camp at Richborough from its new owners Pearson Dorman Long Steel, and proposed to convert it to accommodate up to 3,500 young men (between the ages of 18 and 40) who had fled Nazi persecution in Germany, Austria, Czechoslovakia and other parts of Europe. Ernest Joseph formed a Kitchener Camp Committee which included Sir Robert Waley-Cohen, Professor Norman Bentwich, Harry Sacher and Frank Samuel, a fellow Brigade man, and persuaded the Home Office to admit refugees on a block permit, on condition that they would neither find employment in England, nor become a public charge, and seek eventual re-emigration elsewhere. EMJ conceived the idea of getting the refugees themselves to fit up the camp, 'both for reasons of economy and to maintain morale' amongst men who had gone through the trauma of separation from their families. He used his architects' training to plan the renovation of the camp and organised an advance party of 100 skilled refugee craftsmen to begin the work. By July 1938 the reinstated camp boasted its full complement of 3,500, mostly Jewish refugees, but also including a number of 'non-Aryan' (i.e., *mischling*) Christians who had fled from Nazi Europe. The inmates included amongst their number the 'cream' of the central European Jewish intelligentsia: some 80 doctors, lawyers, university professors, scientists and musicians, as well as youngsters who had not yet had the chance to receive any training. The camp, which was run on collectivist lines, buzzed with educational and cultural activity – not to mention with ideological debate and the inevitable conflicts which arose between men from such disparate backgrounds. A 'Camp University' taught a wide range of courses, English, Hebrew and Spanish, and practical skills such as building, typing, photography and watchmending. The camp produced its own monthly journal *The Kitchener Camp Review*,[34] boasted a library, a cinema provided by Oscar Deutch of the Odeon chain, and an orchestra, directed by the former conductor of the radio orchestra in Stuttgart, a dance band, string quartet and a choir. Entertainments put on by residents of the camp were much in demand during the summer of 1939 throughout the county of Kent.

The efficient organisation at Richborough no doubt owed a great deal to Joseph's years of experience with the JLB and its Summer Camp. The JLB's secretary Jonas May was lent to the Kitchener

Camp in the capacity of Director for the duration of its existence. The Brigade paid his salary with another £300 per annum upkeep for himself and his wife and baby son at Richborough, provided by the Central Council for German Jewry. Jonas' brother, the cartoonist Phineas May,[35] who was also an officer in the Brigade, joined them in Kent, becoming Welfare and Entertainment Officer and editor of the *Review*. So, too, did the London Regimental Sergeant-Major Mick Banks (formerly known as Levy). Nineteen young members of the Richborough Camp attended the JLB Summer Camp in August 1939 and many other refugees paid a visit. The Brigade loaned its camp synagogue for use by the Richborough refugees. The resident camp 'padre' was Reform Rabbi Dr Werner van der Zyl, who was himself a refugee.

The Richborough camp was the only converted army camp used to house refugees set up in Britain on the eve of the Second World War. It lasted for 18 months. Many of its members managed to bring out their families in time and some succeeded in emigrating to the British Colonies, or to Palestine, or America. In July 1939, 50 refugees from the steamship *St Louis* arrived at the camp and they were followed by the 100-odd pupils and staff of the ORT Berlin Technical School in November. On the outbreak of war in 1939, those who remained at Richborough became 'enemy aliens' and were threatened with internment. Aliens Tribunals sat but eventually it was decided to draft the refugees into the Royal Pioneer Corps, a non-combative military auxiliary force, soon nicknamed the 'King's Own Enemy Aliens' by its members. For a brief period, the Kitchener Camp became the first training ground for the Pioneers, under the command of Lord Reading. With the threat of invasion in 1940, the camp was hastily evacuated and JLB involvement came to an end. The remaining civilian population was interned at Ramsay on the Isle of Man and a substantial number of men were deported from there on the notorious SS *Dunera*. The Pioneers, on the other hand, eventually saw frontline service in France in 1940.

Norman Bentwich estimated that 5,000 men passed through the Kitchener Camp in 1939–40 and that up to 15,000 men, women and children were rescued from the Nazis owing to its existence. The crucial role played by Ernest Joseph and the JLB in this enterprise has, until now, not been fully acknowledged.

For the JLB itself, the approach of war in 1939 posed the same sort of dilemma as it had in 1914. Should the Brigade mobilise as a feeder for the British Army? During the inter-war period the relationship with the Territorials had been maintained, despite the partial abandonment of khaki and, indeed, despite the vagaries of Government policy. In 1930 the second Labour Government withdrew its recognition of Cadet units – and the War Office subsidy which went with it. The JLB, represented by Colonel H.L. Nathan (retd), MP, joined a delegation of the Christian Brigades to protest. A compromise was worked out whereby the Brigades formed themselves into a voluntary association: the British National Cadet Association (BNCA). The JLB affiliated to this body, which secured recognition from the Government. However, it took some time before the Cadet grant was reinstated. Once again, this provoked debate within the JLB as to the desirability of accepting War Office funding. Manchester had little compunction and had reaffiliated to the 8th Battalion Lancaster Fusiliers in 1932. One by one the other Provincial Battalions transformed themselves into Cadet units. Glasgow, in particular, became affiliated to the 7th Battalion, the Cameronians (Scottish Rifles), a volunteer force with a long tradition. Liverpool and London held out against such a move. In London, Ernest Joseph, for one, was in favour of militarisation. The ideological arguments were more clear cut than before 1914. He 'felt that in view of the present [political] position, and the necessity for Jews to indicate their willingness to participate in the requirements of the Government, the Brigade should enter the [Cadet] scheme wholeheartedly'.

B.M. Woolf, a member of the Brigade Council and a former secretary of the JLB, was not so sure, given that acceptance of the Cadet grant would most likely imply affiliation to a Territorial unit. He was of the opinion that 'the Brigade should not get more military than at present'. After all 'they should take the long view that the present difficulties were not likely to last for any length of time . . .', and besides 'other cadet units had scuttled out of the Association' (i.e., the Boys' Brigade).

Woolf was in a minority. Joseph, strongly backed up by Lady Swaythling, disagreed. He expressed grave concern at the lack of citizenship in evidence amongst the boys and their parents . . . it was time that the Brigade should come into the open and give every encouragement to its members to join the citizen army. The Brigade's actual task was to make its members loyal and efficient citizens but that the Territorial Association must do the actual recruiting. Those who held strong pascifist [sic] views should part company with the Brigade.[36]

In December 1937 the link between the London JLB and the 8th Battalion Royal Fusiliers which had existed between 1915 and 1930 was restored. £200 per annum was made available from Government funds. However, with Europe rapidly sliding towards war, in April 1938 the War Office hastily set up a committee to consider upgrading the role of the Cadet Force 'as a third line of defence'. The committee recommended that the Territorials be given powers over the operation of the Brigades, that miniature rifles be issued and grants be made as an incentive for the recruitment of both officers and lads into the TA or His Majesty's Forces proper. Co-operation would be repaid by a subsidy of £1,200 for Headquarters administration.

At this stage, the JLB balked. Halsted asserted that the adoption of the scheme 'would militarise the Brigade in a manner which was never intended by those who founded it'. Sir Max Bonn felt 'that it could not be right to make soldiers of youngsters from 12 years of age', and Charles Magnus agreed that the scheme 'would have fatal results'. On the other hand, fears were raised by Lord Swaythling about the bad publicity which could ensue were the *Jews* seen to be shirking their public duty. As ever, the JLB was concerned about its public image and conscious of its role of combating anti-Semitism, a menace which had returned with a vengeance in the 1930s, not only abroad but at home in the guise of Mosley's Blackshirts. As in 1914, so too in the late 1930s, the JLB was worried about the adverse effects of 'militarism' on the recruitment of both officers and lads and upon parents and subscribers. The Headquarters Committee was inclined to withdraw from the BNCA (it is perhaps significant that Ernest Joseph was absent from most of the meetings at which the matter was discussed) but decided that the issue was one for the Jewish communal leadership to address, and referred it to the Rothschilds. Little sympathy for the Brigade's predicament was forthcoming from

New Court however, where 'the feeling was expressed . . . that the Brigade ought to support the [BNC] Association as far as possible, unless the effect on the Brigade would be virtually to smash it'.

In the end, Charles Magnus came up with a compromise. The JLB should affiliate with the BNCA and accept TA interference, on condition that the latter agree to Civil Defence work in the form of Air Raid Precautions (ARP) rather than military training by the Brigade. A programme of training in ARP for JLB officers at Camperdown House was devised in the first instance, with a view to the eventual allocation of officers and seniors to Local Authorities in London and the regions, to disseminate their skills amongst the public at large. ARP lectures were organised at Manchester, Glasgow and Liverpool.

On 26 April 1939 the Government announced the introduction of compulsory military training for men between the ages of 18 and 35. In his capacity as Chief Staff Officer, Magnus lectured Warrant Officers and Sergeants on what he considered to be their clear duty – 'definitely and without qualification' – to volunteer for the TA. Moreover, he asserted, 'if the Brigade suffers a set-back or even goes smash because everyone between the ages of 18 and 35 are in the Territorials, then no one would be more proud than I to tell the world the reason'.[37]

'Doing their duty' was still the Brigade's watchword. Anticipating the Government announcement, Manchester JLB commissioned a recruiting poster to display outside their premises. It is curiously striking how overtly unideological was the debate. It did not appear to be a question of the Jews fighting Hitler as the ultimate threat to their survival as a group. British Jews should merely join up as a public expression of gratitude to Britain, the country 'in which [they] were] fortunate to be free'. Apparently, attitudes had changed little since the First World War.

THE SECOND WORLD WAR, 1939–45

As in 1914–18, the war years 1939–45 severely dislocated JLB activities. Officers, Warrant Officers, NCOs and senior boys joined all of the services, Army, Navy and Air Force, and Civil Defence, and were to be found serving the Empire 'from Iceland to India'. In April 1940 the press reported that there were '87 Officers, Warrant Officers, and N.C.O.s and over 220 lads of the Jewish Lads' Brigade now giving service in the Army or in civilian defence units'. At the same time, 'The first Brigade casualty was reported. Driver Sidney Ratchkind R.A.S.C. (Glasgow Coy)' in France.[38] He was to be followed by many others. At the beginning of the war the *Jewish Chronicle* carried a weekly feature on 'Jews in the Army' with photographs of young Jewish men – and women – who had volunteered for all the Services. Before long it turned into a Roll of Honour, and lists of wounded and missing servicemen and prisoners of war.

All told some 60,000 Jewish men and women, out of an estimated Anglo-Jewish community of 400,000, saw active service in the British Armed Forces in the Second World War. Of these some 14,000 were in the Royal Air Force and 1,500 in the Royal Navy. These figures represent over three per cent of the community, a proportion roughly equal to that of the British population as a whole serving in the forces. They exclude, nevertheless, the 4,000 so-called 'enemy aliens' who formed the Pioneer Corps (1,500 of whom, as we have seen, volunteered at the Richborough refugee camp), the 5,000 who served in the Jewish Brigade from 1944 onwards, a further 30–35,000 Palestinian Jews who served in the Middle East and many others in the Dominion forces. Of the British Jews, it has recently been calculated that at least 2,010 lost their lives.[39]

It is not possible to determine with any real degree of accuracy the numbers of officers and lads of the JLB who served or died in the Second World War. No attempt was made to erect a permanent memorial, as had been the case at the end of the Great War a quarter of a century earlier, at Camperdown House. A handful of names of ex-Brigade members who made the 'supreme sacrifice' may be gleaned from the columns of the *Jewish Chronicle*. Motel Robins, the Brigade Archivist, compiled an incomplete list in the 1970s or 1980s. It shows a total of 44 killed, including 16 pilots in the RAF, and about 180 who served and returned. Of the latter, two, Cyril Goodman and David Spector, served in the Jewish Brigade. Whilst Allan Burke (born Abie Burkovits) of the Manchester JLB, served in the Royal Navy in four separate battleships, rising to the rank of Lieutenant-Commander and Commanding Officer HMS *Damsay*.

He saw action in the Battle of the Atlantic and during the D-Day landings. In 1948 although he 'had never belonged to a Zionist society', Burke volunteered to fight in the Israeli War of Independence. His maritime experience being a rarity and although technically still a 'foreigner' Burke was put in command of an Israeli flotilla which took part in the blockade and bombardment of Gaza, El Arish and Rafa: he subsequently became Chief of Naval Operations and Inspector-General of the Israeli Navy. He was responsible for safely bringing in what became the Israeli Navy's first major warship in an operation clothed in secrecy in 1949.[40]

Casualties sustained by the JLB in the Second World War included Lance-Bombardier Edward Lazarus Levy of the Royal Artillery who was killed in action in Libya in January 1943. Before the war he had been a Lieutenant in the Liverpool JLB as well as a *cheder* teacher at the Princes Road Synagogue. Sergeant Pilot Simon Hirsch of the RAF was 'Previously reported Missing, now believed Killed' in October 1943. He 'had flown over Europe on more than 30 major operations and many minor ones' and was buried in Holland. Originally from Cheetham in Manchester, he was a former Quartermaster Sergeant in the JLB. He left a wife and 18-month-old son.[41]

Whether or not membership of the JLB instilled especial bravery into Jewish lads who joined the services during the Second World War cannot be proven. After all, there are many instances of courageous acts by soldiers who had never been members of any youth organisation. On the other hand, a great deal of testimony supports the view that JLB training did much to equip Jewish boys for the army and to minimise the 'culture shock' frequently experienced by conscripts. To take but one example, David Spector writes:

> Certainly service in the Jewish Lads' Brigade both in the ranks and as an officer was of great help in my subsequent army service. In the JLB I learnt how to manage groups and their welfare and gained general administrative experience at the large summer camps where I acted as Regimental Clerk to the Adjutant. On enlistment I was posted to a new unit in process of formation and within three months had risen to the rank of Sergeant and in charge of the Orderly Room . . . . I was posted yet again as a 2nd Lt. to a new unit and within the year promoted to Battery Operations Captain. Fortunately I did not experience any antisemitism or trouble from my ordinary ranks and it was the spirit of the welfare of the soldiers imbued to me by the JLB that helped.[42]

Ex-JLB officers and lads were rapidly promoted and were awarded gallantry medals in all fields of operation. Again, it is difficult to compute the exact proportion of the nearly 1,000 honours bestowed on British Jews who served in the forces which went to graduates of the JLB. However, the record of Gorbals-born Merchant Navy Junior Ship Engineer Henry Sless was probably unique. He was honoured twice within six months for bravery at sea in 1942–43, earning both the DSC and the MBE. His ship was subjected to heavy air attacks whilst at anchor. His citation reads:

> The ship was hit and fire broke out. The magazine was a mass of flames, and five men were killed. Throughout the attack, Mr Sless remained at his post in the engine-room, and when the magazine was hit, the third engineer officer joined him to help him in speeding up the fire pumps and shutting off steam from the burst pipes.
>
> On the voyage home, which took six weeks, the ship was continually attacked by the enemy.

Twenty-four-year-old Sless was already a veteran. He received his first medal for gallantry for his part in bringing the tanker *Ohio* safely into port at Malta 'in the face of heavy attacks [on the convoy] by day and night from enemy aircraft, submarines, and surface vessels'. On receiving his MBE, Sless told the *Jewish Chronicle*: 'In the Merchant Navy one is always ready to tackle any job, and sticking to duty during dive-bombing is all in the day's work.'

Sless was a former member of both the Jewish Scouts and the JLB in Glasgow.[43]

No less brave were those who manned the Home Front, in the Home Guard, Auxiliary Fire Service and other branches of Civil Defence. One such was 17-year-old David Lazarus from Whitechapel, a former pupil of JFS, who was awarded the George Medal in 1941. According to press reports he

> was on his way to duty during an air raid, when he heard the crash of a bomb that struck an East End block of flats, followed by the cries of trapped and wounded people. Immediately he rushed to the building and began, unaided and with his bare hands, the work of rescuing the injured. He had succeeded in dragging four people from the ruins, and was continuing his work amidst the bursting bombs, when a high wall suddenly collapsed, burying him beneath tons of debris.[44]

Young Lazarus was himself very badly injured but happily recovered after three months in hospital and was able to collect his honour.

Sidney Hart (Hartz), who was a member of the JLB between 1926 and 1939, first in the JFS Company and subsequently as a Warrant Officer in the Gravel Lane, East London Company, joined the Auxiliary Fire Service in May 1939, several months before the outbreak of war. He later recalled that 'Although there were many Jewish people in the A.F.S., there were exceedingly few Jewish professionals'. He decided that 'a Fireman's life was the life for me' and trained to become a full-time fireman. Soon his skills were in demand: 'Of course we had a warm time during the Blitz. I was wounded on the night of 9 January 1941, the night of the Bank and Liverpool Street Station disasters, and was put out of action until March, but was back on full duty in time for the last big air raid on May 10 1941.' By the time he retired after 30 years service Hart had 'worked through the ranks to become a Station Officer' and was probably 'the highest-ranking Jew to have served as a professional fireman'.[45]

As in the Great War, the links between the JLB and the Cadet Force at home were consolidated. The affiliation, under the Army Cadet Force regulations (1941) of the London Battalion, with Lieutenant-Colonel Charles L. Magnus as Commanding Officer, to the Royal Fusiliers (2nd Cadet Battalion) and of the Provincial Companies to their own local Volunteer regiments, underlined the JLB commitment to pre-service training: 12 to 15-year-olds were enrolled in the Brigade and seniors (16–18) encouraged to join the Cadets. In July 1940 it was reported that 'a large number of lads' had joined the Local Defence Volunteers in Stepney, who were then based at Camperdown House.[46] Battle-dress uniform was issued and wartime camps supplied from Ordnance. The War Office grant was awarded on a per capita basis for the number of officers and lads who passed Cadet proficiency examinations. At the end of 1941 the JLB co-operated closely with the AJY in a scheme initiated by the latter's secretary David Mellows to form Cadet units at six Jewish youth clubs under the AJY umbrella in London. These were: Hackney, Stepney, JFS, Victoria, West Central, and the Tower (which subsequently closed). Oxford & St George's had formed its own Cadet unit independently. As his last act for the JLB before his death in April 1943, with 50 years of youth work behind him, Sir Max Bonn undertook delicate negotiations with the War Office and Air Ministry to secure official recognition for the Brigade as the national organisation representing Jewish Cadets and to encourage, as far as possible, the enrolment of Jewish boys in JLB units, securing an enhanced War Office grant in the process. In January 1944 the following directive was laid down: 'The War Office recognises the JLB as a body representing units with a predominantly Jewish membership and is ready to consult with it on all matters in which the JLB might be specially interested, excluding training and organization.'[47] This official recognition encouraged the JLB to appoint Company Chaplains, a practice which had largely lapsed during the war, and Revd Arthur Barnett became Brigade Chaplain in 1945.[48]

The Air Ministry did not follow the War Office lead. This is perhaps surprising given the keen part played by JLB members in the Air Training Corps Scheme for boys aged 16–18 announced in January 1941. Stamford Hill and North London JLB Boys' Clubs 'immediately took the initiative' and started to form their own squadrons. The Hackney Jewish Boys' Club likewise attempted to form a Flight. These volunteers were drafted into the non-denominational No.1020 (2nd Hackney) Squadron on its formation by Flight Lieutenant Algernon Lawrence 'Laurie' Abraham, latterly of the Brigade, and the premises of the North London Club in Amhurst Road were given over to its activities. A second squadron was started in North East London under Flight Lieutenant S. Hyman, another former Brigade officer. Both squadrons had 'a predominantly Jewish membership' and many of their graduates joined the RAF, some serving with distinction.[49]

On the JLB Home Front, London Headquarters was manned throughout the war by the two Ernests, as it had been in 1914–18. They were ably assisted by a small band of stalwarts, including Sir Max Bonn until his sudden death in April 1943, Lord Swaythling, Charles Magnus and the secretaries, Miss Marcus (1940–41) and L.J. Solomon. On top of the loss of personnel to the army, came the mass evacuation, of children especially, from the capital and the start of the Blitz. In October 1939 Camperdown House was requisitioned for use by the LCC Auxiliary Fire Brigade. The 1,200 books belonging to the JLB Library were the first casualties of this change of occupancy. Motel Robins (I.M. Rubenstein) who was in charge of what 'was the largest [library] of its kind within Jewish Youth Club Circles' recalled many years later:

> When hostilities ceased in 1945 . . . both the Library and its complete contents were found to be missing. Eventually, I discovered that the 'National Fire Service' which had taken over our building during the Was [sic] had put these [books] in store in the basement . . . because of a 'fire risk'? They were later found to be severely sodden due to dampnessi [sic] in the basement areas and eventually 'used' as a source of heating up the building. They were all burnt. This information was given to me by an Ex member of the J.L.B. who served during the war as a member of the N.F.S.[50]

Stepney Borough Council took over other spare rooms in September 1940. At that point, the JLB was obliged to decamp offices and Laurie Abraham came to the rescue by offering space at his own premises. In April 1944 Ernest Joseph secured temporary offices at 38 Hallam Street, W1, shared with the AJY, and this arrangement lasted until Camperdown House again became available at the end of the war. Provincial Companies were not so fortunate. Harold House in Liverpool was requisitioned by the Ministry of Labour, and in 1941 was renamed 'West India House', now serving as a hostel for West Indians under the auspices of the YMCA. The JLB had to move to the Princes Road Headquarters of the Jewish Girls' Club. In 1941 the Birmingham Thorpe Street Barracks suffered a direct hit, which effectively put paid to JLB activities in the city for the rest of the war. Tragically, long-standing Commandant Archie B. Solomon's son was killed in action in 1940. In December 1940 the Manchester Headquarters were badly damaged, but the JLB struggled on in a local schoolroom for the following two years, when a private house ('Fernleigh', 435 Cheetham Hill Road) was acquired and converted into a new clubhouse. In 1943 a Drill Hall was built at the back and was opened by Lady Swaythling.

In the middle of the war (April 1943) it was reported that the total strength of the London Battalion was 330 (10 Companies), Manchester 300, Sheffield a very creditable 100 given the size of the Jewish community in the city, Glasgow 75 and Liverpool 60.

However, certainly in the provinces, wartime membership figures were distorted by a significant influx of non-Jewish members, owing to the loss of denominational identity on the transformation of the JLB into Cadet units. Only in London were steps taken late in 1942 to safeguard the Jewish identity of the Brigade. For Sir Max Bonn the restoration of the letters JLB to the name of the London Battalion was indeed 'a matter of principle'. Nevertheless, by 1945 half of the members of the Manchester unit were non-Jews and the Harold House unit in Liverpool consisted 'almost entirely of non-Jewish boys'.[51] Sir Max Bonn also organised a conference of London and provincial representatives in February 1943 and a further meeting was held at the request of E.C.Q. Henriques in Manchester in March 1944, largely as a means of staying in touch. Whilst the war encouraged greater co-ordination with the AJY, culminating in David Mellows' secondment to the Brigade Council in 1945, there was no attempt to reconstitute JLB Companies in the evacuee areas to which the majority of London Jewish schoolchildren were sent.

After interruption in 1940–41, camping activities were resumed on a smaller scale, rationing and transportation difficulties notwithstanding. The pre-war camping ground at Hawkshill, Kingsdown, Walmer was requisitioned by the army, so the London Battalion held camps on the Rothschild estate at Tring in the summer of 1942 and 1943 and at Pirbright – home of the Brigade of Guards – in 1944 and 1945. The nine-day 1942 Tring camp was attended by 198 all ranks, at a charge of 30/– per head for lads and 50/– for officers. Unlike the former peacetime camps, the emphasis was on military training. The training programme consisted of the following subjects:

> Fieldcraft (7 hours)
> Rifle Drill (2 hours)
> Weapon Training (3 hours)
> Physical Training (7 hours)
> Aircraft Recognition
> Map Reading
> Sanitation and Hygiene
> Chemical Warfare (1 hour each)

Army instructors were hired and a veritable 'armoury' of weapons supplied consisting of *inter alia* 'a Tommy Gun, a Browning Automatic Gun . . . Dummy Hand Grenades' and live ammunition. Camp Commandant Magnus conceded that this programme was 'too advanced and too ambitious' for boys who had only been in the Cadet Force for a short period, but felt that it was necessary to 'maintain the lads' interest' and appeal to their imagination.[52]

Weekend camps were held at Stanmore, Middlesex. The 1020 Squadron attended the camps at Tring and in subsequent years held annual training sessions at various aerodromes; Felixstowe (1943, 1945), Bircham Newton (1944) and Locking (1946). Provincial Camps too were held whenever possible, usually by each town separately, but in 1945 and 1946 Manchester and Glasgow joined forces at Blackpool. For the only time in its history, Glasgow had joined the local Church Lads' Brigade in a joint County Camp in 1944.[53] Kosher meat rations were always secured for the Jewish campers by the War Office. In 1942 Manchester abandoned the attempt to hold a camp mainly owing to the impossibility of obtaining kosher food supplies.

Unexpectedly, this restriction of activity 'solved' the Brigade's financial troubles. By 1945 the JLB had not only eliminated its recurring debt at the bank, but careful saving and investment had pushed the accounts well into the black. Brigade finances were in a 'very healthy' state by 1944. The OCA was in abeyance during the war, owing to a large number of members joining up. Headquarters made efforts to keep in contact with ex-Brigade lads in the armed forces, especially those serving overseas. 'Comforts' such as cigarettes, chocolates, and woollens were sent to the troops especially for *Chanuka* and a Ladies Knitting Committee was set up by Lady Swaythling and the wives of officers early on in the war to assist in this effort.

The end of hostilities saw the Brigade much depleted but essentially still intact. Ernest Halsted, who had reached his seventieth birthday in 1943, stepped down after more than 50 years' service to the JLB in December 1945. He nominated Louis Gluckstein MP as his successor and to him fell the task of post-war reconstruction and the challenge of a changed world.

4 · 'Muscular Judaism?': Religion, Zionism and the Brigade

> The Brigade is a practical body, making solely for manliness, and appealing in no way to the tawdry sentimentality of our drawingroom philanthropists . . . [It] prefer[s] to employ the iron rule of discipline rather than the softening influence of female patronage . . . It is in the highest sense of the word religious, for its aim is the physical inculcation of the moral laws on which Judaism is based . . . . The aim of the Brigade, however, is not to impose theocracy upon them . . . [but to set an example by] moral action.[1]

So wrote the *Jewish Chronicle* in 1898. The JLB was undoubtedly a product of its time and place. It may be seen as the Jewish variant of the 'Muscular Christianity' espoused by Thomas Arnold of Rugby, the Evangelical movement and the Salvation Army. It was inspired by it and expressed the same notions of physical fitness and moral rectitude so characteristic of the English public schools, Cadets and youth movements of the late Victorian era. Unlike its Church equivalents however, the JLB did not 'play up' religion. Its activities were not punctuated by Bible reading and hymn singing. Religion was equated with moral behaviour and social action.

The contrast with the Church Brigades did not go unremarked at the time. After all, the other Brigades had grown out of the Sunday School movement: 'The religious element is the ruling principle . . . the various brigades [offer] excellent means of training boys to become loyal and useful members of the Church' noted a correspondent to the *Daily Telegraph* in 1909. 'The only brigade . . . which differs from this view is the Jewish Lads' Brigade, where the religious element is in no sense obtruded, there being no religious instruction and but few synagogue parades.'[2]

In the early years at least, the basic requirements of Jewish law were respected, but never emphasised. This may be explained by the overriding objective of the movement in those days: anglicisation. The officers and gentlemen who ran the Brigade no doubt felt that the sons of immigrants in their charge got 'enough' Judaism at home. Their educational and cultural requirements were more than adequately satisfied by parents, *melamdim* and *rabbonim*. The function of the JLB, on the other hand, was to inculcate *English* values.

The annual Summer Camp, which brought lads and officers together for a week or ten days under canvas, revealed a great deal about the JLB's attitude towards religion. As we have seen, in the early years camp was run on spartan and highly regimented lines. In this regard JLB camp was little different from those run by the other Brigades, Volunteers and Territorials with whom they shared the camp site on farm land near Deal. (Other Jewish youth groups, such as Brady Street copied the format of the JLB camp.) Indeed, there was little distinctly Jewish about the JLB camp. Certainly, a Camp Chaplain was usually, but not always, in attendance. To begin with, at Deal, this was Revd Francis Cohen and he was succeeded by Revd Michael Adler. Adler was appointed Staff Chaplain in succession to Cohen in 1906.[3] Adler also succeeded Cohen as Jewish Chaplain to the Armed Forces and saw service in France between 1915 and 1918. The Revd Leonard M. Simmons of the Manchester Congregation of British Jews (Reform) was the first Chaplain to the Northern Camp at Lytham in 1899. Revd Dr Berendt Salomon, the Danish-born and German-educated rabbi of the Manchester Great Synagogue, was also an early participant. However, the rank of Staff Chaplain to the Northern Brigade was bestowed upon the British-born and educated Revd Reuben Tribich of Bradford's Orthodox congregation, and he soon took on the role of regular Camp Chaplain as well. At the 1904 Lytham camp Tribich delivered a Sabbath morning homily on the subject of 'The True Gentleman' which was thoroughly imbued with the public school spirit. In 1908 the scholar, former Toynbee Hall resident and minister of the Manchester Reform Synagogue, Harry S. Lewis became Northern Camp Chaplain and, in 1910, Staff Chaplain, roles which he fulfilled until his emigration to the USA in 1913. In 1899 the Chief Rabbi himself came down to Deal for the day and, after the departure of Francis Cohen for Australia, he accepted the post of Honorary Chaplain to the national Brigade.

A 'parade for prayer' took place every morning before breakfast and every evening, including, of course, on *Shabbat*. At the very first camp in 1896, the boys were prepared for *Shacharit*: 'all but one lad came down duly provided with his Tephillin and everyone without exception displays his Arbang Confes [sic].'[4] At the Lytham camp in 1904 'Morning service [was] held at 6.15am, conducted by the Chaplain . . . This [was] preceded by a prayer inspection at 5.15, when devotions of the lads in their tents [were] privately seen to by Mr. Tribich'.

Likewise, the Sabbath was observed. On Friday, in 1897,

At sunset the bugler sounded the 'retreat' and the flag [Union Jack] was hauled down. Then evening prayers were chanted in the marquee, the responses being led by the synagogue choristers who are among the rank and file of the Brigade. As it was Friday night, 'Kiddush' was also made by the Chaplain. At 9.30 pm, the 'tattoo' sounded, and a special supper was served out. . . at 'lights out' . . . the sergeant-major [Brock] and the other non-Jews in camp extinguished the lamps.[5]

Orderlies from the Royal Marine Depot at Walmer were brought in to carry out 'the cookery duties of Saturday'. Making and extinguishing fire and cooking are two activities forbidden on the Jewish Sabbath. The bands refrained from playing and the necessary bugle calls were made by the non-Jewish bandmaster, Mr T. Jarvis.

Friday night and Saturday morning services were held in the open field, weather permitting. At Deal in 1900 'A hollow square was formed, at the western side of which a pulpit was erected of drums, covered by a Union Jack, and the colours of the Brigade, a flag of white and blue'.[6]

In the morning, the Chaplain conducted a shortened form of service and read an extract in English from the week's *sedra*. A *Torah* scroll was only brought down for special occasions, such as the very first *barmitzva* celebrated at camp – in the *barmitzva* year of the Deal camp itself, in 1908. The Chaplain never failed to deliver a sermon on the importance of 'king and country . . . race and religion'. The 1900 Lytham camp took place during the Three Weeks, the traditional period of mourning for the destruction of the Temple in

Jerusalem: 'On Saturday evening, being the eve of the Fast of Av, the Book of Lamentations was intoned, and on Sunday morning the full service for the Fast was read.' In 1903, 'boys wishing to fast were given facilities to do so'.[7]

On Saturday morning at the 1899 Deal camp, lads 'were for the most part occupied in making beds, a domestic exercise permitted by the conscience of the strictest sabbatarian, the process in this particular instance being limited to renewing the supplies of straw in the canvas ticks upon which the lads repose at night.'[8]

At first, 'under no consideration should the canteen be opened on Saturday', but in 1901 the camp authorities relented and sanctioned the issuing of tickets which could be exchanged in return for refreshments. This was to get around the religious prohibition of trading on the Sabbath.[9]

Yet, the overall impression given by camp orders, regulations and minutes, is that religious requirements were treated in a more and more perfunctory fashion as the years passed. It should be noted in this connection that boys were not accepted for camp under the age of 13, i.e., *barmitzva* – the age of religious majority.

On the Sabbath at the 1899 camp, after Revd Cohen had 'read the service . . . The whole of the day was given to sport etc, no drill taking place'.[10] Official sports matches were not generally gazetted, but informal cricket games, including officers *v*. lads challenges, did take place on Saturday afternoons. Boys were also expected to participate in the daily 'Bathing Parade' even on the Sabbath, contrary to Orthodox religious law.

Twenty years later, the Grove House Lads' Club in Manchester, 'membership of which [was] restricted to members of the Brigade', was 'open every night and Sunday afternoons, and cricket, football and basket ball games are organised on *Saturday afternoons* [my italics] and week nights'.[11]

On the eve of the Second World War, the Hutchison House Club, based at Camperdown House, was open on Saturday evenings in the summer, before nightfall. It was also suggested that the club also be open 'on the second day of the Holydays, excepting New Year and Passover'. Permission was granted by the Brigade, subject to the agreement of the London Brigade Chaplain. It is doubtful whether he approved.[12]

By the early 1920s there are instances of JLB participation in sports competitions with non-Jewish clubs taking place on Saturday afternoons. This was somewhat ironic, given that one of the original motivations for the founding of the Jewish Athletics Association, to which the Brigade belonged, was to facilitate sports fixtures on Sundays and weekday evenings and thus avoid public desecration of the Jewish Sabbath.

The JLB Employment Bureau was designed to help working boys to keep the Sabbath. However, this rationale was apparently not very compelling in 1905: 'The applicant shall be asked whether he is prepared to work on Saturdays and if so whether his parents have any objection, and no other question on this subject is to be put to him. Best efforts shall be made to obtain him employment whether he is prepared to work on Saturdays or not.'[13] This was hardly a ringing endorsement of the sabbatarian principle. It would have been inconceivable for a Church organisation to permit its members to work on Sundays.

Catering arrangements at camp were not up to the stringent standards of *kashrut* which would be required by Jewish organisations approved by the Chief Rabbinate today. Yet, they apparently satisfied the more relaxed standards which prevailed in Anglo-Jewry in the days of Hermann Adler. The Camp Sub-committee did ensure the supply of meat from a kosher butcher in Petticoat Lane and subsequently in the Harrow Road, which was sent at extra expense down to Deal. Kosher cake was initially provided for *Shabbat*. However, other foodstuffs including bread, biscuits and cheese were mostly supplied by the local farmer, or general English food companies. The main criterion seems to have been cost rather than *kashrut*. Equipment such as cookhouses, boilers and stoves were hired locally, although it does appear that the JLB supplied its own crockery and cutlery new or used from Jewish sources. The Camp Chaplain did not join the 'Fatigue Party' which went down early to set up the camp, nor did he act as *mashgiakh* of the kitchens to ensure that the food was prepared according to the laws of *kashrut*. This is surprising, especially given the fact that, until 1910, the JLB employed two cooks from the Marine Depot at Walmer under the direction of Sergeant Foxworthy to do the catering. The Lytham camp had its own Jewish caterer, Mr Mendes, and obtained its meat from a kosher butcher in Manchester which was apparently 'koshered in camp'. Often, the camp site was taken over by the JLB after being used by a non-Jewish organisation, and equipment shared. In 1899 for instance 'The Camp was taken over from the Boys' Brigade on the *Saturday afternoon* [my italics], and the extra tents were erected during the afternoon by a number of Royal Marines kindly sent by Colonel Maurice'.[14]

Even before the First World War, the JLB was under attack within the Jewish community for apparently sacrificing Jewish tradition to the overriding quest for anglicisation and social acceptance. To some critics the *Jewish* in the Jewish Lads' Brigade was somehow becoming lost. In 1910, Eugene Woolstone, a practising Jew from the West End of London, wrote a letter of complaint to the Jewish press:

> Many like myself, who support financially this Lads' Brigade movement, want to feel assured that these lads will turn out good Jews as well as good Englishmen . . . it surely should be possible . . . to discover some more suitable way of passing the Sabbath than to ask these lads to indulge in athletic sports on that day. The danger is not only that these lads themselves will lose the feeling of reverence for the sanctity of the Sabbath, but further, that many parents will be deterred from permitting their lads joining this movement owing to the fear of their becoming contaminated.[15]

The editor of the *Jewish World* was loath to deprive the young of 'healthy recreation', but reluctantly agreed with his correspondent that 'on the whole, it would be advisable not to give gazette sanction to the playing of games on the seventh day' so as not to 'offend the susceptibilities of any of our co-religionists'. The issue had not been forgotten by the following summer. Rabbi I. Raffalovich of the Liverpool New Hebrew Congregation complained to Captain Yates of the JLB in that city about cricket matches on the Sabbath: 'I have it on reliable authority,' he subsequently informed the *Jewish Chronicle*, 'that scoring and writing are freely indulged in.' He went on:

> such procedure is against traditional usages and would certainly be considered by the parents of the lads, who are mostly orthodox Jews, a breach of the Fourth Commandment . . . I feel positive that the parents . . . would resent this organised Sabbath desecration by their children, and it is but right that they should be made aware of the facts.

He concluded pointedly: 'I would like to ask whether any Christian school or Church Brigade would arrange cricket games on Sunday?' Raffalovich was an immigrant rabbi from Russia who had studied at *yeshiva* in Jerusalem. He was in a position to know the mood amongst foreign-born traditional Jews in Liverpool. However, his protest was not received by Commandant Yates with much sympathy: 'Mr Yates . . . seeks to assure me that . . . this game [of cricket] has been indulged in on the Sabbath for years past without raising objections from any quarter.'

Another correspondent, the Zionist intellectual Isadore Wartski (later Senior Lecturer in Modern Hebrew at the School of Oriental and African Studies at London University), largely siding with Yates, extolled 'The moral of organised games'. Significantly however, Wartski also recognised the very real conflict of cultures which many of the lads experienced, 'the difficulty of obeying a stern orthodox parent and keeping up the *camaraderie* of his school and club'.[16]

The Brigade took the problem seriously and took steps to reassure traditionalist parents. In connection with the 1913 camp, the press reported that 'There are still very many parents who object to camp for fear the religious side is neglected. It is very unfortunate that this idea should be so prevalent.' To counteract this impression, Camp Orders stated that 'Lads should bring a copy of the Authorised Daily Prayer Book (Rev. S. Singer). Parade for Prayers at 7am, with a special service on Friday night'.[17]

Soon after the outbreak of the Great War, 'permission to conduct route marches to Hampstead Heath on Saturday afternoons, for the purpose of performing extended order drill' was refused by HQ: 'The proposal was considered inadvisable as likely to hurt the susceptibilities of strictly conforming Jews.'[18] In 1923 Friday night youth services were started at Camperdown House, in association with the United Synagogue, and the practice was copied in Manchester. In 1924 special High Holyday services attracted some 700 boys. However, the regular *Shabbat* services were sparsely attended and had a chequered career. Whilst the Brigade professed itself to be 'keenly alive to the desirability of encouraging lads to attend religious services',[19] the sentiment was apparently not reciprocated by youngsters in the East End, despite the fact that in organising the services, the economic realities of life in the district were taken into account: 'The form of service has been approved by the Chief Rabbi, and in order to enable working boys to attend it is proposed to hold the service at 7 o'clock [on Friday evening] throughout the year.'[20]

Services at Grove House in Manchester followed suit. In the winter of course, when the days are short, *Shabbat* can commence as early as 3.30pm in London. Evidently, few boys were willing or able to ask their employers if they could leave work early on Friday afternoon. In many cases, their employers too were Jewish. A generational clash within immigrant Jewry, between traditional values and the attractions of English society, was beginning to make itself felt, and the JLB was attempting, none too effectively, to hold the ring between the two. For example, in an effort to boost attendance on Friday nights, it was decided to make 'the main feature prior to the Service . . . a gramophone recital or a lecture on subjects of interest to the lads'. No Orthodox rabbi would give sanction to concerts, live or otherwise, being held on the Sabbath. Nevertheless, for a growing number of boys, the Friday night services at Camperdown House and camp were the only real exposure they had to Judaism, 'for in many of the homes of the lads the Sabbath is forgotten'. The British-born second generation was only too keen to shake off the religious and cultural legacy of its immigrant past. The anglicisation promoted by the JLB was seized upon with eagerness by its members. The 'Yom Kippur' Jew was well and truly in the making.[21]

In the spring of 1928 the JLB issued a flysheet to boost recruitment. It reassured parents that: 'The Jewish Lads' Brigade is the only Jewish Brigade. The members are encouraged to observe their religion. No parades are held on Sabbath and Holydays, and the food supplied at camp and elsewhere is Kosher.'[22] At the AGM eight years later Halsted confessed that

> For many years . . . they had been concerned about the religious training in the Brigade. The average young Officer in the Brigade did not feel himself qualified to deal directly with that side of a boy's life.

Through the AJY, the Brigade had secured the appointment of 'a number of Welfare Officers' connected with the United Synagogue who would make 'the religious side of the work their special duty'.

Nevertheless, the issue of religious observance still rankled at the end of the 1920s. An Orthodox Jew who had spent a weekend with the JLB Summer Camp at Birchington in 1929 was shocked to see 'large numbers of boys [who] travelled from London, smoked cigarettes, wrote and typed in the camp itself on the Sabbath under the very noses of the commanding officers'.[23]

The JLB prudently decided to take no action to contradict this letter in the press. Nor did it take a stand on the issue, but left it up to the conscience of the individual. In 1936, when Maurice Braham, Commandant of the London Summer Camp 'raised the question of closing the canteen on Saturdays, and intimated that whereas he felt that this should be done, he realised that it would involve the Brigade in a certain loss of profit. It was decided to leave the matter entirely to Mr Braham.'[24]

Certainly, JLB activities were not marked out by their religious atmosphere, and their religious content was minimal.[25] At Grove House in Manchester, each evening's activities were rounded off by a service conducted by the Chaplain. It was all of five minutes in duration. Throughout the 1930s the bathing parade and organised games continued to be held on *Shabbat* in camp. At the Northern Camp, cricket and football matches were played between JLB teams and against rival clubs. The *Jewish Chronicle* reported from the 1931 JLB camp that

> During the afternoon, all kinds of games were played on the parade ground, and – Rabbi Kook, please note! – none was more enthusiastic than the Rabbi Chaplain [Rabbi Dr. Morris Ginsberg, Richmond United Synagogue] who joined heartily with the boys in the games. As I watched those youngsters, I thought of the late Chief Rabbi, Dr H. Adler, who, many years ago, in reply to a question put to him, said that 'healthy recreation was permissible on the Sabbath'. There was certainly no breach of the spirit of the Sabbath in this instance.[26]

Presumably, Rav Kook, who had been the spiritual leader of the influential Machzike Hadath Synagogue in East London during the First World War and who went on to become Ashkenazi Chief Rabbi of Palestine under the British Mandate, had ruled against sport on *Shabbat*. The London Beth Din, particularly after the arrival of Yekhezkel Abramsky as Rabbi of the same Machzike Hadath in

1932 and his appointment as *Dayan* in 1935, moved towards more stringent standards of Orthodoxy, such as prevailed in eastern Europe and away from the more relaxed style of the Adlers and their Jewish 'Chaplains' who happily donned dog collars in imitation of their Anglican counterparts.

In August 1933, Rabbi M. Swift, who was also to become a *Dayan* on the London Beth Din, wrote to the *Jewish Chronicle* 'to express openly my disgust at those in whose care is the religious organisation of the Jewish Lads' Brigade, when out of the 430 lads present in their Summer Camp, about 40 performed the daily practice of the Tefilin. Some mornings, I am told, 15 attended.'[27]

According to Allan Burke, afterwards Inspector-General of the Israeli Navy and a keen footballer, the pre-war Manchester JLB football team was 'at that time the only Jewish football team in the country to play on Saturdays'. Issy Pressman and his brother Stanley being 'always on the lookout for new young talent . . . came round to my school and persuaded our headmaster to let them sign me on for the Grove House football team. Two years later I played as goal-keeper in the side which won the Manchester Combination Cup.'[28]

In 1930 the Grove House public speaking section held a debate on the motion 'That the playing of football on the Sabbath is not desirable'. The outcome is not recorded.

Indeed, it was argued, the Brigade actively contributed to the decline in religious observance, which was rapidly accelerating amongst the British-born children of the immigrant generation. This process, encouraged by army service during the First World War, was to be all but completed during the Second, when the Blitz and evacuation took Jewish youngsters out of the East End and away from their Jewish roots, often for good. Wartime training camps boasted even less religious content than their peacetime equivalents, not helped by the absence of a resident chaplain. True, kosher meat was *de rigueur* and camp was liable to be cancelled if no supplies could be obtained, rationing notwithstanding. The Commandant of the 1942 Tring Training Camp reported that

> Prayers were said each morning before breakfast. As there were twenty-five Church of England lads in Camp, these prayers were undenominational. On Friday evening and Saturday mornings, Services were

conducted for the Jewish lads by the Rev. [S.M.] Bromberger assisted by other Officers. On both Sunday mornings, the Church of England lads attended Tring Church in which seats had been reserved for them by the Vicar.[29]

In 1944 the Glasgow unit 'For the first time in the history of the JLB . . . attended a combined camp consisting of Cadets from Lanarkshire, Dumbartonshire and Glasgow'. However, in this instance the 40 Jewish Cadets 'had a special kosher kitchen catered by an Army cook under the supervision of our own Q[uarter] M[aster] Staff. We also had a Mess Marquee to ourselves and a Marquee for morning prayers.'[30]

Similar arrangements were in force at the Manchester Cleveleys camp in the summer of 1942. Here too, despite the claim made on behalf of Glasgow two years later, 150 Jewish boys camped along-side their 150 non-Jewish comrades in the 2nd Cadet Battalion Lancashire Fusiliers (formerly the Jewish Lads' Brigade).

In general, the wartime conversion of JLB Companies into Cadet units tended to dilute their Jewish character. Under the pressure of national emergency, the JLB felt the need to throw in its lot in the national war effort with the population as a whole. It was considered churlish to exclude non-Jewish Cadets and officers who wanted to become members and this policy continued to operate in the JLB Cadet units after the war's end. However, a request by the 2nd Cadet Battalion Royal Fusiliers to be allowed to camp together with the Brigade at Walmer in 1949 was turned down by Head-quarters, after much discussion, 'as a large number of the boys in the 2nd (C) Battalion were not Jewish, and were generally older than the Brigade boys . . . the effect on the Brigade Units would not be good'.[31] Nevertheless, the shortage of officers ensured a heavy reliance on the paid services of non-Jewish wardens, such as Mr Smewin at the North London Club, and PT instructors.

At the annual meeting of the Brigade Council in 1951, Revd Arthur Barnett, the Brigade Chaplain, complained that the 'spiritual and ethical objects of the Brigade' were not being got across to the Jewish community. Stanley Rowe, as a non-Jewish youth worker in Manchester, felt that he would be 'lacking in my duty if I did not point out that [the Spiritual Side] is the very weakest part of our work'. Indeed, it is true that national Annual Reports throughout the 1950s hardly alluded to the religious content of Brigade work. However, the Manchester Annual Report for 1957–59 did comment upon the fact that: 'Modern Jewish youth today jives, listens to pop records, watches "telly", wears jeans and has Perry Como haircuts. There is nothing bad about these things . . . But they are not noticeably Jewish.'[32]

The Brigade was 'misunderstood' by the synagogues and little support was to be found from that quarter. Barnett's suggestion in 1948 that each London Company adopt its own Chaplain, as happened in many cases before the war, was partially acted upon. Rabbi Ginsberg of Richmond Synagogue was brought back and an enthusiastic new face was Revd Saul Amias of Edgware United Synagogue, who had served as an Army Chaplain during the war and was appointed Chaplain to the 2nd Cadet Battalion Royal Fusiliers in 1949. He was fully recruited after expressing his dissatisfaction with 'the religious aspect of the Brigade's work'[33] in 1950. Revd Amias was subsequently made London Regimental Chaplain (1952) and was a regular at Summer Camp in the 1960s and 1970s. In 1948 the practice of appointing an Honorary Chaplain was reinstituted. Chief Rabbi Brodie of the United Synagogue was the first to hold this office and he was gradually joined by the *Haham* of the Spanish and Portuguese community – and, from 1970, by representatives of the Reform and Liberal synagogues. These appointments were more in the nature of patronage rather than implying practical involvement with the day-to-day running of the Brigade.

At camp, the pre-war formula of Prayer Parade and the drumhead service on *Shabbat* was continued. Weekday afternoon and evening prayers, however, disappeared. 'Grace' (i.e., *bensching*) was, it seems, only publicly recited on Friday night and before and after the Inspection Day dinner. In 1947 Camp Commandant Cyril Goodman reported from Walmer that 'The Kosher food arrangements were in accordance with those of pre-war years and no complaints were brought to my notice as regards their adequacy or otherwise. Meat was supplied daily by rail from London by Messrs Barnetts, and proved of good quality.'[34]

Plans drawn up for the 1953 camp included the recommendation that 'no banking facilities be made available on the Saturdays'. Nor was there band practice on *Shabbat*. On the other hand, on the Saturday morning at the Whitsun Camp in 1954 'Prayer Parade in the open was followed by swimming and sun-bathing on the beach'.[35]

Innovations of a quasi-religious nature were: the practice of consecrating the colours, Anglican army-style, and the composition of a special Brigade Prayer and Prayer Book, first mooted by Gluckstein in 1953. Such innovations were clearly in the Reform tradition. In 1954 concern was expressed at Headquarters about the length of the Afternoon Service (i.e., *mincha*) to be recited at the planned Diamond Jubilee Service and a request was sent to the Chief Rabbi for permission to 'abridge' it for the occasion. The answer, not unreasonably, was 'No'. Complaints were heard 'that caps were not provided for the platform guests'[36] at the Jubilee Display to be worn during the prayers in accordance with religious custom.

The secularising trend evident in the JLB stood in stark contrast to the Christian Brigades, whether Anglican, Catholic or Non-conformist, where the teaching of the Gospel remained central to their ethos. The whole question of the relationship of the JLB with Judaism is worth exploring, for what it reveals about the Jewish identity of both officers and lads, and their attitudes to 'ethnicity' and Zionism – increasingly pressing issues with the rise of both Fascism and Communism in the inter-war period.

Of course, Brigade founders Colonel Goldsmid and Francis Cohen were, as we have seen, committed Jews. However, it would be true to say that, even in the early days, JLB officers were not characterised by rigorous Orthodoxy. Where synagogue affiliation can be established, it appears that the majority of London officers were members of the United Synagogue, the ostensibly Orthodox umbrella organisation of 'West End' Jewry under the jurisdiction of the Chief Rabbi. Brigade Commandant, Sir Frederic Nathan, for example, was a member of the New West End Synagogue in Bayswater. Outside the capital, officers largely belonged to synagogues recognising Adler's authority, except, perhaps, in Manchester, where the Manchester Congregation of British Jews (Reform) was influential. However, nominal synagogue affiliation is not necessarily an accurate indicator of personal religious commitment. Indeed, lay leaders of the United Synagogue, who tended to call the tune, were notoriously lax in their personal observance. Financial resources and social connections counted far more than adherence to the standards laid down by the Chief Rabbi.

Goldsmid's successor as Commandant, Lieutenant-Colonel Emanuel Montefiore, was a member of the Council of the West London Synagogue of British Jews. Goldsmid's right hand man in the early days, Major H.B. Lewis-Barned, was also a member of the Council and a former warden of this congregation. Founded in 1840, West London was the first Reform synagogue in Britain. Its establishment thus pre-dated the United Synagogue by 30 years and its credentials were every bit as socially superior as those of its Orthodox rival. Indeed, West London was on a par with the prestigious Spanish and Portuguese Congregation and drew many wealthy members from it. Leading 'Cousinhood' families, including Goldsmids, were founder members of the Reform and by 1870 the congregation had moved into its own magnificent purpose-built synagogue at Upper Berkeley Street. In reality, the United, the Sephardim and the Reform increasingly resembled one another in terms of the social classes from which their membership was drawn and, indeed, in their outward form of worship – if not in the dogma to which they were supposed to subscribe. Whilst the Reform were hardly radical in their innovations, the United and the Sephardim became increasingly anglicised as the years went by.[37] From 1927 to 1931, the JLB accepted invitations not only from Bevis Marks and leading United congregations but also from the West London Synagogue for its Chanuka Parades, despite the disapproval of the Chief Rabbi. In 1934 the parade was held exclusively at the Reform synagogue. Revd Leonard M. Simmons of the Manchester Congregation of British Jews was, as we have seen, a founder member of the JLB in Manchester. The Chanuka Parade and Tea was, from time to time, hosted by the Reform Congregation, for example in 1927.[38]

Thus the religious ethos to which the JLB subscribed from the beginning was a highly anglicised version of Judaism, be it Orthodox or Reform. It had little in common with the Judaism practised by the immigrants. Whilst it would be an exaggeration to assume that the largely Yiddish-speaking newcomers from eastern Europe from the 1880s onwards were uniformly *frum*, it is true to say that what they understood by normative Judaism as it existed in Russia and Poland, bore little resemblance to the genteel variety practised in England. Immigrant Jewry shunned the religious institutions of native Anglo-Jewry, preferring to set up their own *minyanim*, *chevrot* and *shteibels*, where they could recreate the familiar world of the *shtetl* – or at least of urban Warsaw or Odessa whence they had come. *Yiddishkeit* in the immigrant quarters was demonstrative, intense and informally structured. The social gap was as wide as the cultural. Membership of the United Synagogue, even at its East London Synagogue opened in 1877, was beyond the reach of all but the best off East End Jew. The Federation alone attempted to fill the void, not without success.

The leadership of the JLB was as unrepresentative of the religious constituency of immigrant Jewry as it was of its social mix. Only one member of the Executive Committee of 1898, J.M. Lissack, was Federation (he was also secretary of the London Board for Shechita). Later on, the Swaythling family connection with the Federation was to count for little in the context of the religious life of the JLB. Members of independent Orthodox *kehillot* such as the influential East End based Machzike Hadath and the German North London Beth Hamedrash were nowhere in sight. However, the 'bottom line' criterion for the existence of segregated Jewish youth groups was respected in theory at least: that both Brigade staff and members be Jewish. In June 1898 the Executive Committee passed a motion which had been put forward by Jacob Waley Cohen and Herman J. Cohen: 'That the Executive admit only Israelites as officers except in the case of insuperable difficulty in forming a Company without the assistance of a non-Jew intimately connected with an association of a Company.'[39]

However, in practice, non-Jews were appointed officers as we have seen in the case of Captain Baker – who really appointed himself – in Canada. In May 1899 E. Warden Denniss replaced the Jewish Captain S.J. Solomon as commander of the Old Castle Street Company in the East End of London. Denniss informed the Royal Commission on Alien Immigration in 1903 that he was 'the only officer [of the JLB] who [was] not a Jew'.[40] Nevertheless, there was at least one non-Jewish officer in the provinces at that time, George Cecil Kenyon of the Liverpool Company. Kenyon took command of the Company at the 1904 Lytham camp. Sadly, he died in October 1906 at the early age of 32.[41] Non-Jewish instructors for drill, sports and music were employed by the Brigade, such as Bandmaster Jarvis, who served for many years before the First World War.

The JLB took its religious identity seriously, in so far as it bestowed a denominational distinction separate from the Christian Boys' and Church Lads' Brigades. Towards the end of the First World War, when Government policy seemed to be moving in the direction of compulsory Cadet service for teenagers (14–17-year-olds), Sir Frederic Nathan wrote a stern warning letter to the Jewish press:

> I wish to point out clearly to the Community that unless sufficient support is received [for the JLB] . . . the Government will inevitably actively encourage the formation of rival Cadet Corps in the centres of Jewish population, and the lads will be brought under non-Jewish instead of specifically Jewish influence. Thus the first seeds will be sown for their drifting away from Judaism.
>
> Much of the work of the Community in the direction of Jewish educa- tion and religious training must prove useless and become nullified if our young boys are to be drafted into Cadet Corps in which the Jewish element is entirely lacking, and in which they would inevitably be led to disregard the Jewish sabbath and Jewish laws, as well as to attend Christian services.[42]

Whilst the official link with the United Synagogue was maintained in the inter-war period, through Chaplains Michael Adler and his successor (1935–38) Rabbi M. Gollop, who was appointed a *Dayan* at the London Beth Din (he was also Adler's successor as Senior Jewish Chaplain to the forces in 1926), leading personalities in the Brigade were closely identified with Progressive Judaism. The Brigade was not alone in this respect. Other clubs too had Reform links. Lily Montagu, the strongwilled daughter of the first Lord Swaythling (founder of the Federation of Synagogues) instigated the Jewish Religious Union in 1903, the experimental forerunner of the Liberal Movement. Ten years earlier, she had started the West Central Jewish Girls' Club. In 1913 Basil Henriques came down from Oxford to the East End to found the Oxford & St George's Club and Settlement (housed at the Bernhard Baron Settlement in

Berner Street from 1929 onwards). Henriques – or 'the Gaffer' as he was known – an imposing figure, 6 feet 5 inches tall with a distinguished military record, was the very embodiment of 'Muscular Judaism'. His approach to youth work was strongly influenced by Baden-Powell. From the outset, the Settlement was associated with both the West London Reform and Liberal Synagogues.[43]

Ernest Joseph and his wife had been founder members of the Liberal Jewish Synagogue in 1910. Indeed, Joseph's father Nathan had toyed with the Jewish Religious Union, his status as architect to the United Synagogue notwithstanding. Ernest, in turn, became Honorary Architect to the Union of Liberal and Progressive Synagogues and was responsible for the design of their premier building at St John's Wood in 1925, and for its reconstruction after bomb damage in November 1940 (the synagogue was demolished in 1991 and rebuilt behind the reconstituted, largely original, front elevation). Ernest played a prominent role in the affairs of this synagogue, being elected to the Council in 1929, and serving as treasurer between 1936 and 1953 and vice-president from 1953 until his retirement in 1956.

Halsted, by contrast, had family connections with the Bayswater Synagogue where he was married in 1908. Nevertheless, he had some sympathy for the other Ernest's views on religion. Beatrice Harris (née Hallenstein/Halsted) describes her father's attitude towards religion thus: 'My father wasn't at all Orthodox . . . He obviously "thought very Jewish". He must have done . . . He had a stepmother . . . None of his family were [religious] . . . My mother was much more religious – not Orthodox – and so my father went to synagogue to please her.'

Conflict arose between the Brigade and United Synagogue Orthodoxy in 1938. Dayim Gollop, who was minister of Hampstead Synagogue, refused to attend a Brigade dinner at the Mansion House which was not strictly kosher. The holding of a function under JLB auspices at which the food was not supervised by the London Beth Din was not unprecedented. At the 1935 'SS *Camperdown*' Bazaar held at Shell-Mex House, 'the entire catering [was] in the hands of Messrs Wm. Whiteley, Ltd '– the well known Bayswater department store. Apparently, no eyebrows were raised at the time, in public at least. Three years later, however, the new

Chaplain handed in his resignation in protest, complaining that he was not consulted where religious matters were concerned. The fact that he had two sons who were officers in the JLB did not deter him from taking a stand. In June 1938, the JLB had tightened up on matters of *kashrut* at camp at Gollop's request. Apparently, the camp did not provide separate crockery and cutlery for meat and milk foods as was required by Jewish law. Headquarters decided to conform to the *Dayan's* wishes in 1939 at a cost of £180, towards which he had offered to pay. Gollop's lobbying evidently had some effect because in the kitchen at the weekend camping ground at Epping that year 'There were, of course, separate crockery and cutlery for milk and meat, each clearly labelled on different shelves'.[44] A 120-seater camp synagogue tent, donated by Jonas May and fitted out with monies raised by Hampstead Synagogue, had been consecrated by Gollop at Walmer in 1937. Nevertheless, he felt that these concessions had been made 'merely to please him and that he had in fact been considered a nuisance for making complaints at all'.[45] He felt keenly his communal responsibility as Chaplain to ensure that the Brigade 'be conducted on such lines that no orthodox Jewish lad should have any qualms about joining or attending camp and that no orthodox parent should be discouraged from allowing his son to do so'. Halsted well understood the implications of Gollop's resignation: 'This incident has, I think, made it difficult, if not impossible, for any orthodox minister to accept the office of Chaplain in the future . . . a position which requires earnest consideration on our part.'

Nevertheless, he was not prepared to accede to Gollop's request for membership of the Headquarters Committee and thereby greater influence in the running of the Brigade. Given 'the many practical difficulties of really strict adherence to the "din"' and 'the large number of members who were actively opposed to this, there would be constant trouble on minutiae'. Indeed, 'strong and radical differences of opinion exist[ed] among Officers and Lads, concerning the value of these observances.' Therefore 'a stricter adherence to orthodox practice than in the past' was not desirable and Halsted was supported in this view by both Ernest Joseph and Sir Max Bonn. In any case, Halsted asserted that 'from its foundation the Brigade had received no real help or support in religious matters either from its Chaplains or from the ecclesiastical authorities and that the majority of the services arranged by the clergy had been of so stereotyped and unhelpful a nature as to have no spiritual value whatever'.

In the discussion at the Headquarters Committee which followed, B.S. Woolf averred 'that it was against all modern tendencies to do anything which would make the Brigade adhere more strictly to religious observances'. Jonas May, who was himself observant, Eric Jacobi and Charles Magnus disagreed, fearing the harm which could be done to the JLB's reputation through the lack of a Chaplain. They were in a minority, and the organisation did without a Brigade Chaplain until the last year of the Second World War when Revd Arthur Barnett was appointed after the intervention of Rabbi Solomon Schonfeld in his capacity as a member of the Religious Advisory Panel to the BNCC.

The Manchester JLB did not possess an official Chaplain in the inter-war period until the appointment of Revd A. de Souza Pimontel of the Spanish and Portuguese Synagogue in Cheetham Hill Road as Chaplain and Club Warden in 1936. He had first acted as Camp Chaplain the previous year, the first time that a regular qualified Chaplain was appointed to camp staff. During most of the 1920s and 1930s, the role of Chaplain to the Northern Camp was played by a staff officer, usually Isaac Cansino or S. Hyman. Revd Dr S.M. Lehrmann of the Higher Broughton Congregation first acted as Chaplain in 1927 and again in 1929 and 1933. As a member of the Manchester Beth Din, Lehrmann insisted on high standards of religious observance. In 1933 he forbade the JLB boxing team from collecting their shield from the Prince of Wales himself as the ceremony was scheduled for *Shabbat*. Similarly, he disallowed JLB participation at a civic Armistice Parade on a Saturday. Nor was Lehrmann satisfied with the catering arrangements at camp. In the past, the Camp Chaplain had been acting as *shomer*. In March 1934 the Officers' Minute Book stated that 'It was being arranged for Dr Lehrmann to meet Mrs Wellings [the caterer] to discuss the question of Kashruth'. By May, it transpired that the Brigade 'had received a letter from Mrs Wellings stating her inability to comply with the demands of the Beth Din'.[46] It was probably not coincidental that Lehrmann did not act as Camp Chaplain ever again. In 1934 his place was taken by the Revd S.I. Solomons. Solomons and Pimontel were prepared to take a more relaxed view than their predecessor. In 1934 the Brigade celebrated E.C.Q. Henriques' Silver Wedding with a non-supervised vegetarian meal at the Midland Hotel, the favourite venue for the annual Brigade Ball in Manchester. In 1938 – the very year in which Dayan Gollop resigned over the issue in London – Manchester JLB calmly accepted an invitation to dine with the Lord Mayor at the Town Hall: 'Capt. Hyman [the former 'chaplain'] suggested that it would be a nice gesture if all J.L.B. officers were to abstain from eating meat . . . It was finally decided that the Lord Mayors [sic] secretary be informed that J.L.B. officers would not partake of any meat and to see that a suitable menu be arranged.'

After 1945, the connection between the Brigade and Progressive Judaism was continued through Commandant Sir Louis Gluckstein. Indeed, it still exists today through the current Commandant Sir Peter Lazarus who is a former chairman of the St John's Wood Liberal Synagogue. Gluckstein (1897–1979), tall and distinguished looking, was the son of Joseph Gluckstein, one of the founders of J. Lyons & Co. Ltd. of Corner House teashop fame. The Gluckstein family, which originated in Germany and moved to Holland, had started out in the tobacco trade in London in the 1840s (Salmon & Gluckstein).[47] Educated at St Paul's School and Lincoln College, Oxford, Louis became a barrister, a colonel and was Conservative MP for Nottingham East between 1931 and 1945. Later he served on the London County Council and was elected chairman of the Greater London Council in 1968. Gluckstein succeeded Claude Montefiore as president of the Liberal Synagogue and, as its representative on the Board of Deputies, he played a prominent role in the battle at the Board to secure legal recognition of Liberal Judaism for the purpose of appointing marriage secretaries. Since Chief Rabbi Hertz had finally (despite some measure of accommodation during the war years) set his face against recognising the Liberals as 'persons professing the Jewish religion', Gluckstein's efforts proved fruitless. Like the Reformers before them (in 1856) the Liberals were obliged to seek redress through Parliament with a special Marriage Act in 1958.

Perhaps more significantly for our present discussion, the Liberal

Synagogue became, in the words of Geoffrey Alderman, 'a religious refuge for anti-Zionists in the inter-war period'.[48] The association of Liberal Judaism with anti-Zionism inevitably affected public perceptions of the ideological colouration of the JLB.

That the JLB should have come to be associated with those elements in the Anglo-Jewish community who opposed the re-establishment of the Jewish homeland in Palestine – and whose antipathy to the aspirations of the Zionist movement did not, as is popularly assumed, end with the Balfour Declaration (1917), but persisted throughout the period of the British Mandate (1922–48) – is ironic to say the least. As we saw in Chapter 1, Colonel Goldsmid had been a *Chovevei Tsionist* before he founded the Brigade. Indeed, there are striking similarities between the constitution of the English *Chovevei Tsion* and the later JLB. Despite their disagreements, Goldsmid worked with Herzl. He fired his youthful recruits with an uncompromising dual loyalty: 'Israel is my father and Britain my mother' was one of his favourite mottos. Another was 'Loyalty to the Flag for which the sun once stood still, can only deepen our devotion to the Flag upon which the sun never sets'.

In the 1890s the physical fitness of the Jew became an essential prerequisite for the survival and national regeneration of the Jewish people. Mind, body and spirit were to be fused in the Zionist enterprise. At the Second Zionist Congress in Basle in 1898, the physician Dr Max Nordau made his famous plea for 'the physical education of the new generation which will return to us the lost "Muscular Judaism"'. The idea was developed in his article 'Muskeljudentum' published in the *Judische Turnzeitung* in 1900. Centuries of living in the 'sunless' ghetto dominated by the fear of persecution had ruined the health of the Jewish people. The ancient sporting and military tradition evoked by the name of Bar Kokhba had been lost. It was time to 'recreate a Jewry of muscle . . . let us once more become deep-chested, sturdy, sharp-eyed men'.[49] Sporting prowess was the key to the achievement of Jewish self-respect.

As early as 1895 – the same year as the JLB was founded in London – the first Jewish sports club, the Israel Gymnastics Club, was opened in Constantinople, and others followed in Bulgaria in 1897. In response to Nordau's call, the Bar Kokhba Gymnastics Club was started in Berlin the following year. Thus began a network of sports clubs in Germany, Austria and Hungary, Turkey, Bulgaria, Poland and, finally, Palestine (1906) which, after the Sixth Zionist Congress in 1903, were combined into the movement known as the *Judische Turnerschaft* (Union of Jewish Gymastics Clubs). Subsequent Zionist Congresses before the outbreak of the First World War were treated to staged displays (*Schauturnen*) by Jewish gymnasts. The *Turnerschaft*, which published its own journal from 1900, evolved into the modern Maccabi organisation and from the outset was strongly influenced not only by Zionism but, ironically, also by fashionable German Social Darwinist theories and the concept of the *Volk* (transmitted via Martin Buber's philosophy). Certainly, the *Judische Turnerschaft* was closely modelled on the *Deutsche Turnerschaft* and the *Sokol* sports movement in Slavic lands – many of whose adherents operated an exclusionist policy against Jews. So it was, in central Europe at least, that anti-Semitism provided a spur to Jewish youth to set up their own sports organisation and to 'prove' to the Gentiles their physical prowess.

Whilst it is likely that Goldsmid was aware of these developments on the Continent – the Zionist Congresses were widely reported in the *Jewish Chronicle* – my researches have uncovered absolutely no evidence whatsoever that there was ever any interaction between the German Jewish youth groups and the JLB, which, in typically English fashion, was devoid of any *overtly* ideological agenda. Like the British in general, the Anglo-Jewish community looked to the Empire, not to Europe, for inspiration. For their part, the German Jewish organisations were preoccupied with an intense internal debate between the proponents of allegedly superior *Turn*, i.e., gymnastics which was associated with mass participation, discipline and nationalism, and those of '*Englische Sport*', i.e., athletics which was held to be synonymous with individualism and 'bourgeois decadence'. By 1912, however, this conflict had been largely resolved for the Jewish organisations – if not for their German models.

The year 1912 also saw the establishment of the *Judische Wanderbund Blau-Weiss* – the Zionist Scouting organisation modelled on the German *Wandervogel* rather than on Baden-Powell's British formula.[50] *Blau-Weiss* reached its peak membership of 3,000 in the early 1920s and directed its outdoor activities to pioneer settlement (*chalutsiut*) in

Palestine. Independently, a Jewish Scouts organisation was set up in Palestine under the British in 1919.

Meanwhile, in 1921 the World Maccabi Union was formed at Karlsbad 'as an organic part of the Zionist movement' and claimed a membership of nearly 100,000 spread across 22 countries. In 1929 the first international Jewish sports meeting was held in Prague – the forerunner of the quadrennial Maccabiah Games – the 'Jewish Olympics' first held in Palestine in 1932. In 1935 Maccabi head-quarters were transferred from Nazi Germany to London where Selig Brodetsky took over the presidency and a British Maccabi was created in 1936. On the eve of the Second World War the centre of Maccabi activity shifted to *Eretz Yisrael* where it has remained ever since.

By the 1920s, in contrast, the JLB, with its emphasis on patriotic service to the state, had become the natural home of those 'Englishmen of the Mosaic Persuasion' to whom Jewish nationalism was anathema. Certainly, as far as Brigade work was concerned, their political views were not made overt. As Sidney Bunt has commented, these men 'could not persuade their organisations [the AJY as well as the JLB] to adopt an official anti-Zionist policy, but they were able to bring about a non-policy of masterly inactivity'.[51]

The apparently non-committal stance of the Brigade did not pass without comment at the time, even though such attitudes were widespread throughout the communal establishment of the day. The pro-Zionist editor of the *Jewish World*, Leopold Greenberg, wrote as follows in 1929: 'I was surprised to find, a few weeks ago, that the J.L.B band could not play *Hatikvah*. Is it that in the Brigade Jewish Nationalist feelings are quelled or kept submerged? Someone in authority might care to state what attitude the J.L.B takes up on this question.'[52] No response was forthcoming from London Headquarters. Even behind the scenes the subject of Zionism was studiously ignored. One can search in vain through the JLB Minutes for 1948 for some mention of the creation of the State of Israel – a momentous event in modern Jewish history by any standards. By contrast, in November 1948, the Brigade immediately sent a telegram of congratulations to their Majesties King George VI and Queen Elizabeth on the birth of a grandson and Heir Apparent, Prince Charles, later Prince of Wales.

This reluctance to accept the new political realities persisted and, arguably, was reinforced by the experience of the Second World War and the Nazi Holocaust. One-third of world Jewry had been wiped out in the Nazi genocide. But throughout the 1950s the JLB carried on as if nothing had changed. This was no doubt symptomatic of the 'collective amnesia',[53] induced by guilt feelings which enveloped Anglo-Jewry in the immediate post-war period.

In 1950 the World Maccabi Union approached the JLB to cooperate in the organisation of a British team for the first Maccabiah to be held in Israel. Instead of jumping at the opportunity, it was half-heartedly minuted as follows: 'It was decided that, as the Brigade was affiliated to the Association for Jewish Youth, who were represented on the appropriate committee, any assistance that the Brigade could give, could be rendered through this medium.'

Similarly, in January 1951 the AJY asked the JLB to publicise an appeal for the Jerusalem Jewish Youth Centre amongst its members. Headquarters agreed, but not until an assurance had been given that the centre was 'entirely non-political and run on AJY lines'.[54] At the Diamond Jubilee Display at the Seymour Hall in November 1954 'God save the Queen' was preceded by the singing of the traditional hymn *Adon Olam* ('Lord of the Universe'). *Hatikva*, now the national anthem of the State of Israel, was conspicuous by its absence.

In the provinces, on the other hand, the rift between the Zionists and their opponents was largely absent. Manchester Jewry, indeed, had developed a strong Zionist tradition, dating back to Chaim Weizmann's arrival in that city in 1904. In 1932 the Grove House Lads' Club instituted Modern Hebrew classes, because the Manchester Education Committee (the body which oversaw evening classes in the city) refused to sanction teaching of the language on the grounds that it constituted 'a religious matter'. Grove House justified what, for 1932, was a very progressive educational policy thus: '"It is our intention to teach Hebrew as a modern language as it is spoken today in Palestine," said Mr Norman Jacobs, the secretary of the club . . . "We do not intend to introduce any question of religious teaching".'[55]

This may have aroused the interest of the *Daily Express* which published the story, but the *Ivrit* classes were hardly a resounding success. Within a short time they 'had to be dropped for want of support'.[56] Nevertheless, when Weizmann died in 1952 the Manchester JLB cancelled its scheduled ball as a mark of respect for the late President of Israel. In the smaller communities, lack of numbers, especially of children, meant that the youth organisations, Scouts, *Habonim* (see presently), Maccabi and JLB had to work together and often shared the same facilities, schoolroom or synagogue hall.

The fact remains, however, that from the 1930s onwards the Brigade was being increasingly challenged on its own territory, with the appearance and growth of Zionist youth movements in Britain. A youth wing of the English Zionist Federation (EZF) had been set up as far back as 1915. By 1925 it had evolved into the Association of Young Zionist Societies (AYZS) which published its own journal *Young Zionist*. The AYZS aimed to co-ordinate Jewish nationalist activity especially amongst university students. By 1931 it had over 2,000 members organised into 50 societies around the country, just over a half of these being in London. The following of the AYZS was limited however to middle-class, college-educated and largely suburban Jewish youth, rather than to the working class in the East End. However, youthful Zionism received a tremendous boost from the creation of *Habonim* (the Builders) in 1929 by Wellesley Aron. Aron was a Cambridge graduate who had himself been a Boy Scout and a member of Baden-Powell's own troop at Gilwell Park. In 1926, he went to Palestine where he worked for two years at Zionist schools in Tel Aviv and Haifa. He returned to Britain at the request of Weizmann to work for the Zionist Organisation as assistant to Leonard Stein. Aron set up *Habonim* on his own initiative after visiting the various East End clubs and noting their lack of Jewish content. *Habonim* had its headquarters in Canon Street, a stone's throw from the Bernhard Baron Settlement, and within a few years it had become militantly Zionist. In common with the JLB and the clubs, *Habonim* members indulged in athletics and scouting activities. The *gedud* (troop) structure and the division of responsibility between adult leaders and child assistants upon which *Habonim* was organised 'was taken directly from the Boy Scouts'. But the atmosphere, whilst 'never slavishly observant' in a religious sense, was unmistakably Jewish. Hebrew was interspersed with English as the language of command, lectures were held on aspects of Jewish history and culture. In the course of time, summer camp (from 1932 on) became *hachshara* – agricultural training with a view to settlement on *kibbutz* in the Land of Israel. Indeed, with Aron's return to Palestine in 1932, *Habonim* became increasingly radical, secular socialist Zionist, with a greater emphasis on *chalutsiut*. This tendency was encouraged by *shlichim* from the Palestine Labour Party then in London, including the later Mayor of Jerusalem, Teddy Kollek. By 1939 the movement boasted 4,000 members – twice as many as the JLB and its summer camp attracted at least as many participants (1,350 in 1936). In August 1939, on the eve of war, *Habonim* held a huge camp in Bedfordshire consisting of about 1,100 Anglo-Jewish youngsters plus 300 refugees. The *Jewish Chronicle* claimed that it was the 'largest Jewish camp ever held in Britain'. During the Second World War, *Habonim*, rather than the communal establishment, took the initiative in setting up hostels to fill the gap in Jewish education in the evacuation areas in which Jewish children were now dispersed.[57]

In 1935 the Association of Young Zionist Societies merged with the University Zionist Council to form the Federation of Zionist Youth (FZY), which soon claimed to represent perhaps 2,500 members. The FZY came to rival the AJY for the allegiance of Jewish youth. Zionism was becoming fashionable amongst young Anglo-Jewry and its image was arguably more democratic. Indeed, Bunt draws a contrast between the 'Old Order' as represented by the Association *for* Jewish Youth – and the Brigade – and the Federation *of* Zionist Youth created by the young people themselves.

The activities of the Zionist youth movements were stimulated further in the late 1930s with the influx of refugees from central Europe. Many of these had been exposed to Zionism in their countries of origin, especially through the Maccabi organisation, with its militant athletic brand of Jewish activism; *Betar*, a paramilitary Zionist organisation founded in Riga in 1923, (British branch 1938), *Young Poale Tsion* (Workers of Zion, British section 1938) and the revolutionary Marxist inspired *Hashomer Hatsair* (Young Guard) which began in Galicia in 1916 (in England 1939) and was exceptional, amongst the continental Jewish youth movements, in being directly influenced by Baden-Powell in its methods. Some of the refugees were members of *Hechalutz* (the Pioneer) which, originating in Russia at the turn of the century, prepared potential settlers on the *kibbutzim* in Palestine. Agricultural training was of more than academic value to these young people who, after all, had only been admitted to England on condition that they would eventually re-emigrate. Under the impact of events in Germany, an identifiable, if tiny, *Hechalutz* movement appeared in England in 1933. In 1944, *Habonim* amalgamated with *Mishmar Habonim* (the Builders' Watch), the umbrella organisation for *chalutzim* from the continent, and a combined membership of 3,000 was recorded.

With the establishment of the State of Israel, Zionist youth groups in Britain lost some of their most active leaders to *Aliya*. On the other hand, Israeli youth workers began to appear on the scene. *Young Poale Tsion*, in particular, benefited and briefly enjoyed expansion in the early 1950s with a membership of about 700 largely, it would seem, drawn from the Jewish working classes who had had little exposure to other forms of Jewish education. Numbers fell back to around 400 by the end of the decade. A multiplicity of other minor left-wing orientated Zionist youth groups, mirroring trends in Israel, were active in Anglo-Jewry: *Hashomer Hatsair* with 600 members in 1958, *Dror* (150) and *Hanoar Hatsioni* (120).

However, it is Maccabi which has been the most successful of the youth organisations in the Zionist camp since the end of the Second World War. In 1951 its strength was put at 5,000, almost as large as the combined membership of the groups gathered under the AJY umbrella. The Central Maccabi Fund was instrumental in the provision of sports and club facilities, with the opening of the Maccabi Centre in West Hampstead and of a stadium in Hendon in the 1950s. In 1958 the membership of Maccabi had fallen back to 3,500 but it still remained a force to be reckoned with on the Jewish youth scene.[58]

Religious Zionism, however, remained distinct from the predominantly secular and politically left-leaning groups so far described. The British *B'nai Akiva* (Sons of Rabbi Akiva) was founded in 1939 by refugees from the continental movement (1929) dissatisfied with what they saw as a neglect of religious values on the part of *Habonim*. *B'nai Akiva* and its senior equivalents (for those aged 17 and over), *Bachad* (*Brit Chalutzim Dati'im*, Covenant of Religious

Pioneers) and *Torah Ve'avoda* (Torah and Labour), were the youth arm of *Mizrakhi* (*Merkaz Rukhani*, Spiritual Centre), the Orthodox religious Zionist political party in Palestine. In those days, *B'nai Akiva* was 'unmistakably left-wing and Socialist'.[59] Like *Habonim*, *B'nai Akiva* took members, both boys and girls, from the age of nine and became increasingly influential on the Anglo-Jewish scene after the Second World War. In 1951 membership of *B'nai Akiva* was put at 2,000 compared with 3,000 in *Habonim*. *Bachad* boasted 750 members in 14 towns and ran two *hachsharot* farms at Thaxted and Dockenfield, two youth houses and a *Merkaz Limmud* (study centre) in Manchester. By 1958 *B'nai Akiva/Bachad* had almost caught up with *Habonim* in terms of numbers, 2,000 as compared with 2,200, whilst the smaller grouping *Torah Ve'avoda* added a further 500 children to the religious Zionist movement.

As already noted in Chapter 3, the JLB's ranks were severely depleted during the Second World War. In April 1945 the chairman of Harold House in Liverpool, Maurice Rathbone, wrote to Laurie Abraham in London about the state of the Brigade in the north-west:

> Our present position . . . gives us cause for some concern, as the Harold House Unit today consists almost entirely of non-Jewish boys. This is due to a variety of circumstances, including dispersal, evacuation etc. and particularly because of the counter attractions of movements such as Habonim and Bachad, which have drawn a number of lads who might otherwise have come to us.[60]

Unlike *Habonim* which had a successful policy of establishing Jewish hostels for evacuee children in outlying areas, the JLB made no real attempt to reach its displaced clientele during the war years. Instead, in the 1930s and 1940s, in the face of Zionist competition, the JLB stuck to its tried and tested formula. In 1934 Harold M. Lion, a future Brigade Commandant and a member of the West London Reform Synagogue, declared in a speech at the Oxford Union:

> I for one am a British Jew and whilst I have every sympathy with the trials and tribulations of our co-religionists abroad, my loyalty is to England and it seems to me a poor sort of loyalty that discredits its country where one earns one's living, has been educated and had all the advantages of imperialism in the true sense of the word . . . I do not want you to misunderstand me as being anti-Zionist; perhaps the better way of putting it would be to say that one is pro-British.[61]

Harold L. Cohen, a leading benefactor of the Brigade in Liverpool and a member of the Liberal Synagogue in London, was 'on more than one occasion' reported to have said that:

> He was not . . . what for want of a better term was called a Zionist, but for all Jews fortunate enough to live under the aegis of the British Empire . . . it could only be good to assist those Jews who still suffered great disabilities, and even persecution, in some other European countries. It was for them that the work in Palestine was intended.[62]

In contrast, the Zionist youth groups encouraged ideological debate and political activism. They competed with the Communist Party and its Young Communist League (YCL) for the allegiance of young Jewish radicals in the East End of London and the working-class districts of Manchester, Leeds and Glasgow. The secret of CPGB popularity amongst Jews, which reached its culmination in the election of Phil Piratin as MP for the Mile End Division of Stepney in 1945, was undoubtedly its stand against Fascism, both at home and abroad. The 'Battle of Cable Street' (October 1936) became the symbol of a far wider Communist inspired counter-offensive against the Mosleyites, whom the Party identified with home-grown anti-Semitism in general. Propaganda and street activism appealed to working-class Jews dissatisfied with the lukewarm attitude of the established political parties (including Labour) and the low-profile adopted by the Board of Deputies. In the 1930s the Communists went out (and were remarkably successful in) enlisting Jewish support in unabashed 'ethnic' fashion. Their message appealed in particular to the young. In 1934, in keeping with its policy of mobilising above party Popular Fronts against the British Union of Fascists (BUF), the CPGB was instrumental in the creation of the East London Youth Front against Fascism and War (1934). Young Zionists, especially on the left, joined in the common fight against the Far Right, including the Boycott of German Goods campaign spearheaded by the newly formed Jewish Representative Council of 1933. FZY joined the Jewish Peoples' Council against Fascism and anti-Semitism (JPC) created in 1936, despite the misgivings of the Zionist Federation which disapproved of the influence which Communists had in it.[63]

The JLB's strategy to deal with anti-Semitism in the 1920s and

1930s was little different from its response before the First World War: the inculcation of good citizenship and discipline, the latter quality being one which was deemed to be in short supply amongst Jews in general. In his celebrated 'Camp of God' speech in 1928, E. Royalton Kisch, who was one of the earliest supporters of Liberal Judaism,[64] reminded his young audience that

> There are other reasons which lead to an anti-Jewish feeling here, and one of them is . . . the undisciplined and un-Jewish behaviour of some of our fellow Jews . . . Unnecessary showiness of dress; extravagant public displays, intolerance of the views and feelings of others, disrespect of persons and institutions, money-lending and sharp practices in commerce are unfortunately not rare . . . .
>
> We are a conspicuous minority and always in the limelight . . . and the bad impression caused by the wrong-doings of the ten bad men reflects ten-fold upon the many Minyanim of good Jews.[65]

This speech came dangerously close to an apologia for the anti-Semites, whose brand of racial prejudice was far nastier than anything which had confronted the Brigade in its early days. In the aftermath of the Battle of Cable Street, Harold Lion, Officer Commanding the London Regiment, declared:

> The Jews are as worthy citizens as anybody else in this land. We have been disgusted and shocked at the things that have been going on in the East End. They are most undeserved and I am afraid it has been a case of Jew-baiting.
>
> I feel there is nothing like speaking one's mind. Ninety per cent of our fellow Jews are as good a type as anyone else. It is that minimum which belongs to no organisation at all who cause trouble. If we can get every member of the Jewish community into the brigade or a club or some similar organization, I am sure that through the training we give them we shall have no anti-Sematism [sic] whatsoever.[66]

Following an impressive display mounted by the Brigade in March 1937, Lord Reading wrote in glowing terms to Lion:

> I am sure that it must be a lasting satisfaction to you and your officers to realize that your hard work is not wasted but is successfully supplying the best possible answer to antisemitism.

In any case this temporary wave of artificially engendered hostility will pass, but the results of your labours will remain for all to see in the physical and moral development of the next generation.[67]

The assumption that anti-Semitism could be cured by 'good behaviour' on the part of Jews permeated down through the ranks of the Brigade. In an issue of the Brigade journal, *The Advance*, published soon after the coming to power of Hitler in Germany in 1933, Captain P.Levy of the Tottenham Company wrote under the heading 'Anti-Semitism' as follows:

We Jews in England are fortunate to live in a country which has always been extremely tolerant . . . The English have always treated the Jews well; the Jews have, in their turn, always striven to show how they recognise this just treatment . . . by force of example we should demonstrate how unjust and how unreasonable attacks on Jews really are. The charges that the Nazis bring against the Jews can be refuted only in one way: by actually showing that the Jew is neither treacherous, nor deceitful, nor unscrupulous in his greed for gold, nor mean and cunning, nor lacking in any of the nobler motives which the Nazis deny of all Jews . . . .

I would urge upon you the necessity of always living an upright and chivalrous life, as only through such example can anti-semitism be *permanently* destroyed.[68]

The idea that Hitler was amenable to 'gentlemanly' behaviour and the claims of 'justice' was hopelessly naive. English public school notions of sportsmanship and fair play were to be swept away in the maelstrom of the 1930s and 1940s. Captain Rubby Risner, who had grown up with the Brigade and who was something of a writer in its journals, spent a few weeks in Germany in November 1934. Judging from his account published in *The Advance* the following spring, the experience had been nothing less than traumatic. 'Unfortunately,' he wrote, 'the accounts given in the Jewish Press are more or less true . . . . The Jews are completely segregated and ostracised.' (This, before the imposition of the Nuremberg Laws in 1935.) On one occasion, Risner attended a concert held in a grand synagogue: 'The orchestra of thirty sat on a platform just in front of the Ark (the men wearing their skullcaps) and rendered a fine interpretation of Schubert, Mozart, Haydn,

125

Beethoven . . . Thus by playing to Jewish audiences first-class Jewish musicians are able to eke out a livelyhood in the Germany of today.' Yet, even Risner clung to his faith in human nature:

> I came away from Germany with the conviction that if only the common people were given *a sporting chance* [my italics] – before the youth have been poisoned by the teaching [of Nazism] – there will yet be a chance for German Jewry to regain their lost status . . . But the Jews themselves are very pessimistic.[69]

Back in England, it did not do for the Jews to attract attention to themselves by being overly successful. In 1936 the Brigade took the decision to withdraw temporarily from competing for the Prince of Wales Boxing Shield. The JLB had won this trophy an almost embarrassing number of times since its inception in the early 1920s. This remarkable success was attributed 'to the fact that other cadet units could not compare, age for age, with the Jewish boys in physique and fitness, and to the fact that greater care was lavished upon their children by Jewish parents'.

The decision to withdraw may have been hailed as sportsmanlike, but was governed too by other motives. As the veteran Commanding Officer (E.C.Q. Henriques) of the Manchester JLB, which had on several occasions found itself pitted against London in the final for this cup, put it: '[We do] not go out for "pot-hunting", and, indeed, there was a danger in the Jewish clubs always being so successful, so much so that jealousy was perhaps created and non-Jewish clubs would not enter the competitions.'

In December 1939, soon after the outbreak of war, the notorious English Nazi radio propagandist Lord 'Haw-Haw' described the JLB as 'the greatest of Jewish sports organisations' and as in control of British sport.

The Brigade evidently did not subscribe to the philosophy of Benny Leonard, the American Jewish light-weight champion of the world, who asserted that 'the Jewish youth of America should learn the art of boxing, because the ability to handle your fists is perhaps the best insurance against anti-Semitism'.[70] Still less did the Brigade wish to engage in any form of political activism. In April 1933 an organisation styling itself the 'Jewish Lads' Brigade anti-Fascist Group' distributed leaflets outside Camperdown House calling upon members to demonstrate at the May Day rally in Hyde Park. The flyer, signed by the committee's chairman, Joe Levy, and secretary, Miss Green, was headed 'JEWISH LADS' BRIGADE. WHAT ARE WE DOING AGAINST HITLER'S MURDER GANG?'. The answer was provided by Ernest Halsted and his colleagues who swiftly brought an injunction to stop the anti-Fascist committee from printing and disseminating 'defamatory' material in the name of the JLB. In their evidence, the Brigade submitted that 'It had no political object, and was entirely opposed to any form of political agitations [sic] and to the spreading of Communism and class hatred among its members'. Nevertheless, the rather curious spectacle of a Jewish organisation silencing anti-Nazi activity hit national headlines. Perhaps the JLB's stance was not so remarkable after all. They were simply following the example set by the Board of Deputies in the 1930s.[71]

There is some evidence, however, that grassroots JLB members engaged in political activity, despite the disapproval of Headquarters. A few weeks after this court case, the socialist *Daily Worker* reported that 'delegates' from both the JLB and Oxford & St George's, *inter alia*, had participated in elections held at the Workers' Circle House in Aldgate (an organisation with strong Bundist connections) for representatives to the World Youth Anti-War Congress in Paris in September 1933.[72] At the same meeting a youth Anti-War and Anti-Fascist Council for East London was elected.

Motel Robins, long-time Brigade Archivist, recalls:

> If my memory serves me well, and it does, many a demonstration which took place East of Aldgate Pump mainly consisted of alerted members of the working class, Communists, Socialists, and many young Jewish 'teenagers'. They always had a band, which consisted mainly of members of the JLB D/Fife & Bugle Band – of course in MUFTI. If the upper crust were aware of this, I shall never know, but who knows, perhaps the Nelson Eye existed amongst those who cared. Most youth club members took part in the struggle against Fascism. I cannot recall any demonstration taking place at that time organised by the big whigs of the Jewish Community.[73]

Another old comrade from the provinces remembers that:

In the 1930s the band was a very important morale booster for the Jewish community in Liverpool in the period of Fascism. It was a great annual event when the band used to march through Liverpool leading the Companies of the JLB to the trains to go to Deal to Camp . . . and it was a great civic event and it compared . . . to the Christian militant [sic, military] bands and parades . . . .

Of course, it is not unusual for the young to disobey their elders. To read the glowing press reports of the annual JLB Summer Camp and other activities, one would gain the impression that discipline, a virtue so essential to the ethos of the Brigade, as a fundamentally authoritarian movement, was never anything other than impeccable. Only rarely was a lad sent home from camp for 'insubordination' to his superiors. Rarer still is the nature of his offence spelled out. Nevertheless, it appears that the 1919 Deal camp was marked by 'breaches of discipline' on the part of Westminster and the Jews' Free School Companies. In 1933 Captain S. Ansell recalled his impressions of that particular camp as being 'funny'. 'There were strikes: Free School Company one day refused to go on parade, as one of their number was sent home.'[74]

In August 1925 the *Isle of Thanet Gazette* reported that 'two youths hailing from the East End of London', by the names of Aaron Mintz and Hyman Lewis, were hauled before the local magistrates accused of stealing apples and damaging crops in the process. When caught redhanded by a policeman, they admitted their guilt but tried 'to do a deal', asking him 'Can't we settle it?'. In court nevertheless, 'when their names were called out, they came forward, clicked their heels, and stood to attention after the manner of well-trained Brigade boys, and pleaded guilty'. The boys, one of whom earned 10/– a day as a tailor and the other who earned 30/– a week, were each fined 20/– and 10/– costs. Although the press report did not directly say so, they were both members of the JLB.[75]

We have to turn again to the left-wing *Daily Worker* to find another slant on Brigade activities. In August 1933, under the headline 'JEWISH LADS' UNITY IN CAMP' the paper reported that

The Jewish Lads' Brigade annual camp ended with a demonstration which astonished the officers.

Shorter food supply among the 450-odd lads in the camp led to a demonstration in Marquee A on the night of August 12. The officer who tried to quieten them down was jeered and one of the lads was ordered out. The whole section soon followed the lad and their mass demonstration had such an effect that all the lads were provided with sufficient food.

Another concession was forced by demonstration when, on a rainy day, the boys were exempted from wearing shorts.[76]

Of course, this report could be, and probably was, dismissed by the Brigade as 'Communist propaganda'. Perhaps it was exaggerated, given the resentment no doubt felt in radical circles at the attitude of the JLB to anti-Fascist activity. On the other hand, assuming that the report was essentially true, who, one wonders, furnished the *Daily Worker* with it? There must have been at least one 'Bolshie' lad at camp!

Others, naturally, preferred to 'sell out' to the authorities. At the wartime Tring camp (1942) it was noted that 'four N.C.O.'s [sic], appointed themselves Cadet Police, following a complaint of the conduct of some of the lads in Tring'. 'Whereas my first reaction had been to terminate their self-made appointments', confessed Commandant Magnus to HQ

I decided, when I saw them on patrol – and the salutary effect which their presence had on others – that they were serving a very useful purpose. I must confess to have been influenced by the fact that one of the four N.C.O.'s [sic] had been numbered among the offenders the day before. His action confirmed the truth of the adage 'Set a thief to catch a thief'.[77]

Clearly, the drill and discipline demanded by Brigade membership was not to the liking of all Jewish boys. The writer, Louis Golding, who was claimed as an illustrious alumnus, to the extent of penning – an entirely irrelevant – preface to the 1925 JLB Annual Report, admitted to having lasted precisely one evening in the Manchester Company! Other young Jews, who were politically conscious were, as we have seen, attracted to Zionism or Communism. Traditionalists preferred the more sedate intellectual atmosphere of Rabbi Julius Jung's Sinai League, founded under the auspices of the Federation of Synagogues in 1915. Other Orthodox, non-Zionist youth groups later appeared on the scene; *Ezra*, attached to the *Agudat Yisrael*, non-Zionist political party in Israel, and *Ben Zakkai*, associated with the Adath Yisrael Synagogue and the Union of Orthodox Hebrew Congregations, led by Rabbi Schonfeld in England. These groups differed from *B'nai Akiva* in that boys and girls were segregated for all social activities. In 1958 *Ezra* was reckoned to have a total membership of 1,000. After the end of the war, the Reform movement began to develop its own youth programme; the newly formed Federation of Liberal and Progressive Youth Groups had 400 members in 1951 and 550 in 1958, and the Reform Synagogues of Great Britain Youth Association some 500. Other non-ideological groups which appeared in the 1950s included the Federation of Jewish Youth Societies (1,200), Jewish Youth Study Groups (300) and the *B'nai Brith* Youth Organisation (BBYO) (400) in 1958. Jewish youngsters simply seeking an outlet for their energies joined the Jewish Scout Troops, which offered all of the attractions of the Great Outdoors without the rigorous regime insisted upon by the JLB. In 1951 there were nine troops with about 500 members; in 1958, 1,500 plus 350 Jewish Girl Guides. No figures exist for the number of Jewish children who joined non-Jewish youth movements, the Scouts in particular, nor indeed for the, presumably, large number who remained outside the orbit of any of the youth organisations. In 1937 the *Jewish Chronicle* estimated that of some 15–18,000 young Jews in London alone, only 6–7,000 were affiliated to a youth group. In 1951, the paper's correspondent Joseph Finklestone, later foreign editor, found that 'about half of the children and youth between the ages of nine and 21 belong[ed] to some kind of youth movement – a total somewhere in the region of 30,000'. There was undoubtedly much truth in the allegation of Jewish 'individualism'.[78]

Yet despite all this, the JLB still managed to attract a substantial following between the wars – and continues to do so today. Discipline and moral training may go in and out of fashion, but the Brigade has continued to flourish. It has been suggested that perhaps this was because of the fact that the JLB succeeded in being an organisation where young Jews could socialise and perpetuate their 'ethnic' identity in a form which was secular and non-nationalistic without being anti-religious. As Basil Henriques put it in 1942: 'The club movement, which includes the JLB, need not be ashamed of its aims, which are to produce good citizens of the Jewish religion. We are proud of both these objects. But, unlike the [sic] Habonim, the clubs are non-political. They contain members of every shade of English and Jewish political thought.'[79]

After the Second World War, the official connection with the mainstream United Synagogue was conscientiously maintained, the personal Reform convictions of influential elements on London Headquarters notwithstanding. Saul Amias, who succeeded Revd Barnett as Chaplain in 1955, tactfully ensured that normative Orthodox standards prevailed in the JLB's public life. He encouraged religious observance at camp, reinstituting evening prayers and introducing *kiddushim* in 1969; he organised *kashrut* and made sure that Brigade events did not clash with incompatible dates in the Jewish calendar. His article entitled 'Torah in Tentland' which was published in the *Jewish Chronicle* in 1952 was reprinted by Headquarters for Brigade-wide distribution. Amias' conscientiousness was not always rewarded, however. A printed programme for the 1966 Summer Camp declared in bold capitals that 'football, cricket, netball, pushball, volley ball – tug-o-war' would all take place on 'Saturday July 30th' and that 'Inter platoon sports finals' would follow on 'Saturday, August 6th'. Camp Commandant Josh Manches took the view that 'Anything we did in Camp on *Shabbat* was all right because it was in our own home'. But competitions with outside bodies were not permitted. Care was taken not to offend the religious, but the fact that many members did not conform to Orthodox standards was necessarily tolerated. For example, camps, especially weekend camps in the winter, would begin at 3 o'clock on Friday afternoon, to ensure that participants could arrive before *Shabbat*: 'The fact that people turned up at 6 or 7 or 8 was besides the point.' Manches recalls that, on another occasion,

They were selling icecream in Camp . . . and [Rabbi M] Ginsberg [the Chaplain] came to me and said 'You know *that* icecream is not kosher' . . . . He said 'I didn't see it . . . but I think you ought to know'. It was too late to do anything about it . . . he was a wise man . . . It was sufficient for us to make sure [that it did not happen again.]

Nevertheless, by 1981 the Brigade could claim '[W]e are an Orthodox movement with kosher food in Camps always'.[80] The 1987–88 Annual Report stated that 'Camps, indeed all Brigade activities, are carried out in a Jewish atmosphere. All food served is strictly kosher and JLGB encourages its members to take pride in their Jewish heritage.'

When a possibility arose in 1959 to move the JLB offices to the Liberal-inspired Bernhard Baron Settlement, Revd Amias dissuaded the Committee on the grounds that such a 'move would be mis-interpreted'. However, in 1966, when this option arose once again, Amias' misgivings were brushed aside. The JLB operated out of the Settlement from 1967–75. Indeed, from 1975–84 the office was based at the St John's Wood Liberal Synagogue and Amias regularly attended Headquarters meetings there.

In 1970 the Brigade received a request in writing from Judge King-Hamilton, president of the West London Reform Synagogue, to appoint the Senior Rabbi of that synagogue, John Rayner, who was also chairman of the Council of Reform and Liberal Rabbis, to the post of Honorary Brigade Chaplain alongside the Chief Rabbi and Haham. Revd Amias conveyed Chief Rabbi Jakobovits' opinion that 'the appointment was not necessary and that the Reform and Liberal Synagogues [could] be assured that they would be consulted on any matters affecting members of the Brigade who were also members of their Synagogues'.

Such a stance was unacceptable to the Progressives, who sought the communal legitimacy which such a largely symbolic role in the Brigade would bestow. Moreover, a refusal to concur would not only be interpreted as rudeness but would be to ignore the reality on the ground. The Brigade, after all, contained many children from Reform families, and some of its Companies operated on Reform premises, both in London and Manchester. The minutes of the following Headquarters meeting tersely noted 'that Rabbi Rayner had been appointed an Hon. Brigade Chaplain and the Chief Rabbi had been advised'.[81] This appointment was soon followed by that of other Progressive religious leaders: Hugo Gryn, Sidney Brichto, J.J. Kokotek, Dov Marmur and Tony Bayfield.

However, largely through the efforts of Revd Amias and of his successor, the current (1993) Chaplain Alan Greenbat, the Brigade has attempted to adhere to more stringent religious standards and this policy has, to some extent, paid off. The movement has succeeded in penetrating into Orthodox schools through its administration of the Duke of Edinburgh Award Scheme. Youngsters at the Hasmonean High Schools, Beis Shammai and connected with Lubavitch-Chabad are currently participating in the scheme, including its Expedition Section. Children of primary school age participating in the new Challenge Award for Jewish Youth are required to complete a Jewish Heritage Section which has received the endorsement of the United Synagogue Board of Education – which helped in its design – and of the Chief Rabbi, now Dr Jonathan Sacks, himself.

Even so, the Brigade has continued to take a liberal line on the admission of members to its ranks. According to Brigade Secretary Charles Kay, 'Any child whose parents claim to be Jewish, we will accept as such. We do not require a *ketuba*'.[82] In other words, in contrast to all of the Jewish schools in Britain (bar one Reform school), the JLB does not insist that its intake be of proven *halakhic* Jewish status, i.e., Jewish through the maternal line. In the context of contemporary Anglo-Jewish youth work, inclusivism is seen to be a virtue which outweighs religious exactitude. However, inclusivism has its limits. Leaving aside exceptional circumstances during the Second World War, the JLB has never tolerated the dilution of its identity by the deliberate inclusion of non-Jewish members. Whilst the occasional non-Jewish club leader or officer was still to be found (such as Edward S. McCulla in Liverpool and Stanley Rowe in Manchester) and, more often, the non-Jewish sports instructor, the overwhelming feeling of Jewish parents whose children went to Brigade, that they should mix with other Jewish children, was respected. This feeling was very well expressed in 1958 when the Manchester JLB hosted a social visit, including dancing, by members of the Gentile Flixton Youth Club and the latter planned to reciprocate this hospitality. The local *Jewish Gazette* published a letter of protest from Revd G. Wulwik of the Prestwich Jewish community which stated that 'This is a matter which is the vital concern of every Jewish parent, and it is up to the religious and lay leaders of our community to bring pressure to bear upon the Jewish Lads' Brigade to arrange for responsible control which will ensure that in future the brigade's club truly lives up to its name as a Jewish club'.[83]

This somewhat sensitive issue was taken up in the general local press, to the obvious embarrassment of the Council of Manchester and Salford Jews which suppressed discussion at its meetings. The 'bottom-line' function of a Jewish youth organisation to socialise its members within the Jewish community and thus hold back the tide of assimilation and intermarriage had come well and truly to the fore. This was at a time when, in the opinion of an 'outsider', Stanley Rowe, 'The majority of members of the J.L.B had . . . no interest at all in religion and this . . . was the fault of the parents'.[84]

In Liverpool, ten years later, 'The biggest bone of contention' at the Dunbabin Road Jewish Youth Centre was 'the admission of some 30 non-Jewish members, about 5 per cent of the total membership'.[85] Some of the Jewish members of the club apparently 'strongly' disapproved.

By the 1980s the rate of intermarriage in Anglo-Jewry had reached an estimated one in three. The Jewish youth club served as one of the last outposts of Jewish life for those children from non-practising backgrounds – the large majority – who attended neither a Jewish day school nor part time Hebrew classes. Statistical surveys and market research have consistently shown that most Jewish parents still want their children to mix with and eventually to marry other Jews, even if they cannot rationally explain why they feel this way. The JLB has certainly done its bit to satisfy this demand.

Eventually, and wisely in the interests of its own self-preservation, the JLB came to terms with the existence of, and finally embraced the State of Israel, but the process took a decade. In 1958 the Israeli Ambassador to London, Eliahu Elath, inspected the JLB camp at Walmer. The invitation was extended by Commandant Harold Lion, but the initiative had come from Jonas May. Headquarters Committee 'applauded the news', welcomed the anticipated publicity, and invited the Ambassador to write the foreword to the Annual Report. His flattering words concerning the 'noble tradition of the Brigade' carried an unconscious irony. It was just as well that the Ambassador had been insufficiently briefed on the history of the Brigade. In any case, bygones were bygones.

In July 1962 ten chosen officers, led by Major Jack Wagman (prominent as the head of the Norwood Orphanage), warrant officers and senior sergeants, made an official visit to Israel on behalf of the Brigade. They spent three weeks touring the country, hosted by the Zionist 'Bridge in Britain' programme, and the venture, despite some organisational teething troubles, was deemed a great success.[86] The JLB reciprocated by inviting Israeli youth leaders and students to attend Summer Camp and assisted in organising a Cotswold camp for a group of Israeli teenagers – who all promptly caught colds in the English summer of 1962. Contacts were forged with the Israeli Cadet Force, Gadna. Henceforth, the appearance of contingents of the JLB at Israeli Independence Day celebrations and, indeed, the playing of *Hatikva* together with 'God save the Queen' became unremarkable events in the Brigade calendar. As CO London Regiment, Josh Manches had been responsible for introducing the playing of *Hatikva* in the late 1960s 'because of the pressure from parents who found it very, very odd' that the anthem was omitted. He recalls:

> I was the first person that introduced at our Camp playing . . . *HaTikva*
> . . . I remember so clearly that Swaythling was very much opposed to
> it . . . he said that we are a British unit here and we don't play the national
> anthem of foreign countries . . . Certainly, we did not want to give the
> impression that we were under any instructions or any control from
> Israel . . . The only time we ever played at Camp before that the Israeli
> national anthem was when we had their Ambassador . . . Swaythling
> said that that's the time when you play[ed] the national anthem, a
> foreign national anthem.

By Manches' time, a public demonstration of affection for Israel no longer posed a psychological threat to the stability of Anglo-Jewish life.

On 1 June 1967 an emergency meeting of the Headquarters Committee was called on account of the crisis in Israel which went down in history as the Six Day War. Lord Swaythling did not attend but made known his view that 'the J.L.B. had never taken any part in politics or political issues. [and] He did not see that Brigade personnel would have any difficulty in rendering such help as they wished in their private capacities.'

Swaythling's opinion, however, was not shared by other members of the Headquarters Committee. Ellis Stanning, for one, felt that

The situation could well deteriorate and there were clear indications that thousands of young people and the vast majority of the community were taking a personal responsibility to assist Israel during the crisis. Non-Jewish Organisations, the Press and public opinion was largely more than sympathetic towards Israel . . . whilst the Brigade could avoid involvement, it would have to take the consequences.[87]

Josh Manches agreed 'that the publication of an unhelpful attitude or of a less than sufficient interest would cost the Brigade virtually all support in the community'. Clearly, events had run ahead of the Brigade and whilst political 'association with the Jewish Agency', i.e., the Zionists, could not be countenanced, it was deemed essential that it be seen to stand behind the Board of Deputies in positive general support for the State of Israel in her hour of need. In fact, at least 11 young men, mostly officers from the London Regiment, volunteered for war work in Israel. The 1966–67 Annual Report noted that 'large numbers of Brigade young people responded to appeals for help at the time of the June War, some in this country and others as volunteers in Israel. The Brigade is maintaining contact with those volunteers who have not yet returned home'.[88]

By the time of the Yom Kippur War in October 1973 there was no longer any question about Brigade 'sympathy' for Israel and the need for its 'positive and practical' expression throughout the organisation.[89] The JLB internalised support for the Jewish State in a typically non-ideological fashion which, in keeping with its tradition, appealed to the sense of duty of its members.

In the end, it must be said that the existence of a religiously inclusive and non-ideological movement like the Brigade, well suits the non-ideological character of the Anglo-Jewish community. Perhaps this is one of the secrets of its survival.

5 · 'The Lasses': The Brigade since 1945

In 1955 the JLB celebrated its Diamond Jubilee. In London, it was marked in November 1954 by a professionally produced pageant in the West End held before a distinguished audience including the Secretary of State for Air and the Marquess of Reading. This was followed in January 1955 by a Service of Rededication at the New Synagogue in Stamford Hill attended by Chief Rabbi Israel Brodie and other communal dignitaries. A public display also took place at the Free Trade Hall in Manchester, and in Glasgow a special dinner was arranged.

Behind the 'glitz', however, the Brigade had fallen upon hard times. Post-war Britain was a land of austerity, with rationing and reconstruction the order of the day. Money was tight and the ideal of voluntary service was lost in an age of compulsory National Service and state intervention in the social sphere. The advent of the first majority Labour Government in 1945 was a landmark in the development of the welfare state. From 1944, under the Butler Education Act, the Ministry of Education, Local Authorities and the LCC were obliged to provide club and recreational amenities for young people. The professional social worker and youth leader appeared on the scene.

The JLB, in common with other youth organisations in the voluntary sector, suffered a severe decline in the late 1940s and 1950s. Income dropped whilst expenditure, not helped by post-war inflation, increased. The Brigade went into serious overdraft, to the tune of some £3,000 by 1952. Gluckstein admitted to the Brigade Council in 1950 that 'the Brigade was . . . far from paying its way'. By 1953 the financial situation was 'extremely grave'.[1] In an attempt to

137

salvage the situation, the Brigade Council was radically expanded, Headquarters Committee enlarged by one third and a series of sub-committees were set up at Headquarters, one devoted entirely to public relations, and a professional publicity agent was consulted about how to launch an effective appeal. In 1949, 10,000 copies of an Appeal Brochure with a dedication from the Chief Rabbi were mailed to prospective subscribers. The graphic artist Abram Games, an ex-member of the Clapton JLB, designed a striking new cover for the Annual Report in 1950. The London Regimental magazine was re-launched thrice yearly under the title *Advance Again!* in the Coronation year (1953). The OCA began to publish its newsletter in 1951, but this was soon incorporated into *Advance Again!*, which became the journal of the whole Brigade. In 1951, £650 was spent on making a 15-minute feature film to show to potential members, officers and patrons. This was a self-conscious attempt 'to combat the competition from other organisations', i.e., *Habonim*, Maccabi and *B'nai Akiva*. As we saw in the previous chapter, the Zionist groups continued to thrive and, if anything, to expand under the momentous impact of both the Holocaust and the creation of the State of Israel. By comparison, the image of the Brigade appeared ill-defined and its objectives obscure. Despite extensive preparations, including the composing of a suitable 'brief' to accompany the presentation, the results of the film promotion were desultory. From 1950 to 1953 the Stock Exchange Dramatic and Operatic Society donated the proceeds of its opening night to the JLB, but in the last year ticket sales slumped and the enterprise was not repeated. A bazaar held in 1953 at Woburn House, the Jewish communal offices in London, and opened by Princess Alice, Countess of Athlone, raised over £1,000 but did not solve the JLB's financial problems. According to the Treasurers: 'In the early months of the year [1953] it had been necessary to sell yet more of the few remaining available securities and the threat of being unable to find enough ready money to carry on had become very real.'

A new departure was the staging of a professional charity boxing display at the Royal Albert Hall in 1955 which raised about £2,500. Despite dances, theatricals, bazaars and raffles, the JLB overdraft inexorably rose, reaching £6,000 in 1958. 'A major problem,' noted the financial report to Headquarters in 1961, 'was the loss each year of old and loyal subscribers who were not being replaced.'[2]

In 1958 the Brigade Council was informed that the overdraft had reached £9,000, income amounted to only £3,000 per annum, expenditure to 'at least £12,000', making a total deficit of £5,000. The Camperdown House Trust, through Ernest Joseph, was forced, somewhat reluctantly, to come to the rescue. The Brigade was largely kept afloat through the generosity of the Trust and its careful husbandry of investments, which had accrued over a long period since before the First World War, when the Trust had been established independently of the Brigade to oversee the purchase and construction of Camperdown House. In 1962 the deficit was temporarily cleared largely through monies given under the terms of Harold Lion's will (he died in 1961). Nevertheless, the JLB remained in a precarious financial situation until the mid-1960s.

Added to this, the JLB was failing to attract young blood, both officers and lads. After six years of war and the continuation of call-up until 1963, ex-servicemen were anxious to get back to civilian life, their families, to complete their disrupted education and build up their businesses. There was little time to be spared for luxury extra activities, such as giving up the two evenings a week necessary for running a JLB Company. In 1953 the Brigade Council was informed that not a single new officer had been commissioned for a whole year. Nor were businesses so free with their generosity as they had been in the old days. The Treasurers informed Headquarters Committee in September 1953 that 'The appeal to firms for gifts of food-stuffs for Camp had been a failure. Only one gift having been received as a result of 50 letters.'[3]

Yet the failure to attract officers was regarded as the most pressing problem faced by the Brigade after the war. The Annual Report for 1951 bemoaned the fact that: 'The spirit of service which attracted young men to the J.L.B. in pre-war days seems to be entirely lacking, and it is left to a generation too far removed from the boys themselves to carry out the work . . . [To satisfy] the crying need for manpower in the service of Youth.'[4]

Thus the JLB was thrown back on the dedication of the old guard whose loyalty had not diminished but whose health and energy were declining. Stalwarts from the pre-war days manned the Headquarters Committee or were brought back in at the grass roots. The average age of the staff was between 60 and 70. Inevitably, the JLB suffered many bereavements in this period: Ernest Halsted, E.C.Q. Henriques, Benjamin Strump, Archie Solomon and Harry Berly all passed away. Ernest Joseph, however, remained active on the Headquarters Committee almost until the last. He died in 1960 with 62 years of JLB activity behind him. At the same time, the lads themselves were getting younger and fewer in number. This latter trend was partly, but not entirely, due to the shortage of officers.

Other factors, however, compounded the Brigade's recruitment problems. One was the unpopularity of military-style organisations after the war. Significantly, the Boys' Brigade was not seriously affected, largely owing to its avoidance of War Office affiliation on the eve of the war. In August 1950 a *Jewish Chronicle* editorial wondered whether

> Those responsible for the organisation of the [JL] Brigade might . . . consider whether it would not be advisable for a body that so hotly resents any suggestion of 'militarism' to eschew the use of military titles to which some of the holders have no legitimate claim. The leader of a company of boys should be able to enforce discipline without finding it necessary to call himself 'Captain' or 'Lieutenant'.[5]

Naturally enough, the Brigade was loath to give up such a fundamental part of its character. When challenged on the point in the increasingly egalitarian post-war period, Brigade leaders protested the unimportance of the use of military rank in the organisation, and, indeed, the uniform which went with it. The fact remains however that the military trappings were somehow felt to be essential to the ethos of the Brigade. The debate over 'image' was to come to a head in the 1960s and 1970s. In the immediate aftermath of war, what was more important was the slowness of the Brigade to react to the current unpopularity of things military by clinging to the connection with the War Office. It retained the connection with the Cadet Force until the Army Cadet Force (ACF) itself severed the link in 1950 (June in London, August in Manchester) – despite the negative effect on its image. The Glasgow JLB's attachment to the 7th Battalion, the Cameronians was not ended until as late as 1954. In reality, the JLB as a separate entity ceased to exist in Glasgow after the war. In 1981 Ralph Delmonte recalled that when he had come on the scene 'the Brigade in Glasgow [had] deteriorated to the extent that it became in the early 50's [sic] non existent . . . the last few remaining members joined a Cadet Force in . . . Yorkhill . . . and . . . the Jewish Lads' Brigade as such ceased to exist'.[6]

Even under Delmonte's leadership, a semi-military connection endured through attachment to the 154th Field Ambulance Royal Army Medical Corps (TA). Indeed, from 1946 to 1950 the Brigade operated parallel JLB Company and Cadet units in each area, the former, consisting of 12–15-year-olds, acting as a feeder for the latter (15–18) and ultimately for the forces. Brigade sections reverted to the pre-war uniform of cap (beret), belt and haversack, whilst the Cadets were dressed in khaki. In 1953 the uniform for seniors was modified to 'battledress, with flashes, web-belt, and peak cap'. The officer in charge of the 2nd Cadet Battalion, the Royal Fusiliers, Major L. Maurice Dale (who had been awarded the Military Cross for bravery during the war), reported in October 1947 'that he was finding that Jewish boys and officers were not keen to join the Cadet Force and that the present proportion of the Battalion was about half Jewish'.[7]

Similar reluctance to join the Cadets was encountered in Manchester, where the ACF was by 1950 'lessening in popularity'. Attempts to establish Cadet Companies in Birmingham and Newcastle after the war were discouraged on the grounds that there was no demand. In March 1950 Major Dale gave the strength of his Battalion 'as 9 officers and 100 lads, 25% being of Jewish faith'.[8] By this point, the City of London Army Cadet Force had decided to amalgamate units and link them with the Territorial Army. The JLB did not consider it worth holding out for a separate Jewish unit for 25 boys.

As as result of 'considerable pressure from company officers',[9] Junior Sections, catering for boys between the ages of 10 and 12, were started in many Companies. The problem of retaining the interest of the older boys remained. A Company for senior boys of over 15½ years was started at the North London Headquarters in 1952. On the other hand, it was announced at the Brigade Council meeting that year that the general age for recruitment was being lowered to 11 years and three months. This was compared with 13 before the First World War.

Another problem for the Brigade was posed by the dispersion of the Jewish community itself after the war. The drift to the suburbs, both in London and the provinces, perceptible in the 1920s and 1930s, became a flood in the 1950s and 1960s. The Blitz and evacuation had decimated the old Jewish East End. An estimated 30,000 Jews remained in the area in 1945, compared with at least 100,000 in 1914. The immigrant community was in the process of breaking up and East End Jewry went into irreversible decline. The second and third generations were moving out, especially to the Boroughs of Barnet in the north-west and Redbridge in the north-east, often leaving the ageing immigrants behind. Only one JLB Company was revived in Stepney after the war and this had 'difficulties in obtaining recruits'.[10] Soon, Camperdown House lost its *raison d'être* as the centre of activity. Even the club encountered 'difficulties . . . in maintaining . . . numbers'. The Camperdown House Masonic Lodge and the 2nd Cadet Battalion Royal Fusiliers, with its 'Rose and Crown' social club, still met there. In 1953 Brigade-Major George H. Lang estimated that 'In the past, three-quarters of the total membership of the Brigade came from East London' but that only a 'few of the Brigade's 400 members in London' now hailed from that area. The HQ building became a drain on resources. In 1952 the Camperdown House Trust decided to lease out the whole building to the Territorials and the Brigade was obliged to find other offices. After a long search, they found suitable premises at 75 Baker Street which they leased from 1953 until 1956. These offices were 'not easy to find . . . [being] tucked away at the back of a non-descript building opposite the palatial Baker Street head offices of a well-known chain-store [Marks & Spencer]'.

Even so, for reasons of economy, the Brigade decided to transfer operations to the North London Club in Amhurst Road. In the early 1950s, the North London Club remained adequately patronised as many Jews were still to be found in Stamford Hill, Tottenham and Stoke Newington. Nevertheless, the problem of finding local headquarters to fill the void left by Camperdown House remained. Annual Reports declared that it was Brigade policy to open a series of centres in north-west and north-east London to function as both JLB headquarters and youth clubs. This objective was only partially met by the acquisition of 197 Earlham Road, Forest Gate in 1954. This project ran into legal difficulties; within two years the Brigade was forced to cut its losses and sell the building. Another ill-fated venture followed: the purchase in 1957 of Ilford Cottage, Mansfield Road, reputedly the first house in Ilford, and its conversion into a new Hutchison House Club and Headquarters for the Ilford Company. This centre, too, only lasted for two years, for reasons which will be discussed below. In any case, no similar centre was secured in north-west London which, no doubt, accounts for the failure of the JLB to make a real impact in that growing Jewish area of the capital for many years after 1945.

Camperdown House had been 'not only the head but also the heart'[11] of the JLB and without it the organisation enjoyed a nomadic existence. With the closure of the North London Club at the end of 1959, the Brigade was obliged to be satisfied with modest offices at Woburn House and a basement store in the Finchley Road.

Wider social changes also militated against the revival of the Brigade. The raising of the school leaving age from 14 to 16 did not necessarily mean that young people had less free time for extra-curricula activities, despite the pressures of homework and the increasing need for academic qualifications. After all, a seven-hour school day was less onerous than a 12-hour working day in a factory or shop. More significant were the widening opportunities, in part created by better education, available to the young after the war. By the 1960s, young people by and large had the spending power to exercise choice. The high-minded charitable side of youth work which had predominated in Victorian times was no longer relevant. Children no longer needed to escape the squalor of inner city streets and grinding poverty. The summer camp was no longer their only chance of a summer holiday. On the contrary, as parents, especially white-collar Jewish professionals, moved to the suburbs and became more affluent, they could afford to take their children on holiday with them. Holidays abroad became more commonplace. Teenagers developed more sophisticated tastes and became more demanding. The new danger was boredom and apathy, not poverty. The role of the youth club had to change subtly to meet these new challenges.

In 1950 the JLB had a total of only 725 members compared with 2,000 in the 1930s and 4,000 before 1914. This included 500 from London, Manchester 100, Newcastle 50, Glasgow 45 and Birmingham 40. By the end of December 1956, the London Battalion was parading '15 officers, 15 Warrant Officers, 59 N.C.O's and 169 Cadets', figures which were regarded as being 'disturbingly low'.[12] In 1958 London Companies had an average attendance of 23, there being about 320 boys in all. Attendance at Summer Camp (at Walmer) shrank from 1,000 to an average of about 400 all ranks. This was despite the fact that camp was still heavily subsidised by Headquarters. Lads were charged £4 10s for ten days in 1954. Many parents could no doubt have afforded to pay more. Camp ran at a considerable loss.

Conditions at camp were made less spartan. An electric generator was installed for lighting at night. Proper showers (supplied with cold water, granted) and closed latrines were introduced and, in 1947, Bathing Parade was moved from morning to afternoon, following a 45-minute compulsory rest period after lunch. Proper beds rather than sleeping bags were purchased for the 1958 camp and chests of draws provided for the boys' clothing. The sea off Walmer tended to be cold and rough; Cyril Goodman, the Camp Commandant that year, reported that

> Swimming is not too good at Walmer and a large number of boys who attended the compulsory parade did not in fact do more than paddle; they were not forced to enter the water.
>
> It is a matter for consideration whether, despite the tradition attaching to the compulsory bathing parade, it would not be advisable, in future camps, for the swimming parade to be a voluntary one.[13]

In 1947 Summer Camp was attended by only 130 all ranks, from London alone. From 1948 onwards the Walmer camp effectively became the National Camp of the JLB. Provincial Companies, led by Manchester, came south to join their metropolitan brethren. In 1951 Manchester solicitor Vivian Steinart became the first provincial National Camp Commandant and in 1952 the tradition of a public display held before the Mayor of Deal was instituted. However, the concept of a Northern Camp was revived for five years between 1956 and 1961 when Manchester joined with Sheffield to camp at Nash Court Boys' Training Centre in Shropshire and subsequently on the Wirral. (In the late 1940s and early 1950s, too, individual Cadet units attended local non-Jewish Cadet camps in their region.) Subsidies were provided by London Headquarters to keep travel costs down, but disputes frequently arose between London and Manchester over the extent of funding as the pre-war fixed capitation grant was not fully restored. The 400 all ranks total at camp in 1950 included 80 from Manchester, 20 each from Birmingham and Newcastle and a modest six from Glasgow. The lack of numbers meant that Companies had to be combined under unfamiliar officers for the purposes of camp. This posed problems for discipline. Camp Commandant E.E. Goodson reported that 'a number of individual cases of bad discipline occurred which were dealt with suitably . . . There is evidence that the standard of work and the standard of instruction in the various companies is poor.'[14]

For a long time after the end of the war JLB uniform was still subsidised, except for officers who were asked to pay for their regulation blue battledress from 1954 onwards. However, in 1960 a major policy decision was reached. Blue battledress was introduced as standard wear for all recruits, to be paid for outright by them. Nevertheless, there was concern that the cost of uniform was discouraging enrolment in the poorer areas of London, particularly in the north-east, and a system of 'assessment' was introduced. Poor boys thereby continued to be subsidised although it is unclear whether or not many took advantage of this. In 1961 boys were charged 6d a week Company subs.

London Companies were revived and new ones created after 1945. In north-west London and Middlesex: Brondesbury (1947–55), Edgware (1948–50, restarted 1953), St John's Wood (1954–56), Golders Green (c.1948, restarted 1959), Finchley (1948–49, restarted 1956), Wembley (1959, renamed Kenton 1962), Maida Vale (1960), and Stanmore (1965). In north London: Finsbury Park (1947, renamed Stamford Hill 1953, revived as Finsbury Park 1959), Clapton (1949, revived 1951), Southgate and Palmers Green (1960), Hackney (revived 1964), Dalston and Tottenham (both dates unavailable). In east London and Essex: Ilford (February 1948, revived 1956), Leigh-on-Sea (March 1948), Bethnal Green (1949), Leytonstone (1950–56, restarted 1957–63), Bow (1950, restarted 1957–59), East Ham (1950), Stepney Lads' Club (1950–55), East London (at Rutland Street School, 1953), Highams Park and Chingford (1953–56), Romford (1965), Tower Hamlets (1966) – an amalgamation of East End

145

Companies, Wanstead and Woodford (1966). In the west of the capital: Ealing (April 1948), Marble Arch (1953), Central (1960) and New West End (merged with Hammersmith, 1961). Finally, the south: New Cross (April 1948), Norwood and Streatham (1948), Brixton (revived c.1948), Richmond (1950–55), Woolwich (1951, amalgamated with New Cross, 1951–56), and Croydon (1955).

A pattern of post-war JLB development was emerging. The concentration of strength was in the areas of secondary Jewish settlement to the east and north-east. The weakness in north-west London was striking and was no doubt due, as I have already suggested, largely to the failure of the Brigade to establish a Headquarters in this district. Other youth organisations, most notably Maccabi and the Zionist groups, succeeded in penetrating the area. The Brady Maccabi club at Compayne Gardens, West Hampstead was opened in 1937. Suburban synagogues affiliated to the United Synagogue and the Reform movement began their own youth clubs. The *B'nai Brith* Youth Organisation (BBYO/A) which was started during the war, expanded its activities in the 1950s, organising events hosted in private houses, rather than dependent on club premises. The *B'nai Brith* Hillel Foundation had been founded in the 1930s and in 1955 opened its first purpose-built Hillel House for students in central London. This activity was aimed at an older age group however. By contrast, the Golders Green and Finchley JLB Companies had collapsed by 1952 (Finchley was amalgamated with Brondesbury) and Edgware had a chequered history, although 'one of the largest units of the [London] Regiment'[15] in 1955 – despite the fact that these areas boasted a growing Jewish population which tended to be better off economically speaking than its counterpart in Redbridge. However, perhaps this comparative affluence militated against the influence of the Brigade in the north-west London suburbs, where it may have been perceived by parents in this period as a no-longer-needed and best-forgotten 'hang-over' from the poverty stricken heyday of the Jewish East End. The JLB's chaplain Revd Arthur Barnett recognised the urgent need for the Brigade to compete on the youth club level, but his was an isola-ted voice on the Brigade Council in the early 1950s.

In 1956 Cyril H. Davis, a member of the Headquarters Committee, produced a 'private' memorandum setting out various options for the reorganisation of the Brigade, in response to changing circumstances. These options were: 'OFFICERS VIS-A-VIS PAID PERSONNEL, CLUBS VIS-A-VIS COMPANIES, SUMMER CAMPS VIS-A-VIS WEEK-END CAMPS.'[16]

The basic problem was that the Brigade was not holding its own in the face of competition from other youth organisations using the latest social work 'know-how' – professional club leaders rather than volunteers, attractive club facilities with a relaxed style of discipline, a wide variety of activities, and frequent 'week-ends' in schools or youth centres around the country, and not under canvas. The JLB formula of voluntary service, military discipline and spartan summer camp no longer appealed to the vast majority of Jewish youth. Like the Boys' Brigade and the Church Lads' Brigade, it was looking decidedly old-fashioned by the 'Swinging Sixties'.

Professional club managers were employed at the North London and Ilford Hutchison House Clubs (1957) with little marked success in either case. In 1959 the decision was taken to close down both clubs and to sell the buildings. Cyril Davis, for one, had reached the conclusion that 'It was apparent that the J.L.B. Clubs were making no contribution to Company work and . . . that although this disproved the wisdom of the decision to locate Clubs by area it was none the less the answer which had been gained from practical experience'.[17]

In Manchester it seems that greater progress was made towards integrating the JLB with club life. The Manchester JLB and Club Annual Report for 1953–54 set out a coherent philosophy for youth training. It stated 'We feel young people have four main needs. They are (1) The need to belong. (2) The creative instinct and recognition of achievement. (3) Opportunities for new experiences. (4) Discipline' and expanded upon the benefits bestowed by club membership in all these directions for 'the ordinary young people without too much talent' as well as for the 'stars'.[18] Although unsigned, it is more than likely that these observations were written by Stanley Rowe, the first fully trained professional social worker to be employed by the JLB. In 1955 he was followed by Charles Kay in London. Rowe presided over the Manchester JLB and Club between 1954 and 1969 and was a dynamic force for its development. Under his leadership, the Brigade and Club spawned a multiplicity of activities; music, drama, art, photography and film-making sections, public speaking and discussion groups. The traditional Brigade emphasis on social service was translated into practical action: manning hospitals at Christmas, decorating pensioners' flats and fundraising for good causes. The club 'adopted' a refugee child at the Ockenden children's home and raised money to support him until he reached the age of 15. The youngsters also 'adopted' an elephant in the Kenyan National Park in Nairobi – a neat reworking of the old Imperial Mission which the Brigade in its Victorian phase took so seriously. The range of sports on offer was widened to include fencing, weightlifting, badminton, judo, gymnastics and tennis. Rowe became a nationally recognised pioneering youth worker. Students training to be youth leaders and social workers visited and spent time at the Manchester JLB and Club which was fast becoming a model of its kind. It consciously adopted a policy of training its own senior members and voluntary youth leaders 'on the job'. Manchester also achieved a first in its creation of a Club Members' Committee designed to participate in the running of the club and from which it was hoped future leaders would be recruited. This was a departure from the hierarchical and adult chain of command which had always characterised the Brigade. In 1956 a Junior JLB, catering for the 8–12 age range, was also started in Manchester.[19]

Manchester JLB had been reconstituted at Elizabeth Street under the command of Vivian Steinart. These premises, however, were no longer in the right area to serve the Jewish community and if the decision to sell up and move had not been taken in 1957 'Headquarters . . . would have found itself in a year or two in the middle of an industrial estate'. The final straw had been £300 worth of damage caused by vandals in August 1956. Having sold the old site for £22,000, JLB Manchester moved to temporary accommodation at Middleton Road, in the former Nathan Laski Hall, home to the local Maccabi and to amateur theatricals. The hall was 'in a very derelict condition'.[20] A building fund was launched and in 1960 a modern youth centre costing £30,000 was opened on the site by Princess Alexandra. It was named Henriques House after the pre-war Manchester Brigade Commandant.

However, the problems did not end there despite the fact that the

JLB and Club had some 600 members in 1964. In that year alone the premises were burgled twice, complaints were constantly voiced that youth work was treated as the 'Cinderella' of the Jewish community and about parental 'apathy', and the Club laboured under a mounting deficit. Even though Manchester JLB was 'the most successful club in the community', it was nevertheless affected by the general trend in the city that 'one out of every two youngsters who joined a club left within a short time'. In 1961 it was estimated 'that in the greater Manchester area there were 3,200 young people between the ages of 14 and 21, but only about 36 per cent took part in some sort of Jewish activity. "The numbers are decreasing year by year".'[21]

In 1963 a new Company was formed at the Jackson Row Reform Synagogue, at Prestwich (1964) and at Cheetham (1965). Vivian Steinart retired in 1964 and was replaced by Ronald A. Bentwood. In 1968, under a new Constitution, the activities of the Brigade and Club were separated.

Over on the west coast at Liverpool, the derequisitioning of Harold House in 1948 notwithstanding, there was no immediate sign of a JLB revival. Headquarters in London, basing themselves on a dubious legal claim, threatened the Harold House Committee with being in breach of the terms of their Trust Deed. Finally, in 1958, the Liverpool Company was restarted under local businessman and would-be Liberal Councillor Albert Globe, largely as a means of re-establishing the JLB claim on monies raised from the projected sale of Harold House – which by the mid-1950s was situated in a run down part of Liverpool in which few Jews remained. The drift from Brownlow Hill to Childwall had begun before the war, and Chatham Street now found itself in the centre of a new campus development for Liverpool University. Prolonged negotiations with Government, municipality and university were set in motion to ensure a suitable level of compensation for the enforced removal of the club from the area. In the end, two-thirds of the £140,000 required to build a new purpose-built centre was picked up from public funds. A new Harold House Club and Community Centre, designed by architect Ferdinand Elter, was duly opened in Dunbabin Road in 1965. It became the home for all of the Jewish youth organisations in the city.[22] The Liverpool JLB, under Albert

Globe, Henry S. Tenser (1965) and Bernard Caplan (1965 on), enjoyed rapid expansion in the Merseyside Battalion (Liverpool, Fairfield, Crosby and Southport Companies) and was to prove a source of new ideas for the Brigade as a whole in the following decades.

In Glasgow, Benjamin Strump retired in 1947 to be replaced by Major Louis Blint who himself had already clocked up 30 years service with the Brigade, starting as a boy bugler in 1907 at the age of 10. His own son, Leslie Blint, became Commanding Officer of the Glasgow Junior Brigade Company which in 1949 had 45 members. In 1952 the Glasgow Jewish Pipe Band headed the Glasgow contingent at the National Remembrance Parade in London and was inspected by the Duke of Edinburgh. By 1961 Glasgow, some 80 strong, had spawned three Companies: the Glasgow (renamed Shawlands, 1961), Giffnock (1957) and Clarkston (1958, restarted December 1971), under clothing businessman Ralph Delmonte. Delmonte joined the JLB in 1933 aged 15. He rebuilt the JLB in 1954, on his return from the army and six years in Canada. At his first parade only four boys showed up. Under his leadership, the Glasgow JLB's traditional venue in Butterbiggins Road on the South Side was relinquished in the mid-1950s in favour of 52 Thistle Street, G5. A Parents' Association and OCA were started and fundraising events, including an annual Company variety review entitled 'It's all for fun!', were held. A new JLB centre, funded with the aid of Sir Isaac Wolfson (of Great Universal Stores and an old JLB boy who had certainly 'made good') and the Scottish Jewish whisky magnate Sir Maurice Bloch, was opened at 65 Albert Road, Pollokshields in 1961. Wolfson and Bloch had come to the rescue of the Glasgow JLB which had spent years in fruitless efforts to raise money to establish its own purpose-built headquarters. Delmonte remembered how he 'also approached Sir Morris Bloche [sic] and he asked me how much Mr Woolfson [sic] gave as a donation to the building fund and I said that the Woolfson [sic] Foundation had indeed sent £2,000, and Sir Morris Bloche says make my donation 2,000 guineas'.[23]

Thus it was that plans to build or purchase new premises in the provinces were carried out independently of London Headquarters and the funding was largely by local initiative. In Glasgow, in 1968, a new extension was opened with the aid of Wolfson and Sir Isidore Walton, the chairman and managing director of Scottish Metropolitan

Property. Nevertheless, the Albert Road site did not stay in use for more than 25 years, reflecting the shrinkage of Glasgow Jewry. In 1986 it was sold to a Moslem organisation and the JLB decamped to the hall of the Netherlee and Clarkston Hebrew Congregation, where it is today commanded by Pamela Livingston (see below) who herself joined the Brigade in the 1960s.

Birmingham Company was re-established in June 1949 under Michael V. Solomon and H.E. Solomon, probably the sons of the founder Archie Solomon, and boasted the grand total of 26 all ranks in 1952. From 1957 they met at new headquarters, in a converted room in the caretaker's building at the Hebrew Schools in St Luke's Road, from where most of the members were recruited. Birmingham also boasted an OCA with 70 members in 1950. Likewise at Sheffield, the Company was reformed in November 1952 under Captain L. Newman, son of the founder. Nineteen boys joined with their headquarters at Psalter House. Despite their modest numbers the lads were apparently 'keen as mustard': 'There is one small boy whose father brings him ten miles in his car every Monday, waits until his son has finished, and then takes him back home a further ten miles.' However, the 1960–61 Annual Report stated that the Sheffield Company had 'been through a very difficult year. A complete reorganization is in hand and it is hoped that a small cadre of enthusiasts will grow into something more in keeping with the size of the Sheffield Community.'[24] By the following year, Sheffield had disappeared.

A new Company was started at the Leazes Park Synagogue in Newcastle in January 1949, on the initiative of a group of ex-servicemen, with 25 boys. This figure rose to 50. Geoffrey C. Rossman took command. However, it had collapsed by 1951. Two abortive attempts were made to restart the Brigade in Newcastle, in 1969 by Tony Abrahams, a London officer temporarily in the city on business, and again in 1979–81 by Sam Ogus. Despite the support of Rabbi Y. Fine locally, this initiative foundered apparently because Newcastle Jewry did not have enough young people to sustain more than one youth group, the Maccabi.[25]

In 1959 a short-lived Company was started at Carmel College near Wallingford in Oxfordshire, the only Jewish public school in Britain, with the assistance of founder and headmaster Rabbi Kopel Rosen.

151

Finally, in October 1959, the Leeds Company was re-established with the help of a group of Jewish ex-servicemen, after a lapse of more than 40 years. But the moving spirit was Anthony Lander, a student at Leeds University, who had been active in the recently revived JLB in his home town of Liverpool. The first parade was held at the Moortown Estate Talmud Torah. Fourteen boys between the ages of 10 and 12, all from the immediate neighbourhood of Moortown, were enrolled under the command of Jacob (Jack) Kudlatz. Despite Lander's persistance, the Leeds Company foundered, never managing to achieve a roll of more than 20 boys. The chief obstacle, as he informed Charles Kay in London, was the inaccessible and not very salubrious location of the Talmud Torah: 'It is one of those places where "I wouldn't let my Hymie go there by himself at night"'. But no alternative accommodation appeared to be forthcoming. None of the local synagogues in the now more fashionable parts of Jewish Leeds were willing to come to the rescue. Lander, who was himself religiously observant, vented his frustration: 'It seems that but for the local Talmud Torah, there is no other suitable place in the whole of Leeds . . . a strange contrast to L[iver]pool with ½ of the size of community.'[26] Almost immediately Kudlatz was obliged to return to his native city of Glasgow for family reasons. By 1961 the Leeds Company had collapsed and no further attempt was made to revive it until the mid-1970s.

Leeds aside, by the early 1960s the JLB was showing signs of revival. It benefited from the provision of new community centres in Manchester, Liverpool and Glasgow. Numbers at Summer Camp rose to between 450 and 600. An advertising agency was brought in by Ellis Stanning to revamp the JLB's Annual Report and provide a more professional approach to publicity. Parents' Associations were established at some of the more active Companies, numbering 10 in 1962. These, together with the London Regimental Aid Committee started by Ilford parents in the early 1960s, were to play an increasing role in fundraising in the years to come. Manchester Battalion initiated overseas holidays, Switzerland being a favourite destination in the late 1950s. A greater variety of activities were on offer at Summer Camp, including a day trip to Calais in 1962 (when two-thirds of the boys were sea-sick during a particularly rough crossing), nature study trips, canoeing, fencing, climbing, archery and riding.

A greater accent was placed on entertainment, such as barbecues, filmshows, a treasure hunt and funfair. The well-known actor and JLB old boy Ron Moody joined the lads at the 1962 camp, just as another old boy, Alfred Marks, had done exactly a decade earlier. Indeed, by the 1950s, the list of popular figures, actors, comics, musicians and bandleaders, as well as professional boxers and managers who had started out in the JLB – and its bands in particular – was growing. These included Vic Herman, Mick Fox, Lew Lazar and Al Phillips (the 'Aldgate Tiger'), all boxers, Abram Games, the artist who designed posters for the Festival of Britain, Phil Moss and Sonny Rose, the bandleaders, Sim Saville, who played with the London Philharmonic, TV drummer Mickey Greene and filmstar, the late Marty Feldman. Perhaps the best known graduates of the JLB today are TV scriptwriters Marks and Gran.

By 1960 a total of five bands were in operation: the London Regimental Drum and Fife Band and Bugle Band; the Manchester Bugle and Silver Bands and, of course, the Scottish Glasgow Bagpipe Band. This was recreated in 1955 through the generosity of Sir Maurice Bloch who provided five brand new sets of bagpipes, five drums and a silver mace for the bandmaster to wield. The Norwood Brass Band was also revived after the Second World War but eventually went out of existence. The short-lived Highams Park and Chingford Company formed its own bugle band in the 1950s. But its failure to survive after a brief flowering and the outlay on instruments required put Headquarters off encouraging any similar local ventures.

Weekend camping became increasingly popular. Such camps were held for the London Battalions at Epping until 1950 and thereafter at Walmer and attracted some 250–400 boys each season. Motel Robins and Harry Berly continued to do the quartermastering. A Coronation Camp was held at Walmer at Whitsun 1953 attended by 138 all ranks. Lads were presented with a special souvenir certificate. A new facility was provided in the shape of the Max J. Bonn Memorial Centre at Bracklesham Bay, Sussex where regular training courses were held. Later on, camps were also held at Grange Farm in Essex and at the under-utilised Ernest Halsted Memorial Playing Fields in Buckhurst Hill. Brady's Skeet House was first hired in 1962. Traditional Brigade activities were reactivated: an annual sports meeting at Parliament Hill Fields, a boxing tournament and the Banner and Drill Competition. So too was the Chanuka Parade. In 1956[27] the JLB became one of the first participating organisations in the newly created Duke of Edinburgh Award Scheme, which encouraged outdoor pursuits and set tough tests for youngsters. In 1958 the Brigade created a Special Activities Section (SAS) to train older lads to participate in the scheme. The idea of putting on 'tough' activities to keep the interest of seniors had been piloted at that year's Summer Camp and proved very popular. The handpicked 'Commandos' were issued with a suitable 'working battledress' and sent off on weekend army-style 'endurance tests' to increase their stamina. In 1961 the first Duke of Edinburgh's Award Scheme Gold Standards were won by members of Finchley Company and they were honoured by an invitation to St James Palace to receive their badges from the Duke himself. An internal proficiency badge scheme, on the lines of that pioneered by the Scouts, was also introduced in the mid-1960s. In 1960 the first JLB Swimming Gala since the war was held at the Marshall Street baths in the West End of London. A West End march was instituted as well as an experimental river cruise for the London Battalion. In 1961 a special City march was followed by tea at the Guildhall hosted by the Jewish Lord Mayor, Sir Bernard Waley-Cohen. Parades were also held at the Wellington Barracks, at the Tower of London (from 1966) and at the Royal Naval College, Greenwich, through the intervention of Lieutenant-Colonel Maurice Dale. In addition to regularly forming Guards of Honour at communal events, another new date in the JLB calendar was the Association of Jewish Ex-Servicemen's (AJEX) parade, which took place on the Sunday following the national Remembrance Day ceremony at the Cenotaph in Whitehall. A contingent of the JLB headed by a massed JLB band became a regular sight at this event. OCAs in London, Glasgow, Manchester and Birmingham continued to hold reunions and dinner-dances. In 1951 the Manchester Company reported that at its annual ball 'the presentation of debutantes was reintroduced'. However in 1955 this practice was abandoned. The reason, the Press was informed: 'Times have evened out and there should be no snobbery.'[28]

THE MOVE TO CO-EDUCATION

The Jewish mother has an extraordinary affection for her children, and how proud they are to see the boys in cap, belt, and haversack! One mother . . . had actually five sons going to Camp – and a sixth was coming along. The height of her ambition would evidently not be reached till a 'Lasses' Brigade' was formed, when she could send her daughters to Camp as well.[29]

Thus reported the *Jewish World* in 1908. Another half century was to elapse before this ambition was to be fulfilled.

As noted earlier, separate Jewish youth clubs for girls preceded those for boys. Lily Montagu was the pioneer in this field. Nevertheless, the JLB did not follow the precedent set by the Christian uniformed youth movements. As early as 1900, the Boys' Brigade had set up the Girls' Guildry in Scotland. In 1901 the Church Girls' Brigade was formed, and in the following year the Girls' Life Brigade (the forerunner of the Girls' Brigade) began. Of far more significance was the creation of the Girl Guides. In 1909 a group of girls appeared at the first big Scout rally held at Crystal Palace. They demanded to be inspected by Baden-Powell. Reluctantly he agreed and in 1910 the first Girl Guide companies were started under the direction of his sister Agnes. However, it was his wife, Olave Baden-Powell, who was really responsible for the development of the movement during the First World War. It is often said that votes for women were secured by female labour during the Great War and not by the campaigns of the Suffragettes. Lady Baden-Powell emerged as Chief Guide in 1918 and her subsequent influence on the scouting movement was every bit as great as that of her husband.[30]

The JLB had its own lady patron, Gladys, Lady Swaythling, the daughter of the founder, Colonel Goldsmid. For over half a century Gladys generously supported the Brigade, opening her house at Kensington Court for meetings and organising fundraising events – especially the grand balls in the 1930s. She mobilised her extensive contacts at court and in society on behalf of the Brigade and was a frequent and charming speaker at public displays. In 1921 she was made a Vice-President of the Brigade and later, as President, presided over an organisation composed entirely of men (other women were not appointed to the Brigade Council until 1951). She became the first woman guest of honour at the Maccabeans Chanuka Dinner in 1954. However, it seems that Gladys, who died in 1965 at the age of 85, never suggested that girls be admitted to the Brigade. This is perhaps surprising, given her involvement on the Council of the Girl Guides and the NSPCC and her concern to free housewives from the drudgery of domestic labour, through her patronage for over 20 years of the Electrical Association for Women. This body was set up to educate women in the use of domestic electrical appliances for cooking and heating. Apparently, Gladys was one of the first women in Britain to install an electric cooker in her kitchen.[31] She was made an OBE in the Coronation Honours List of 1953. Nevertheless, the admission of girls to the JLB was to be left, as we shall see presently, to her daughter-in-law, the second wife of the third Lord Swaythling, the former Mrs Jean Knox.

An entry in the Brigade Minutes in June 1901 states:

> It was decided to enrol the following ladies as honorary Members of the Brigade with the rank of Nursing Sister:-
>
> Mrs A.E. Goldsmid, Mrs E. Montefiore, Mrs Lewis-Barned, Mrs Cecil Sebag-Montefiore, Mrs Grunwald, Miss G. Davis, Miss [Nettie] Adler, Miss C[armel] Goldsmid, Mrs L. Montagu [Gladys, later Lady Swaythling], Mrs A.E. Franklin, Miss Olga D'Avigdor, and Miss Hannah Hyams.

A year later we read that:

> Upon the suggestion of the Commandant [Goldsmid] the principle of affiliating to the Brigade Classes for the instruction of Jewish Girls in First Aid, Ambulance and Nursing was approved. The Commandant arranged to consult the Managers of Jewish Girls Clubs & Schools as to the best means of organising such instruction.[32]

Whether or not there was any connection with this resolution passed in London, the Manchester Battalion formed 'a Ladies' Ambulance Class' in 1903, an enterprise which the local Annual Report deemed 'to be as useful as it may seem novel'. The class, it continued,

> consist[ed] of 30 young ladies who are instructed weekly in First Aid by Dr. [S] Finkelstein [Brigade Medical Officer] and Dr. Messulam. This entails no tax on the Battalion's funds, but is, on the contrary, a source

of extra revenue, and promises to be still more so in the future . . . some of these ladies teach physical culture to some of the girls attending the evening classes held at the Jews' School, and hereby help to do (though as yet on a small scale) for the girls what the Jewish Lads' Brigade is doing for our boys.[33]

Unlike the Brigade, however, the 'Ladies' Ambulance Class' was not open to public inspection which was, no doubt, considered to be undignified.

Similarly, the wives of officers played a role in fundraising for the Brigade behind the scenes. At the very least, they tolerated their husbands spending much of their spare time on Brigade work and loyally accompanied them on Inspection Day at camp. In 1909 a Ladies Committee headed by Mrs Leopold de Rothschild organised the first Brigade Ball.

The Manchester JLB, however, owed its existence to the initiative of the daughter of a local communal worker, Lewis Glass. In about 1899 Katie Glass, later Mrs Matz:

was a teacher at the Manchester Jews' School . . . and when she learned of the formation of the Brigade in London she thought that her class of boys would also be interested. She asked the late Rev Mr [L.M.]. Simmonds [Simmons], Minister of the Congregation of British Jews [Reform], to obtain details for her, and formed a corps at the school.[34]

Thus began a lifelong career of Jewish communal service. Mrs Matz, who taught for 11 years at the school before her marriage, was a founder member of WIZO (Womens' International Zionist Organisation). Early meetings took place at Rebecca Sieff's home in Didsbury. Mrs Matz's long association with the Manchester Daughters of Zion and its Old Girls' Union was recognised by the bestowal of the title of Honorary Life President in the 1950s. She was also made honorary vice-president of the Manchester and Salford Women's Zionist Council and president of the Ladies' Distress Society. Mrs Matz was the first lady associate of the Manchester Jewish Working Mens' Club, where she organised a gymastics class.

By the 1930s girls were present on the periphery of JLB activity. The North London Jewish Girls' Club (founded 1912), under the control of the indomitable Miss Isobel Aarons, began to send a contingent to camp at Walmer at the same time as the lads.

However, the boys and girls were strictly segregated. In 1935 the club had about 200 members. The North London girls occasionally took part in JLB public displays from 1930 onwards, presenting their own features. Young women were also recruited to run the Camperdown House Playcentre (1931) before the Second World War. The nursery was under the direction of an all-women's committee headed by Mrs Hannah F. Halsted (died 1936), wife of the Commandant. Jewish women who had risen to prominence in public life, such as LCC councillor Nettie Adler (daughter of Chief Rabbi Hermann Adler) and Miriam Moses, who became Mayor of Stepney in 1931, took an interest in the social work side of Camperdown House. In Manchester, Mrs Henriques, wife of the Commmandant, was president of the Jewish Girls' Club in Bury New Road, amongst her other public activities. In 1936 a Ladies' Committee was set up in Manchester for fundraising purposes. It was chaired by Mrs Steinart, the wife of Henriques' post-war successor, assisted by Mrs L. Finburgh. During the Second World War, as we have seen, the London JLB Ladies Committee knitted woollens and sent 'comforts' to the troops. This was indicative of the expanded role of women in the voluntary sector stimulated by the war. Jewish women made a specific contribution to voluntary war service through the creation of the League of Jewish Women in 1943.

On the eve of the war, Manchester JLB received a request for the formation of a Jewish Girls' Brigade in the city. The writer, now unknown, was referred to the Jewish Girls' Club. However, after the war a Girls' Section was formed (in 1947) at the JLB Club in Manchester and had about 80 members aged 14–18. A unit of the Girls' Training Corps existed alongside for a short time, but never had more than about 20 members. The girls were represented at camp in the early 1950s. Vivian Steinart claimed the credit for suggesting this idea and asserted that 'it was a great success, particularly as it kept the boys in camp at night where mixed activities were arranged rather than them having to go into town'.[35] Nevertheless, the presence of girls clearly caused some 'discipline' problems. In discussion at Headquarters, it was agreed 'that the girls from Manchester should only be in Walmer if a Camp site for them could be found away from the Brigade site'.[36] In Glasgow, a Girls' Training Corps was set up by Miss Zelda Blint (later Mail), daughter of the Commanding Officer, in 1949 and, with nearly 60 members, sent a contingent to camp at Walmer in 1951. The corps lasted for ten years until Mrs Mail's retirement in 1957.

However, it was the newly founded Liverpool Company (1958) which must take the credit for introducing girls into the Brigade proper. In April 1963 the Merseyside Battalion applied for permission to form a junior (9–11) and a girls' section. At the Headquarters meeting of 1 July 1963 both requests were 'unanimously' accepted. The experiment in Liverpool would be reviewed at the end of six months with the possibility of its being imitated elsewhere. The Liverpool 'Jewish Girls' Auxiliary Brigade' was to be an integral part of the Battalion, staffed by 'lady officers' who would have the right to serve on the local headquarters committee alongside their male counterparts. As for their uniform, the girls were to wear:

Navy Battle Blouse with similar badges and embellishments as the other Companies in the battalion, wearing a distinguishing colour (pink?) behind the lions [JLB insignia]. White shirt, black tie, navy beret, with appropriate badge . . . navy skirt, black shoes, white ankle socks or black stockings according to age.[37]

The first parade was held on 2 September 1963 in the Max Morris Hall of the Greenbank Drive Synagogue. Phyllis Abrams, chairman of the Parents' Association, recalled: 'There were three officers – Pearl Malits (Harris), Rita Applebaum and Victoria Tenser. They were in the uniform of the J.L.G.B. Thirty-five girls attended ages 10–16 but only one girl wore the new uniform (Faith Choueke) (Applebaum)'.

By October 1963 there were 50 girls in the Company, aged 10½ upwards and they were 'holding parades and doing drill, knotting and first aid'. 'Painting, hairdressing and beauty culture, cooking and rug-making' were soon added. 'On Sunday 1st December 1963, the Merseyside Battalion was visited by Lord Swaythling who after inspecting the battalion – at which all the girls were in uniform – gave the official accolade of National recognition to the first girls' company in the country.'[38]

In 1964, 25 girls from Merseyside attended Summer Camp accompanied by three lady officers under Mrs Rita Applebaum, and two helpers, housed in a separate compound which was out of bounds to the boys. The Liverpool Companies now boasted nearly 200 boys and girls, with 15 male officers and four female.

The experiment in Liverpool was a success. The presence of the girls apparently 'created a sense of competition within the battalion and assisted recruiting'.[39] Ilford was the first London Company to follow suit and attracted 35 female recruits in February 1964. About 20 girls from Ilford and 12 from Stamford Hill joined the Liverpool contingent at the 1964 camp. According to press reports, females accounted for 68 out of the 485-strong camp. The girls joined in most of the activities put on for the boys. They shared mess and turned out with the boys for inspection, and their officers were invited to join the officers' mess. Moreover, 'The girls took part in an "assault course", which consisted of scaling the cliffs up to the camp . . . Not only did they beat the boys for the time of their climb – but they shattered the Brigade record!'[40]

After almost 70 years, the all-male domination of the JLB had finally been broken. Why did it take so long for girls to be admitted to the Brigade? In 1937, Otto Schiff, who had been one of the founders of the North London Girls' Club recalled: 'Ideas had not been very advanced twenty-five years ago, and when mixed activities had been suggested, the more Orthodox section of the Community thought that they were trying to "plant immorality" in the young people.'[41] Miss Aarons herself remembered that her club was the first of its kind to hold mixed social events: 'It was not without great difficulty that members of the committee consented to holding mixed concerts. The suggestion of mixed dances was held in great horror – (Laughter) – and those who put forward the suggestions were not looked upon with favour; but they won in the end.'[42]

Traditional religious attitudes which demand the segregation of the sexes may have been a factor preventing the JLB from including girls. Nevertheless, as we saw in Chapter 4, the JLB itself did not adhere strictly to religious requirements throughout most of its history. In any case, Orthodox Judaism does not forbid social activities for girls provided that they are *segregated*. Basil Henriques, his liberalism in matters religious notwithstanding, was equally opposed to mixed clubs. The Oxford & St George's Girls' Club was established in 1915 and remained distinct under the leadership of his future wife Rose Loewe. Joint activities were conducted under close supervision. The Brady Street Girls' Club, established under Lady Janner's patronage in 1925, was likewise kept separate from the Brady Boys.[43]

Perhaps a more likely explanation is to be found in what social historians have dubbed the 'cult of masculinity', that is, the male public school notions of 'muscular Christianity' and of 'Christian manliness' which so inspired the uniformed youth movements in the late nineteenth century. By definition, women were necessarily excluded. Even so, the Boys' Brigade had pioneered the Girls' Guildry (1900), which provided the inspiration for the Girls' Life Brigade (1902) and, more importantly, for Baden-Powell's Girl Guides. (The very first Girls' Brigade was actually formed independently in Dublin in 1893, within the Irish Protestant Churches, but never spread to the mainland.) In 1965, the Girls' Guildry and the Girls' Life Brigade, together with the Girls' Brigade of Ireland, amalgamated to form the national Girls' Brigade, two years *after* the creation of the Jewish Girls' Brigade. In any case, none of the Christian youth movements, including the Scouts, advocated *mixed* companies before the 1960s (just as co-educational schooling came into vogue in this period). Boys' and girls' camps were, and still are, kept well apart. Thus, in respect to 'feminism', as in other 'progressive' aspects of youth work, the JLGB was ahead of its Gentile counterparts.

Until the late 1930s, mixed dances, in the JLB and the other uniformed groups, were only for officers and were held at 'respectable' venues. For the JLB this meant smart hotels rather than synagogue halls; the use of the latter for such events ran the risk of offending religious opinion. In the 1920s regular fortnightly dances organised by the Warrant Officers' Mess were held at Camperdown House, with an average attendance of 500–600. 'Many marriages resulted from them.' In 1938 the *Jewish Chronicle* reported that 'visits were interchanged' and 'two dances were organised'[44] at the JLB and North London Girls' camps at Walmer.

In March 1962, Sam Ogus reported to Headquarters that 'he had . . . been asked by certain parents whether the Brigade would form a Jewish Girls' Brigade, and the Chairman [Lord Swaythling] said [the third] Lady Swaythling had some time previously made a similar comment and, perhaps at some future date, something might be done to bring this into being'.[45]

'A Good Jew and a Good Englishman'

When the initiative came from Liverpool to establish a Girls' Section, Lady Swaythling immediately offered her assistance. She secured qualified women trainers for the girls and was active behind the scenes. However, it was the Liverpool JLB Parents' Association which must take the credit for bringing girls into the Brigade. It is not perhaps irrelevant to note at this point that the old Harold House in Chatham Street had been reopened as a mixed club in 1948. In the late 1980s, Mrs Phyllis Abrams recalled:

> Although I was not 'in uniform' – with a husband and two sons greatly involved – it was my pleasure to be part of [the JLB . . .] as Chairman of the parents' committee – secretary of the Management – and self-appointed publicity officer – having some influence at the time with the local Jewish press.
>
> It was therefore with great delight . . . that – at an Officer's Mess Dinner at Bloch's Hotel in Southport towards the end of 1962 – in his after-dinner-speech – the Commanding Officer of the time – Brigade Col Albert Globe said that he had recently attended a meeting in London – and so pleased were they by the progress of the Provincial Companies – they were considering setting up Girls Units.
>
> I was delighted and featured this in my monthly report to the press. However, I was somewhat deflated when – a few days after going to press, to [sic] receive a visit from the adjutant of the Brigade – who (to put it into modern jargon) told me 'I had leaked confidential information.'
>
> The project he said was in its early stages and certainly no decision would be made in the near future.
>
> However, I like to think my 'indescretion' [sic] moved things along somewhat – because within a short time we heard that London had agreed to allow Liverpool to form a Girls Unit – which would be a proto-type and would influence their decision on forming girls units in London and the provinces. So like in 1897 [sic; in fact, Liverpool were the first provincial Company in 1898] – WE WERE FIRST AGAIN![46]

Back in 1950 the JLB was unable to secure an Inspecting Officer for Summer Camp. Stuart Montagu, the third Lord Swaythling, suggested that Headquarters might like to ask his wife to step in. After all, she held the rank of Major-General in the British Army. During the Second World War she was made Chief Controller and

Director of the ATS.[47] The proposal was not taken up at the time. Certainly, the military credentials of the former Mrs Jean Knox, who had acquired her title upon marriage to Lord Swaythling in 1945, were never in dispute. However, unlike his divorced first wife who was a granddaughter of Marcus Samuel, Lord Bearsted, Jean Knox was not Jewish. Nevertheless, in 1965 both taboos were broken, when Lady Swaythling became the first woman to inspect the combined Jewish Lads' and Girls' Brigade at Summer Camp.

Thereon, the trend to co-education was unstoppable. Secretary Charles Kay recalls that the Brigade was 'put under pressure' by the Liverpool parents who were insistent that their daughters should be catered for. Lord Swaythling 'resisted' the proposal, but there was little other opposition to the idea in London. Only one member of the Brigade Council, Tom Phillips, formally objected and resigned. Where Liverpool trod, other Companies quickly followed and, within a year, Girls' Companies had been formed in every region. By 1973 'girls' Companies constituted about one-third of the Brigade's strength'. The girls undoubtedly boosted numbers. In that year the London Regiment consisted of 584 boys and 343 girls. Liverpool, in 1965 had 140 boys and 120 girls. Growth was especially noticeable at Summer Camp, where attendance grew to a post-war high of about 1,000 at the Queen's Silver Jubilee Summer Camp in 1977.

Still the boys and girls remained apart; in Edgware for instance the boys met at the Edgware United Synagogue and the girls at the Reform (Stonegrove). In 1964 the local press reported that the Edgware JGB 'GIRLS LEARN JUDO FOR SELF PROTECTION'.[48] Attempts were made to limit mixed activities to Summer Camp; in 1964 Josh Manches, Commanding Officer of the London Regiment, issued an Order to this effect and it was made applicable to the provinces. In 1965 the first all-girls weekend camp was held by the London Companies. Brigade competitions, notably the Annual Banner Competition, included separate events for boys and girls. In 1965 the Brixton Girls came out overall winners in this competition and in 1968 the prestigious Brigade Award of Honour was won by a girl for the first time, Sally Baum of Ilford. In 1966 a Drum and Fife Band was formed for girls of the Liverpool and Manchester Battalions. Tower Hamlets Girls also formed their own band. Whilst in Glasgow, the JGB joined with *Habonim* to form an all-female football team. It was certainly noticeable how the girls were encouraged and keen to participate in 'masculine' sports activities.

Summer Camp posed its own special problems. After the 1966 camp, its Commandant Albert Globe reflected on

> the problems of running the Camps for boys and girls and their continuing membership meant that each year one was providing for children that much older. The girls . . . were . . . now three years older than when they had first attended [Camp] and there were quite large numbers of young men and women concerned. The developing situation needed careful thought.[49]

The problem, in essence, was how to control natural adolescent interest in the opposite sex. At the 1967 camp, where a separate Girls' Battalion under the command of a woman officer was formed for the first time, provision was made for 'a more free interchange' whereby older girls, over the age of 16, were permitted 'to meet their fiances or boyfriends' socially under supervision. In 1968 a new marquee was created, designated the '16–25 Lounge', as a social centre for all ranks over the age of 16. Nevertheless, 'problems of discipline especially of older boys and girls'[50] remained. A newsletter printed for the 1979–80 Winter Camp at Crowborough categorically stated as follows:

> CAMP RULES – OK?
> Unless you want to risk being sent home, there will be:-
> *NO* SMOKING IN ANY HUTS
> *NO* DRINKING OF ALCOHOL
> *NO* BOYS IN GIRLS' HUTS
> *NO* GIRLS IN BOYS' HUTS[51]

However, the romantic instincts of the boys and girls were quickly turned into a virtue. In 1964 the first 'all-Brigade' wedding took place in London, between Derek Posner, Bandmaster of the London Brigade, and Lorraine Arbisman of the Palmers Green Company.[52] In September 1967 no fewer than three separate engagements were announced in Glasgow. During 1971, *Brigade* featured a column entitled 'Young Marrieds who met through the Brigade'. Meanwhile, in 1971, the girls won 'equal rights to do fatigues at Camp'.[53] But their aspiration to see a woman National Summer Camp Commandant had yet to be fulfilled. Women Camp Commandants arrived in

1978: Sylvia Littlestone (Summer Camp) and Betty Morris (Winter Camp, 1978–79). In 1983 Mrs Littlestone was promoted to CO London Regiment, again, the first woman to hold that rank. Pamela Livingston was the first woman CO in the provinces, also in the 1980s.

In 1974 the name of the organisation was formally altered from the 'Jewish Lads' Brigade' and 'Jewish Girls' Brigade' to the 'Jewish Lads' & Girls' Brigade'. Fully mixed Companies were only a matter of time. Many clubs with boys and girls sections had for a long time, in effect, held mixed activities. At Henriques House in Manchester, for example, it was reported in 1960 that 'Before they are 15 the boys tend to withdraw from the Brigade, the girls from the Guides, both becoming members of the mixed youth club; and save for certain activities, they share a common programme'.[54]

In 1966 permission was given to the London Regiment to hold a mixed Whitsun Camp. 180 all ranks attended including 40 girls. In May 1976 the first combined boys' and girls' Company was formed at Kingston-upon-Thames in South London. By 1979 small provincial Companies, Birmingham and Fylde (Blackpool) as well as the Manchester Hillock and Whitefield Companies, had combined units under one officer. In the early 1980s the boys' and girls' Companies gradually merged into mixed units throughout the Brigade. Mixed junior units, ages 8½–11, were started in London. The bands too, including the Waltham Forest Girls' Band, began to recruit members of both sexes. This development took place on a very low key level, almost as a natural evolution, which provoked no real discussion at the top.

The first Duke of Edinburgh's Gold Standard won by a JLB girl from London Regiment was presented at Buckingham Palace in 1968. In the same year the need to co-opt women onto the Headquarter's Committee, to take a special interest in the Girls' Companies, was recognised. In 1970 Beatrice Harris, daughter of the late Commandant Ernest Halsted, wife of one Brigade officer Stanley Harris and sister of two others, Edward and Victor Halsted, became the first woman to be invited to serve on the Committee. She was soon followed by Mrs Linda Greenbury, first wife of Edward Greenbury (himself currently Deputy Commandant and Chairman of the Brigade Council), and a niece of H.J. 'Josh' Manches. These two women soon formed a special sub-committee to study the question of a new uniform to replace the battledress and sought the advice of a professional dress designer, as well as canvassing the opinions of the members themselves. In 1975 women were made eligible for membership of the OCA and within a short time Hilda Alberg became its Secretary. The advent of women in the Brigade had clearly given it a new lease of life and resulted in a fundamental overhaul of its image.

THE JEWISH LADS' & GIRLS' BRIGADE TODAY

The 1968–69 Annual Report marked a turning point in the image of the Brigade, which had appointed its first Public Relations Officer, R. Alexander Porter. Adopting the catchy slogan of 'Setting about the Seventies', the report was a self-conscious attempt to give the organisation a new look. As Lord Swaythling put it in the Introduction: 'Quite simply, the idea is to bring the JLB a little more up to date. The time for change has come because change is all around us and, if we fail to read the signs, we shall be left behind.'[55]

Throughout the 1970s the report was fronted with a sophisticated silhouette photograph of a Brigade Boy and Girl walking together into the sunset. The old staid 'company style' report of times past was replaced by a snappy 'Scrapbook' of events, profusely illustrated. For the first time, the opinions of 'the rank and file' were solicited and published. This apparent democratisation revealed mixed feelings on a number of subjects: the need for the retention of uniform, military rank and drill, for the continued segregation of the sexes and the importance of community service. A Working Party was set up under Josh Manches, who was Commandant between 1972 and 1984, to look into these issues with a view to 'radical' change. Manches was conscious that '[S]ociety has become so non-conformist and permissive that there are few restraints on the younger generation to live by standards that were sacrosanct just a very few years ago'.[56]

However, the findings of the Working Party, following in the footsteps of the influential Haynes Report (1964) on the future of the Boys' Brigade, including a desire amongst the egalitarian-minded

166

youth of the 1970s for the abolition of rank, were too much for Headquarters. Abolishing the military trappings in the face of current fashion would, it was recognised, vitiate the special character of the Brigade. Such radical change was resisted and the 'regimental tradition' clung on to. Only minor reforms such as a reduction of the number of medals awarded – regarded by Manches as 'unseemly and an anachronism'[57] – as well as a reduction in the number of honorary ranks and the abolition of khaki uniform and flashes for the SAS, and its renaming as the Advanced Training Group, were introduced. In recent years, the Brigade has subtly adapted to new trends, but without compromising its essential character. In the long run, this has been a wise policy, as evidenced by the continuing popularity of the JLB.

The introduction of girls was a successful experiment in reviving the fortunes of the Brigade and giving it a new lease of life. In 1973 the Brigade's future was secured in another fundamental respect too. The sale of Camperdown House for demolition and office development of the site fetched £650,000. This, taken together with wise investment over the years by the Trustees, ensured that the JLGB no longer needed to rely to the same extent on grant aid from public and communal sources, subscriptions or general fundraising. The Camperdown House Trust, under the chairmanship of Sir Louis Gluckstein, became the principal and a handsome benefactor of the Brigade. Monies were forthcoming, for example, for an ambitious scheme to purchase the freehold of and develop a new campsite, an ambition long cherished by the Brigade (the Deal site was leased from the Seaside Camps for London Boys). After years of searching, the Trust finally purchased a site at Stoke Hammond in Buckinghamshire in 1976. Unfortunately, the project proved too costly due to the high inflation of the 1970s and had to be abandoned. The annual Brigade budget grew from £89,000 (total turnover) in 1974 to nearly £330,000 in 1989. The Brigade became an incorporated company limited by guarantee in 1981. This took place after a conference held in London at which the 'Restructuring of the Brigade' was debated and various constitutional reforms recommended. The system of elections to the Brigade Council was found to be outmoded: 'Although there are currently some 150 subscribers and 250 officers, very few attend Annual General Meetings to the extent that the quorum of ten is barely reached.' This being the case it was 'likely that those most motivated to attend and to vote at Annual General Meetings may be any vociferous and dissident group which is politically active, however small and unrepresentative it may be of the Brigade and the silent majority'.[58] The solution envisaged was effectively to turn the Brigade Council into a 'Board of Directors' with responsibility for good management of the 'Company'. For the purposes of registration, 'Membership of the Company' was to be limited to 450 officers and subscribers with voting rights.

The Parents' Associations and the London Regimental Aid Committee played an increasingly important role in fundraising for the Brigade, organising social events for their members. In 1979 a special Trust Deed was drawn up to eliminate conflict which arose over the control of PA funds by the Brigade. The JLB Parents' Association was registered separately with the Charity Commission. The branch of the OCA in London, under Ernest Woolf's direction, grew to an all time high of about 500 members in the mid-1970s. Both in London and the provinces, especially in Liverpool (formed 1975) and Glasgow, the OCA continued to be active on the fundraising side. Methods adopted for fundraising did not always meet with the approval of Headquarters. The Glasgow OCA, for example, seemed to be partial to 'card sessions'. Objections were raised locally to what amounted to 'gambling' on Brigade premises! The OCA were thereupon obliged to remove their activities elsewhere.

A solution to the loss of Camperdown House as a focus for Brigade activities was not found until the mid-1980s. From 1965 to that date, a series of premises were used as offices. In 1965 the Brigade moved from Woburn House back to the East End, to the Old Boys' Club at 241–43 Mile End Road. On the club's removal from the neighbourhood, the Brigade moved (1967) into the Bernhard Baron Settlement at 33 Henriques (formerly Berners) Street, only to be forced out again for the same reason early in 1972. The JLB then moved on to the Brady Club. In 1975 the office finally moved out of the East End for good and, as noted already in Chapter 4, took up residence in the St John's Wood Liberal Synagogue at 28 St John's Wood Road, NW8. In 1983 the Camperdown House Trust finally purchased a new Headquarters for the Brigade in South Woodford. The one-storey former Nonconformist chapel which today houses the Brigade administration was renamed 'Camperdown' to create a symbolic link with its more illustrious predecessor.

In 1967 the general subsidy for Summer Camp was finally abolished, reflecting the growing affluence of large sections of the membership. Nevertheless, a system of assessment was introduced whereby needy families would still be able to send their children to camp for a reduced fee or for free. Jack Wagman, the Principal of Norwood, undertook this delicate work, and Norwood discreetly underwrote the majority of these cases. Norwood's help was publicly acknowledged for the first time in the 1977–78 Annual Report. Indeed, in 1978 some 10 per cent of London children attending Summer Camp had to be helped in this way. Pockets of poverty still existed within metropolitan Jewry, especially in Hackney and to a lesser extent in Redbridge – and still do. The social ideals underlying Brigade work have by no means disappeared.

In 1982, 12 mentally handicapped Jewish youngsters were taken to Summer Camp and, by 1988, a JLGB Company had been formed at Ravenswood Village, the Jewish home for the mentally handicapped. In Manchester, the Delamere Forest School for children with learning difficulties formed its own JLGB Company as 'part of my curriculum', in the words· of its headmaster.[59] Every effort is made to include the disabled and the socially disadvantaged in the life of the Brigade.

In 1990, with the coming of *glasnost* and, as it turned out, the crumbling of the Soviet Union, 37 young Russian Jews were able to attend the JLGB Summer Camp by special invitation.

Despite the abolition of the subsidy, numbers at camp grew steadily from 709 in 1965 to 914 in 1974, approximately 3:2 boys to girls. Conditions at camp became more comfortable. In 1967 the traditional palliasses were replaced by 'foam rubber mattresses and/or sleeping bags' to be purchased by the boys and girls themselves. With the move from the old Deal site in 1984, Summer Camp began to be held at 'ready made' camps, usually schools or army bases, where tents were almost permanent structures, with concrete floors and proper beds. Camp activities became ever more sophisticated, including in 1970, for instance, 'films, a "Hill Billy Hick" night, a professional variety show, a Fashion show and a "Magical Mystery tour"'.[60] Occasional displays by RAF helicopter and parachute troops were also organised. Weekend and off-season camps grew ever more popular; a London Regimental Camp at Crowborough, Sussex in the winter of 1973 attracted some 550 plus participants. By 1986 even driving lessons were being laid on at the Winter Camp.

The overall strength (rank and file) of the Brigade grew to 1,300 in 1973. Of this figure, the 30-odd London Companies accounted for 927, including 584 boys and 343 girls; Liverpool for 170, Glasgow 135, Manchester 100 and Birmingham about 40. The relative weakness of Manchester, given the size of the Jewish community in the city, was marked. Short-lived Companies were started at Brighton in the summer of 1973 and later at Bournemouth. Today, small Companies also exist at Southend (c.1975), Fylde, near Blackpool (January 1976), Southport (1962) and Nottingham. The current strength of the Brigade is estimated to be about 2,000 'divided almost equally between boys and girls'.[61] This figure includes the Junior Companies, the 8–11 age group, which exist in most areas. There are about 300 adult helpers. The OCA has about 500 members.

A Company in Colonel Goldsmid's Cardiff base was recreated in May 1977 under Captains Laurence Cohen and Irving Rose. Cohen, a Cardiff-based chartered accountant, was appointed to the rank of Commanding Officer of the Provincial Regiment in 1990. But it was Noel Egerton, a non-Jewish policeman who had served in the Jewish Brigade in Italy during the Second World War, who was instrumental in re-establishing the Welsh Company and was recruited as Warrant Officer and drill instructor.[62] Cardiff Company had about 25 members, boys and girls, in 1977. The Company initially met at the Rhydypenau Primary School, but, after a year, moved to the Sherman Hall at Penylan Synagogue. Numbers grew in the early 1980s to about 70, including a Bantam unit of 15 children aged 9–11. Until the advent of Maccabi in 1990 the JLB, under Captain Neil Schwartz (1990), was the only Jewish youth organisation in Wales.

The revival of Leeds in May 1974, after a lapse of more than half a century, was of greater significance. The initiative was taken by school teacher David Wilson, an ex-London officer who had moved to Leeds – the third centre of Jewish population in Britain after London and Manchester, with an estimated community of 15,000 in the 1970s. The new unit had an initial roll of 50, half boys and half girls. The Girls' Company was initiated by Mr Wilson's wife, Rosalind, with the assistance of Devra Applebaum, a student at Leeds University and the daughter of the late Rita Applebaum, who had pioneered the Girls' Companies in Liverpool.

In 1976 there were 22 Boys' Companies in London and 17 Girls' Companies. Of these, a total of 13 were to be found in north London, 11 in north-west London and Middlesex, and east London and Essex respectively. None of the 'east' London Companies were based in the old East End, but in the newer suburbs of Ilford, Gants Hill, Chigwell and Woodford. Likewise, no Companies had survived in the metropolitan West End. Three Companies existed in south London, the most active centre being at Kingston; the old Brixton Company started by Phineas May in 1926 was renamed Croydon in 1987. In addition, there were five bands. Today, there are seven, including the London Regimental Pipe Band, successor to the Glasgow Bagpipe Band. Today, too, there are 26 Companies in London, including juniors and bands. Of this total, the majority are in the eastern suburbs (12), nine are in north-west London, three in the south and two in the north. Junior and Senior Companies exist at Southend and as far afield as Watford. There is also a thriving Company at the Ravenswood special needs centre in Berkshire.

The trend towards 'professionalisation' continued at Headquarters, with the appointment of Richard Weber as Development Officer in 1973. More paid secretarial staff were also engaged. Community service, such as helping out in hospitals, old age homes and orphanages, became an accepted Brigade activity. A shortlived Brigade journal entitled *Brigade* and subsequently *Brigade Standard* lasted from 1970 to 1976. The annual Summer Camp *Tent Times*, which was an altogether less expensive venture, has, by contrast, endured.

Lord Swaythling officially retired as Commandant at the 75th Anniversary 'Cavalcade' display at the Royal Albert Hall in December 1972. The link with the Goldsmid/Swaythling families, which stretched back to the very beginnings of the Brigade, began to wain. His son David Montagu remained a Paymaster until 1980, but was never active on the officer side of Brigade work, his association with the AJY notwithstanding. The family connection was briefly revived

171

in 1986–87 when Major-General Sir James d'Avigdor Goldsmid, a distant relative of Colonel Albert Goldsmid, and the highest ranking Jew in the British Army to date, was made Commandant. His brother Sir Henry was a Trustee of the Brigade. An ancestor, Elim Henry d'Avigdor, was a close associate of the Colonel's in the foundation of *Chovevei Tsion* in the 1890s. Conservative MP for Lichfield and Tamworth (1970–74) and prominent in the world of horseracing, Jackie, as he was called, had been appointed to serve on the Brigade Council and Headquarters Committee in 1977, but died in office in 1987. A newspaper obituary described him as 'Tall, dark and of military bearing, a sleek Mayfair bachelor who drove a Bentley . . . [He] undoubtedly had style'.[63]

No other Commandant in recent years could claim such aristocratic connections. Nearly all of the post-war Commandants, in fact, have been 'trade' gentlemen who had made good in business; the Glucksteins in catering, Harold Lion in merchant shipping, Josh Manches in furniture and double glazing. Indeed, Josh Manches was the first Brigade Commmandant who had 'come up through the ranks'. His parents had 'met on the boat' coming over from Russia, although they did not settle in the East End, but in Bermondsey. Manches was briefly a sergeant in the Southwark Company as a boy, but fell out with his Commanding Officer and left. He returned to the movement as an adult in 1954 on the invitation of Harold Lion and, after commanding Clapton and Dalston, and Chigwell Companies, he quickly gained promotion to CO London Regiment and took on responsibility for organising the annual Summer Camp. Edward M. Young, who succeeded Manches for a short time (1984–86), had been responsible for building up the Edgware Company ('the Edgware Hundred') into the largest Company in the Brigade. He was very definitely 'new money' having founded the Young's evening wear business and subsequently taking over the British franchise of the Paris wedding dress company Pronuptia. The current incumbent, Sir Peter Lazarus, a former top civil servant – a Permanent Secretary at the Department of Transport – does, however, have family connections with the Brigade. He is a great-nephew of Ernest Halsted and his father Kenneth Lazarus was Brigade Treasurer in the 1950s.

An 80th Anniversary 'Cavalcade' was held at the Royal Albert Hall in 1976 in the presence of the Duke of Edinburgh. The years 1976–77 were the high watermark of Brigade strength in the post-Second World War period. Numbers at Summer Camp shrank from about 1,000 at the Silver Jubilee Camp, as we have seen, to only 289 all ranks in 1983. Declining attendances at what was supposed to be the highlight of the Brigade's annual calendar forced a radical rethink. The campsite at Deal which had been in use since the 1930s was finally abandoned. In 1984, according to that year's Annual Report 'members were offered the choice of a number of adventure-based camps during the school summer holidays'. A glossy colour advertising brochure was produced. However: 'It was a necessary experiment but, although attendance increased marginally overall, the changed concept has not produced an adequate answer and the Brigade will need to review the arrangements to be made in 1985.'[64]

In 1985 an entirely new formula was tried. For the first time in the history of the JLB, Summer Camp was not held under canvas, but indoors at the Sibford School at Banbury near Oxford. Numbers increased to about 300 and the school was used again for the following two summers. In 1988 the JLGB returned to Kent, to the Dibgate army base near Folkstone and remained there until 1992. The 1993 camp was held at the East Mersea Youth Camp near Colchester in Essex. Attendances have risen again to about 500 all ranks. Winter Camps have, if anything, proved more popular, attracting an average of 400 each year.

The quest for new ideas to appeal to today's young people continues. In the late 1980s the Brigade consciously set out to bring more young Jewish people into its orbit than merely its own immediate constituency. As the only Jewish Operating Authority for the Duke of Edinburgh Award Scheme, the JLGB has been responsible for organising training programmes at many Jewish schools (147 participating pupils at JFS alone in 1992), youth clubs and in outlying communities. By 1992, 250 Brigade members and 300 other young people had been enrolled on the DEA scheme. In 1987 the JLGB launched its Challenge Award for Jewish Youth, its own equivalent to the Duke of Edinburgh Award Scheme for the 8–13 age group. Participating youngsters gain proficiency in five sections: Hobbies, Health & Safety, Physical Activity, Jewish Heritage and Citizenship.

They are also required to set themselves a 'challenge', some task which they think 'is beyond them physically, emotionally or intellectually'.[65] In 1992, 250 children were taking part. In 1990 a new Adventure Training Unit was established for the older members, equivalent to the old SAS.

All of these activities now come under the aegis of the JLGB Outreach-Kiruv project which was launched in 1989. This is a scheme for Associate Membership for young people through their school, *cheder* or other youth group, or from outlying Jewish communities, to participate in the life of the Brigade without their having to go into uniform. Indeed, the Brigade has made pains to emphasise that there are many support roles which adults can play without donning uniform. Nevertheless, at least one outsider, *Jewish Chronicle* reporter Jack Shamash, is not entirely convinced. 'The Brigade,' he wrote in 1990, 'is still very militaristic despite its attempts . . . to soften its Image.'[66] A full-time Project Youthworker, Lester Harris, was taken on in 1989 to develop Outreach-Kiruv. In 1992 it was estimated that some 2,500 children were being reached by the Brigade through this Kiruv work. In addition to the DEA, the Brigade has become an Operating Authority for the Government-sponsored National Inter-Action Computing Award Scheme (NICAS) which, with the support of industry and validation by the Royal Society of Arts, aims to promote computer literacy amongst the young.

Democratisation of the Brigade's decision-making structure has been actively explored in recent years. Late in 1984 Michelle Kaye, a member of the London Regimental Brass Band and a Business Studies student, was commissioned by the Brigade to write a report on 'The Communication Structure' of the JLGB. Her findings were hardly flattering. 'On the whole,' she wrote, 'the communication system of the Jewish Lads' and Girls' Brigade is not of a very high standard . . . there is much room for improvement. The officers involved should be younger and an age limit should be introduced as there is for the children.' This situation, she recommended, could be rectified by more training courses for officers and regular meetings between them and with Headquarters. In this way, a clearer definition and understanding of officers' responsibilities could be arrived at. Overall, however, 'The original concept of the Brigade appears to need modernising. The organisation is not at the same standard as it was in its earlier days and the same can be said for the quality of the staff within the ranks of the organisation.'[67]

It says a great deal for the honesty of the Brigade leadership that Miss Kaye's critical appraisal was taken seriously. Gerry Fifer, CO of the Provincial Regiment, who had been one of the commissioners of the report, issued new 'Regimental Management' guidelines in 1986, which set out clearly the duties of every rank. The 1987–88 Annual Report noted 'JLGB recognises the value of giving young people a role in decision-making processes and the chance to shape the face of their own organisation. The involvement of young people in arranging and co-ordinating events is central to the Brigade's thinking.'[68]

Under the Outreach-Kiruv programme, the Brigade initiated the National Volunteer Organisation of Youth (NVOY) in 1991 but the results were 'very disappointing'. Now, the JLGB is actively co-operating with the Jewish Board of Deputies, the AJY, Maccabi and the Zionist Youth Council, to create a National Jewish Youth Assembly where, in the context of voluntary service, the young may be given a voice in the affairs of the Jewish community. It is planned that youth delegates from across the country, aged 15 to 18, will be elected by their peers to represent their organisation on the Assembly.[69]

Clearly, the Brigade's strategy in recent years has been to seek to enlarge its clientele by appealing to a wider age group and to a broader cross section of the Jewish community. The advent of Outreach-Kiruv, which is costing around 10 per cent of the annual Brigade budget (today totalling about £340,000), has not, it is admitted, been 'universally accepted within the JLGB'. As a current publicity leaflet puts it

> [Outreach-Kiruv] is seen as competing for limited resources, and a distraction from the activities of the uniformed Brigade. However, the Outreach-Kiruv activities themselves are valued, and used for the benefit of JLGB boys and girls.
>
> The Brigade's official policy is that its Objects permit, and encourage provision of leisure-time pursuits for all Jewish young people, whether members of the Brigade or not, in order to do the greatest good for the greatest number.

175

It is considered that the uniformed Brigade has, in fact, benefited from the Outreach-Kiruv programme.[70]

In the marketing language so popular in the 1980s 'The Brigade as "a product" was well defined but care [sh]ould be taken with "the packaging"'.[71] Certainly, the JLGB has come a long way since its foundation in late Victorian England. Yet, the social imperative which underlies its work and the dedication of its founders and leaders is alive and well today. Paradoxically, the insistence on rank, which has always marked out the Brigade from the clubs, has proven to be the glue binding officer and member together in a common sense of community. The caring atmosphere of comradeship, devoid of ideological overtones, retains a perennial appeal. Summer Camp, sport and voluntary service still provide fun and tremendous benefit for Jewish boys and girls from all over the country. On the threshold of its second century, the character of the JLGB continues to evolve whilst remaining true to its unique Anglo-Jewish tradition.

Notes

Sources are normally cited in the case of direct quotations only. Secondary books, pamphlets and articles are cited in full in the bibliographical notes.

PREFACE

1. My title is borrowed from the only article on the JLB published in an academic journal to date: Richard A. Voeltz, '"A Good Jew and a Good Englishman": The Jewish Lads' Brigade, 1894–1922', *Journal of Contemporary History*, Vol.23 (1988), pp.119–27.
2. John Springhall with Brian Fraser and Michael Hoare, *Sure and Stedfast: A History of the Boys' Brigade* (London 1983, 2nd edn 1991), p.16.
3. Letter to Harvey Livingston, Glasgow, 20 May 1986, JLB Provincial Box File P/O D, Glasgow.

CHAPTER 1

1. Copy typescript of letter by Gladys Swaythling, sent to *JC*(?), 1954(?), in JLB GEN/26, materials collected by Dr I.S. Gold for lecture on Col. Goldsmid, 1966.
2. Springhall.
3. Unpub. paper by Simon Bernstein, '"Ironing out the Ghetto Bend": a History of the Jewish Lads' Brigade, its aims and influences', undergraduate research project, supervised by Dr Lionel Kochan, Oxford 1984.
4. *JC* 3 April 1891, p.7.
5. Bunt, p.15; Eugene C. Black, Ch.5.
6. *JC* 13 March 1891, p.5; *EJ* 'Military Service'.
7. JLB First Annual Report, p.7, W.A. Smith to Rev. F.L. Cohen, 13 March 1891.
8. *JC* 1 April 1904, pp.9–10 (obituary); Emden, *Jews of Britain* and *TJHSE* 1939, Hyamson, Bermant; unpub. paper by Dr I.S. Gold in JLB GEN/26; entry by Cecil Roth in *EJ* inaccurate.
9. Lowenthal (ed.), *Herzl Diaries*, pp.82–3.
10. Emden, pp.141–2.
11. Stern, *First American Jewish Families*; Hyamson; 'David Salisbury Franks', *EJ*.
12. *Herzl Diaries*, op.cit.

13. See note 1 above.
14. Alderman (1992), p.205; Henriques, pp.27–31 on Cardiff.
15. JC 1 April 1904.
16. Daily Graphic 10 March 1892, quoted in Fraenkel.
17. Fraenkel, Sokolow, Vol.I, pp.217, 233–47.
18. Letter from Sir Henry D'Avigdor-Goldsmid to Dr Gold, 2 Feb. 1972 in JLB GEN/26.
19. Stuart Cohen, pp.7, 26–9, 35–6; Hein.
20. Fraenkel, p.146.
21. Bentwich, TJHSE, p.56; Ronald Goodman. Cyril Goodman's wife was the first woman member in 1951.
22. No records relating to the JLB's origins have survived in the Maccabaeans Archives now at Southampton University. Emanuel Toff's recollections differed in some essentials from the standard version; a meeting of apprentices was called at the Jewish Working Men's Club in Great Alie Street, the first drill at Swan Street School and only afterwards at Gravel Lane. The first inspection took place at JFS. See E.J. Toff, 'Memoirs', The Advance July–Aug. 1933, p.5.
23. JC 22 Feb. 1895, p.14.
24. Ibid.
25. JLB First Annual Report, pp.33–4.
26. JC 5 April 1895, p.12.
27. Toff, The Advance, op.cit., note 22.
28. Algernon Lesser, 'In the Beginning', The Advance Jan.–March 1935, p.5.
29. JC 21 Aug. 1896, pp.14-15.
30. JC 4 Aug. 1899, p.5.
31. JC 21 Aug. 1896, pp.14–15.
32. Eugene C. Black, p.143; Toff, The Advance Oct.–Dec. 1934, p.5.
33. JG 6 Feb. 1925 (obituary); S. Hyam, 'The History of the Liverpool Company', The Advance Sept.–Oct.1932, p.5 (including some inaccuracies).
34. JLB First Annual Report (1898), p.32.
35. JC 25 Nov. 1898, 13 Jan. 1899, 9 May 1899.
36. JC 18 March 1904.
37. JC 4 March, 8 Jan. 1904.
38. South African Jewish Chronicle 15 April 1904, pp.439–41, 29 April 1904, pp.483–4, 487–9. I am grateful to John Simon of Cape Town for this material and must also acknowledge debt to the late Sam Ogus for assembling the South Africa cuttings from the JC.
39. JC 20 May 1904.
40. Op. cit., note 28.
41. JLB First Annual Report, pp.28–9; JLB Minutes 15 May 1902; JC 23 May 1902.
42. Gerry Black, p.340.
43. JLB Minutes, 25 Sept. 1902.
44. Livshin thesis, p.142.
45. Manchester JLB First Annual Report 1899–1903, pp.24–5.
46. JC 11 Aug. 1899, p.25.
47. Jewish World (JW) 9 April 1909; Manchester Central Reference Library, MS 130, Officers' Minutes Meetings Book 1908–12, 16 Aug. 1909.
48. Livshin thesis, p.150.

49. On Bradford see Oswald M. Stroud, *The Story of the Stroud Family* (privately printed, Bradford 1970–74), p.85, AJ MS 116/51. Acknowledgements to Anne Kershen for this reference.
50. Collins, pp.83, 115–16, 173, 206, 220.
51. *JC* 9 Dec. 1904, p.36.
52. Transcript of interview with Ralph Delmonte, 2 Feb. 1981, p.1, in JLB Provincial Box Files P/O D, Glasgow.
53. Ibid., Bert Firestone to Motel Robins, 1 Feb. 1987.
54. Ibid., unsigned typescript by Gerald Strump, n.d., *c*.1980. Extract from dissertation by Brian Fraser of Glasgow University on Boys' Brigade, p.411 in JLB GEN/129.
55. JLB Minutes, 11 July 1907.
56. Louis E. Wigoder, Leeds to Sam Ogus, London, 3 Feb. 1981 in Provincial Box Files P/O C, Dublin.
57. J. Salter to Motel Robins, 7 Sept. 1985 in ibid.
58. JLB Annual Report 1902–3, p.14–15.
59. See Ch. 2 below.
60. As Goldsmid affectionately called them.
61. JLB Annual Report 1902–3, p.5; *JW* 1 Aug. 1902.
62. *JW* 31 July 1908, p.15.
63. Evidence of Captain E. Warden Denniss, 30 March 1903, *Royal Commission on Alien Immigration 1903*, PP 1903, ix (Cd.1742), para. 18279.
64. JLB Annual Report 1901–2, p.2.
65. JLB Minutes, 15 May 1902.
66. JLB Minutes, 19 April 1906.
67. On Joseph see Magnus, *EMJ* and for the Josephs' architectural legacy see Kadish (ed.), *Building Jerusalem*; 'Camperdown House Trust', unsigned memo by Ernest Joseph, 23 May 1960 in JLB Letters File LETT/7.
68. 'Camperdown House' brochure for opening, 16 Dec. 1913, p.17; copy in JLB/GEN/27 and at Jews' College Library, London; Magnus, *EMJ*, pp.40–2. The important personage being Admiral Viscount Duncan of Camperdown. See Cyril Goodman's Introduction, p.xxii, above.

CHAPTER 2

1. *JC*, JLB Supplement, 27 Oct. 1972, p.ii. According to Charles Kay, this story is probably apocryphal.
2. Joe Rose, 'Our officers in the early days', *Advance Again* Oct. 1957, p.27.
3. JLB Minutes, 5 April 1899.
4. See Springhall, Rosenthal, 'disembodied' quote below from Rosenthal, p.7.
5. The earliest mention of this phrase which I have been able to trace is in the JLB Annual Report 1901–2, p.7 (only known copy in Stanley Rowe papers AJ MS 223 4/13) where it is used as an 'advertising slogan'. The evidence presented by Captain E.Warden Denniss to the *Royal Commission on Alien Immigration 1903* attributes it to Goldsmid himself; PP 1903, ix (Cd.1742), para. 18279, 30 March 1903.
6. *JC* 22 Feb. 1895, p.6.
7. Manchester JLB Annual Report 1899–1903, p.26.
8. Camp Orders Book 1901–2, 28 July 1902, JLB GEN/82.

9. *JC* 12 Feb. 1897, p.17.
10. *JC* 8 July 1898, p.19.
11. *JC* 6 Oct. 1905, p.7.
12. *JC* 12 Feb. 1897, p.17.
13. JLB Minutes, 7 Feb. 1900.
14. JLB GEN/78, HQ Staff Minutes 1897–98, 27 March 1898; JLB Minutes, 21 Sept., 4 Oct. 1899.
15. Manchester JLB Annual Report 1899–1903, p.29.
16. Manchester JLB, Officers Minutes Meetings Book 1908–12, 14 June 1909, MCRL MS 130.
17. *Royal Commission on Alien Immigration*, op. cit., para. 818, 1 May 1902. Entry in JLB Camp Orders Book 1901–2, JLB GEN/82, 31 July 1901, refers to census at camp.
18. JLB Minutes, 23 May 1902.
19. *JC* 24 Jan. 1902, pp.12–14.
20. JLB Minutes, 4 Feb. 1906 (AGM).
21. *JW* 28 Jan. 1910.
22. *Daily Telegraph (DT)* 22 Jan. 1910.
23. *JW* 28 Jan. 1910.
24. *JW* 19 April 1912.
25. Bunt, pp.46–7.
26. JLB Minutes, 6 July 1898.
27. JLB correspondence file LETT/7, Hutchison House Minutes, 24 July 1905.
28. JLB Minutes, 23 Jan., 6, 13 Feb. 1905; *DT* 11 Nov. 1908.
29. JLB Minutes, 11 Jan. 1906.
30. *DT* 1 Aug. 1908; *JC* 6 Nov. 1909, 15 Dec. 1933 (obituary).
31. On respective strength of Scouts and Brigades see *Newcastle Journal* 23 Sept. 1909; Warren.
32. *JC* 13 March 1909; one copy of *Hackney Review* in JLB GEN/125; JLB Minutes, 23 June 1909.
33. Baden-Powell's announcement of retirement widely reported in press, see JLB press cuttings book for Jan. 1910. Nevertheless, in common with many proponents of the Imperial Mission of the day, Baden-Powell internalised racist and anti-Jewish prejudices, see Rosenthal, Ch.9, esp. pp.267–72.
34. See Summers, Warren.
35. JLB Minutes, 10 Dec. 1900.
36. *JC* 4 Feb. 1898, p.33.
37. See Springhall and Rosenthal.
38. See Bernstein and Warren (on B-P).
39. JLB Minutes, 13 July 1910, 13 March 1911; *JC* 11 Oct. 1912.
40. *JC* 1 April 1904, pp.9–10.
41. *JC* and *JW* 26 June 1908.
42. JLB Minutes, 9 Nov. 1915; JLB Minutes, 4 July 1916.
43. Adler, *British Jewry Book of Honour*, p.3.
44. JLB GEN/114 and tape of interview, 27 April 1990.
45. *JC* 15 Aug. 1913, pp.15,18; JLB ALB/4 (WWI Roll of Honour), *British Jewry Book of Honour*.
46. Schechtman, Vol.I, Ch.14; Jabotinsky, Gilner. Statistics arrived at by cross-referencing Adler with JLB Roll of Honour.

47. Ben Levinson, Manchester to Motel Robins, 4 Nov, 9 Dec. 1985 in JLB Provincial Box File, Manchester PO/E.
48. *JC* 30 March 1962 (obituary).
49. Information provided by David Jacobs, his great nephew and grandson of Alex Jacob. Julius gets a mention in Menachem Begin's memoirs, *The Revolt* (1979), Futura paperback edition, pp.298–9.
50. Roth, *TJHSE*, Vol.15 (1945); 'Military Service', *EJ*; Revd F.L. Cohen, 'Jews in the Army and Militia', *JC* 22 April 1904, p.10.
51. See Holmes, pp.66–70; Rosenthal, Ch.5.
52. See Kosmin on Jewish war dead; Bush, and Kadish, *Bolsheviks and British Jews*, Ch.5, on conscription question.
53. Bush, p.148; Ernest Woolf, 'A lifetime with the JLB', transcript of interview on tape, 19 Dec. 1989. Acknowledgements to Anne Kershen.
54. *JC* 11 Sept. 1914, p.11, 7 Aug. 1914, p.14.
55. JLB Annual Report 1917; *JC* 16 Aug. 1918, p.14.
56. Interview with Beatrice Harris, daughter of Hallenstein, 22 Dec. 1993, tape.

CHAPTER 3

1. J. Salter to Motel Robins, 7 Sept. 1985, JLB Provincial Box File P/O C, Dublin.
2. *JC* 6 June 1919.
3. JLB Annual Report 1921, p.12; JLB Minutes, 3 Nov. 1919, 11 Jan. 1920; *JW* 5 Nov. 1919; *JG* 7 May 1920; *JC* 25 Feb. 1921.
4. JLB Minutes, 2 Jan. 1922.
5. Quoted in *JW* 22 May 1930.
6. I.e., Springhall.
7. E. Royalton Kisch, *The Camp of God, An Address to the Jewish Lads' Brigade, Delivered at the London Regimental Camp, Birchington-on-Sea, 11th August 1928*, JLB GEN/5.
8. JLB Annual Report 1934, pp.8–9.
9. L/Sgt R. Risner, Bayswater Co., 'From Strength to Strength', *The Reveille*, Dec. 1922, pp.10–11.
10. Manchester JLB, Officers Minutes, 2 June 1924, 1, 2 Aug. 1932.
11. 'Charles', 'phone-in' on Spectrum Radio, 26 July 1993, tape; Livshin thesis, pp.146–7.
12. *Di Tsait* 11 March 1922.
13. Undated press cuttings, JLB press cuttings book, probably *JC*.
14. David Hudaly, 'The JLB in Liverpool: A Survey' (published but n.d. and source not stated). Acknowledgements to Joe Wolfman.
15. See *EMJ*.
16. *Brixton Free Press* 1 May 1936.
17. JLB Minutes, 13 Nov. 1938.
18. On Leeds see Cesarani (1989), p.66, and Wilcock.
19. JLB Annual Report 1924, p.7.
20. Except in Manchester, 1926.
21. Obituary of Cohen, *JC* 31 July 1936.
22. *Liverpool Jewish Gazette*, Harold House Supplement, 9 Oct. 1964, p.ii. Acknowledgements to Joe Wolfman.
23. JLB Minutes, 13 May 1926.

24. *JC* 5 Feb. 1932.
25. *The Advance* July–Aug. 1932, p.8.
26. JLB Minutes, 2 Nov. 1936, 7, 13 Nov. 1938.
27. *Manchester Guardian* 9 April 1932; *The Times* 29 Nov. 1932; *EMJ*, pp.41–2.
28. Manchester JLB, Officers Minutes, 5 Sept. 1938.
29. *JC* 19 Aug. 1927.
30. JLB Minutes, 9 Dec. 1935; Annual Report 1936, p.5.
31. Letter from Motel Robins to Charles Kay, 5 Jan. 1993, kindly passed on to me. Also JLB GEN/152 and GEN/177.
32. JLB Minutes, 13 Nov. 1938.
33. On Richborough see: Norman Bentwich, *They Found Refuge*, Ch.7; Tylor-Baumel, who entirely ignores the role played by the JLB; *EMJ*, pp.87–99, 'morale' quote, p.90; Kitchener Camp Committee brochure 'Some victims of the Nazi Terror' (n.d., ?1939), in JLB GEN/8; 'The Romance of Richborough', unsigned in GEN/136. European precedents for the Kitchener Camp were to be found in Belgium and Switzerland after Nov. 1938, and the Westerbork camp in Holland was modelled upon it.
34. Bound numbers 1–7 (March–Sept. 1939) in JLB GEN/8.
35. 'Phineas L. May b.1906', handwritten reminiscences (n.d., ?1939), acknowledgements to Anne Kershen. Also tape of interview, 19 Dec. 1989. Besides his collection of cartoons, May kept a personal diary of life at Richborough which is still in his possession.
36. This section based on JLB Minutes 2, 8 Nov. 1936, 25 April, 30 May, 22 Aug., 3 Oct. 1938.
37. JLB Minutes, enc. dated 7 May 1939.
38. *JC* 26 April 1940; JLB Minutes, 21 Jan. 1941, 1 April 1940.
39. See Brodie (1946–47) and Henry Morris, *We will remember them* (London, 1989) which belatedly attempts to fulfil the same function for the Second World War that *The British Jewry Book of Honour* did for the First. Motel Robins' list is in JLB ALB/25 but is unreliable. If JLB membership lists for the pre-1939 period existed it would be possible to cross reference them with Morris' Roll of Honour.
40. JLB GEN/148 on Allan Burke; *Jerusalem Post* 5 March 1986.
41. *JC* 6 March, 29 Oct. 1943 and both listed in Morris.
42. Letter to the author, 29 Nov. 1993.
43. *JC* 15 Jan., 30 July 1943. See also Brodie, op. cit., p.56.
44. *JC* 6 Dec. 1940, 14 Feb. 1941.
45. 'The Life and Times of Sidney Hart' (n.d., *c*.1980) in JLB GEN/139; *JC* 5 Dec. 1958.
46. JLB Minutes, 1 July 1940.
47. JLB Minutes, 27 Jan., 4 May 1944; JLB Annual Report 1940–46, p.6.
48. See Ch. 4 below.
49. *JC* 9 May 1941; JLB Annual Report 1940–46, p.29; JLB GEN/211.
50. JLB GEN/116.
51. JLB Minutes, 14 April 1943, 11 Nov. 1942; *JC* 20 Aug. 1943; letter from Maurice Rathbone, Liverpool to A.L. Abraham, London, 15 May 1945, enc. in JLB Minutes. See also Ch. 4 below.
52. 'Report [of Camp] 2nd Cadet Battalion, The Royal Fusiliers Rgt.(JLB)', Aug. 1942, by Charles Magnus, enc. in JLB Minutes.
53. JLB Minutes, 4 May 1944.

CHAPTER 4

1. *JC* 8 July 1898, p.19.
2. *DT* 24 Aug. 1909. The writer was making the case for secularisation of the Church Brigades, to bring them into line with the Boy Scouts.
3. *JW* 5 Aug. 1904. Adler acted as Camp Chaplain from 1900, except in 1904 when Cohen came back briefly.
4. *JC* 21 Aug. 1896, pp.14–15.
5. *JW* 5 Aug. 1904; *JC* 20 Aug. 1897, p.14.
6. *JC* 24 Aug. 1900, pp.12–13.
7. *JC* 10 Aug. 1900, p.17, 7 Aug. 1903, pp.16–17.
8. *JC* 18 Aug. 1899, p.23.
9. JLB GEN/79, Camp Sub-committee Minutes 1898–1910, 21 May 1900, 11 July 1901.
10. JLB GEN/16, 'Report of 1899 Camp' (anon.).
11. JLB Annual Report 1919, p.46.
12. JLB Minutes, 5 June 1939.
13. JLB Minutes, 23 Jan., 6 Feb. 1905.
14. *JC* n.d. [Aug.] 1906; JLB GEN/16, Camp Report, op. cit.
15. *JC, JW* 12 Aug. 1910, plus editorial comment in latter.
16. *JC* 4 Aug 1911, p.12, 25 Aug. 1911, pp.20, 22.
17. *JC* 1 Aug. 1913, p.28.
18. JLB Minutes, 19 Nov. 1914.
19. JLB Annual Report 1926, p.16.
20. *JG* 2 Nov. 1923.
21. *JG* 14 Nov. 1930; *JC* 20 Aug. 1931; *JW* 28 Sept. 1933.
22. *Jewish Graphic* 30 April 1928.
23. *JC* 19 June 1936, 23 Aug. 1929, letter from Maurice Goodman of Stamford Hill.
24. JLB Minutes, 6 July 1936.
25. Manchester JLB Annual Report 1936, p.12. See Livshin on this issue.
26. *JC* 20 Aug. 1931.
27. *JC* 18 Aug. 1933.
28. Allan Burke to Motel Robins, 26 Feb. 1987, JLB GEN/148; Manchester JLB Annual Report 1930, p.5.
29. 'Report . . .', Aug. 1942, by Charles Magnus, enc. in JLB Minutes, 16 Sept. 1942.
30. 'JLB Glasgow' by Cpt. Louis Blint, enc. with JLB Minutes, 11 Sept. 1944.
31. JLB Minutes, 11 April 1949.
32. JLB Minutes, 13 Nov. 1951; Stanley Rowe, 'JLB & Club, consideration of future needs, Jan. 1959' in AJ MS 223 4/1/2; Manchester JLB Annual Report 1957–59, p.4.
33. JLB Minutes, 22 Nov. 1950.
34. 'JLB' (Camp) by Cyril Goodman, 16 Oct. 1947, enc. in JLB Minutes.
35. JLB Minutes, 11 Nov. 1952; 'Report on Whitsun Camp 1954 by Camp Commandant Brigade Major M. Lyons', enc. in JLB Minutes.
36. JLB Minutes, 6 Dec. 1954.
37. See Alderman (1987 and 1992).
38. JLB Minutes, 20 Sept., 7 Nov. 1927.

39. JLB Minutes, 1 June 1898.
40. *Royal Commission on Alien Immigration*, op. cit., para. 18269.
41. *JW* 9 Nov. 1906 (obituary).
42. *JC* and *JW* c.Sept. 1918 (JLB press cuttings book).
43. On the Reform connection see Kershen (ed.), *150 Years of Progressive Judaism*, esp. Rigal on 'The Settlement Synagogue', pp.28–33; *EMJ*, pp.77–80; Umansky on Liberal services devised by Lily Montagu at her West Central Jewish Girls' Club, pp.121–5; Loewe on Henriques; *The Bernhard Baron St George's Jewish Settlement: Fiftieth Anniversary Review 1914–1964*, copy in JLB GEN/194. Interview with Beatrice Harris, 22 Dec. 1993, tape.
44. *JC* 29 Nov. 1935, 7 July 1939. Copies of menu and tableplan – with Gollop's name included – for Mansion House Dinner, 13 Oct. 1938, in JLB GEN/58.
45. JLB Minutes, 4 July, 5 Dec. 1938, latter enc. 'Report of Interview with Dayan M. Gollop, 16 November 1938'.
46. Manchester JLB, Officers' Minutes, 5 March, 7 May 1934, 31 Jan. 1938.
47. *JC* 19 Nov. 1954, 2 Nov. 1979 (obituary).
48. See Alderman (1992), pp.360–1 re Liberal marriages, p.353 re Zionism; Shimoni (1986) on the anti-Zionist Jewish Fellowship, pp.102–6.
49. See Eisen, pp.248–9; *EJ* entries on 'Nordau' and 'Maccabi World Union'. I am grateful to Richard Cohen of the Hebrew University who first suggested a possible link between English 'Muscular Christianity' and Nordau's 'Muscular Judaism' in a discussion around my paper at the World Congress of Jewish Studies in Jerusalem, June 1993.
50. See Eisen, Rinott, *EJ* 'Blau-Weiss'.
51. Bunt, p.102.
52. *JW* 22 Aug. 1929. Evidently, the Glasgow JLB bagpipe band had learnt to play *Hatikva* in honour of Viscount Allenby at the 1935 Jubilee Camp, see *Manchester Guardian* 7 May 1935.
53. Alderman (1992), p.310.
54. JLB Minutes, 12 Oct. 1949, 30 Jan. 1951. Recollection of Josh Manches, 26 Oct. 1993.
55. *Daily Express* 11 April 1932.
56. *Manchester Guardian* 9 April 1932.
57. See Mendelsson on *Habonim*, quotes from Ch.1, p.14, note 19, Ch.6, p.3, and Bunt, p.87 ('Slavishly observant'). Also Silman-Cheong, *Wellesley Aron*; Kalman on FZY and Shimoni in *Studies in Contemporary Jewry*, *Vol.II* on PZ. I am grateful to David Mendelsson, Gideon Shimoni and Matthew Kalman for their assistance.
58. Joseph Finklestone, 'The Youth Movement', *JC* 2 Nov. 1951; David Pela, 'World Youth Convention', *JC* 25 July 1958.
59. Mendelsson, Ch.5, p.21.
60. Letter, 26 April 1945, enc. in JLB Minutes.
61. Cited in Bunt, Ch.3.
62. *The Times* 28 July 1936.
63. See Srebrnik on CP and Kalman on Young Zionists.
64. *JC* 28 July 1967 (obituary).
65. JLB GEN/5.
66. 'Jew-baiting', 'Cutting from local press' (Woolwich), JLB press cuttings book, 6 Nov. 1936.

67. 16 March 1937, JLB LETT/2.
68. *The Advance* May–June 1933, pp.5, 7.
69. *The Advance* April–June 1935, p.3.
70. *JC* 27 March, 8 May, 11 Sept. 1936 on boxing; 8 Dec. 1939 on 'Haw-Haw'.
71. E.g. *The Times, Evening News, Star*, 1 May 1933.
72. *Daily Worker* 19 Sept. 1933.
73. Motel Robins to Charles Kay, 5 Jan. 1993, kindly passed on to me; 'Ray', 'phone-in' on Spectrum Radio, 26 July 1993, tape.
74. *The Reveille* June 1922, pp.10–11; *The Advance* Jan.–Feb. 1933, p.2.
75. *Isle of Thanet Gazette*, 15 Aug. 1925.
76. *Daily Worker* 18 Aug. 1933.
77. Charles Magnus, 'Report. . .', Aug. 1942, op. cit.
78. Op. cit., note 58 above.
79. *JC* 30 Jan. 1942.
80. JLB GEN/186; interview with Josh Manches, 22 Dec. 1993, tape; Sam Ogus to Cllr Benjamin Abrahams, Newcastle-upon-Tyne, 13 March 1981, JLB Provincial Box Files P/O J, Newcastle.
81. JLB Minutes, 20 July 1959, 11 Feb., 9 July 1970.
82. In recorded discussion at Motel Robins' house, Hove, 26 Aug. 1993.
83. Reported in *Stretford and Urmston News Telegraph* (Manchester), 11, 18 July 1958; *JC* 11 July 1958.
84. *JC* 17 April 1959.
85. *JC* Meir Persoff, 14 July 1967.
86. 'Tour Diary' by Paul Newland in JLB/91; interview with Josh Manches, 22 Dec. 1993, tape.
87. Emergency Meeting of HQ Committee, 1 June 1967, JLB Minutes.
88. JLB Annual Report 1966–67, p.4.
89. JLB Minutes, 30 Oct. 1973.

CHAPTER 5

1. JLB Minutes, 19 March 1950, 4 Feb. 1953.
2. JLB Minutes, 25 May 1954, 10 July 1961.
3. JLB Minutes, 8 Sept. 1953.
4. Annual Report 1951, p.29.
5. *JC* 18 Aug. 1950.
6. JLB Provincial Box Files P/O D, Glasgow.
7. JLB Minutes, 25 Nov. 1953, 16 Oct. 1947. JLB GEN/183 on Dale.
8. JLB Minutes, 7 March 1950, 19 March 1950 (Brigade Council).
9. JLB Minutes, 12 Oct. 1949.
10. JLB Minutes, 24 June 1947.
11. *JC* 19 Nov. 1954 (JLB Supplement), 6 March 1953; JLB Minutes, 28 April 1958, 9 Sept. 1956.
12. JLB Minutes, 19 Dec. 1956.
13. Report on 1947 camp dated 16 Oct. 1947, enc. with Minutes.
14. 'Report on Camp 1950', 17 Aug. 1950, enc. with Minutes.
15. Annual Report 1954–55, p.12; Bunt, Ch.7, on other post-war youth organisations.

16. 'Notes for a Meeting to discuss Brigade Organisation to be held through the hospitality of Mr Cyril H. Davis . . . on 9.9.56.', enc. with Minutes. It is unclear from the context whether or not Mr Davis was in fact the author.
17. JLB Minutes, 14 Jan. 1959.
18. (Manchester JLB) Annual Report, p.5.
19. Stanley Rowe recently deposited archive AJ MS 223 at Southampton University.
20. Annual Report 1957–58, p.15; *Manchester Evening Chronicle* 2 Aug., 7 Dec. 1956; David Mellows, 'Jewish Youth Work in Manchester', 20 April 1958, AJ MS 147.
21. *JC* 11 Oct. 1963, 23 Nov. 1962; Jack Levy, Chairman, Youth Committee, Council of Manchester and Salford Jews, quoted in *JC* 10 March 1961.
22. *Liverpool Echo* 20 Dec. 1966; *Liverpool Jewish Gazette*, Supplement, 9 Oct. 1964.
23. Op. cit., note 6 above.
24. Annual Report 1952, p.32; ibid., 1960–61, p.14.
25. JLB Provincial Box File P/O J, Newcastle. Evidently, the Brigade held little appeal for the strictly Orthodox Jewish community in Gateshead.
26. Lander probably to Charles Kay, draft letters, 7, 29 Feb. 1960, JLB Provincial Box File P/O F, Leeds.
27. In 1959, as a result of the setting up of the SAS, the JLB was recognised as an 'experimenting body' under the Duke of Edinburgh Awards Scheme.
28. Annual Report 1951, p.28; *Manchester Daily Dispatch* 2 Nov. 1955.
29. *JW* 31 July 1908.
30. See Springhall (1979 and 1983), Rosenthal and Jeal.
31. *JC* 12 June 1953, 15 Jan. 1965 (obituary).
32. JLB Minutes, 6 June 1901, 25 Sept. 1902.
33. Manchester JLB Annual Report 1899–1903, pp.14, 31.
34. *JC* 29 Feb. 1952, 1 March 1957.
35. Manchester JLB, Officers' Minutes, 10 July 1939; Steinart, Hale to Motel Robins, Hove, 7 May 1986, JLB Provincial Box File P/O E, Manchester.
36. JLB Minutes, 8 Sept. 1953.
37. Memo enc. with Minutes dated 1 July 1963, JLB Minutes, 8 Oct. 1963.
38. Typescript article by Phyllis Abrams to Clive Nagus, Liverpool (n.d., *c.* 1988). Acknowledgements to Joe Wolfman.
39. JLB Minutes, 4 Feb. 1964.
40. *East Kent Mercury* 6 Aug. 1964.
41. *JC* 5 March 1937.
42. *Hackney Gazette* 23 March 1938.
43. See Henriques, *Indiscretions*, pp.77–80; Yogi Meir, talk on East End Clubs, London Museum of Jewish Life, Research Group, 7 Dec. 1993.
44. *JC* 12 Aug. 1938.
45. JLB Minutes, 21 March 1962.
46. Op. cit., note 38 above.
47. *DT* 31 May 1950, 10 Jan. 1990 (Swaythling obituary). Charles Kay and Motel Robins, tape of interview, 26 Aug. 1993.
48. *Hendon & Finchley Times* 20 Nov. 1964.
49. JLB Minutes, 31 Aug. 1966.
50. JLB Minutes, 12 April 1967, 13 Jan. 1969.

51. JLB GEN/36.
52. *Hackney Gazette* 18 Aug. 1964.
53. *Glasgow Evening Citizen* 13 Sept. 1967; JLB Annual Report 1971, p.3.
54. *Manchester Jewish Gazette* 23 Dec. 1960.
55. JLB Annual Report 1968–69, p.2.
56. JLB Annual Report 1977–78, Introduction.
57. JLB Minutes, 5 March 1975; tape of interview with Josh Manches, 22 Dec. 1993.
58. Conference Programme, 24 May 1981, JLB GEN/110.
59. 'Outreach-Kiruv' publicity leaflet, June 1992.
60. JLB Minutes, 13 Feb. 1967, 9 July 1970.
61. Information supplied by Edward Greenbury, Dec. 1993.
62. *CAJEX* Sept. 1977, p.44, acknowledgements to Jonathan Dubow; *Company Call* (Cardiff Company newsletter), Nov. 1978, on Noel Egerton, JLB *Advance* File.
63. *DT* 10 Sept. 1987; Manches, in interview, 22 Dec. 1993.
64. JLB GEN/158 (brochure); JLB Annual Report 1983–84, p.3.
65. 'Give it a Try!' publicity leaflet (n.d., 1990s).
66. *JC* 7 Dec. 1990, p.36.
67. Michelle Kaye, *The Communication Structure of the Jewish Lads' & Girls' Brigade* (1985), p.10, in JLB GEN/7.
68. JLB GEN/134; JLB Annual Report 1987–88, p.3.
69. Op. cit., note 59 above; *JC* 15 Oct. 1993.
70. Op. cit., note 59 above.
71. 'Draft notes of Central Awareness Year Committee', 25 July 1988, JLB GEN/176.

Note on Sources

When Brigade Headquarters Committee met for the first time after the outbreak of the Second World War,[1] almost the first item reported was the removal of the Brigade records from Camperdown House to the safety of a bank vault in Manchester. Such foresight – rare indeed – ensured the survival of a rich archive without which this history could not have been written. The JLGB is an organisation deeply conscious of its own tradition and, as such, has carefully preserved both published and unpublished material dating right back to the beginning of its history. *The National Brigade Archive* has now (1994) been deposited in Anglo-Jewish Archives at the *Hartley Library, Southampton University*, where it will be open to inspection by written permission from the Brigade Secretary. Southampton University is still adding to its Judaica collection, and would be interested in receiving further materials relating to the history of the JLGB.

The collection consists firstly of a complete set of Minute Books of the national movement (except for the very first book which has gone missing within the past ten years). There is a very valuable original Register of Officers before 1908, a Headquarters Staff Minute Book 1897–98 and a Camp Orders Book from 1901–2. There is a series of Annual Reports, with a few gaps in the early years and in the 1920s and 1930s.

Another incomplete set of national Annual Reports is included in the *Stanley Rowe Collection* (MS 223) which was bequeathed to the Hartley Library on Rowe's death in 1993[2] and has only recently been catalogued. The Rowe collection also contains a Manchester JLB Annual Report 1899–1903 as well as a series of Grove House Lads' Club and Manchester JLB Annual Reports from 1928–38 and 1957–70. The rare 1899–1903 Manchester Report plus a further set of national

Annual Reports is available at the *Manchester Central Reference Library* (MS 130).

In Manchester, too, is to be found a separate series of Manchester JLB Officers' Minute Books dating from 1908–39, as well as the Minutes and correspondence of the Grove House Lads' Club from 1916–34. The Rowe papers, which run to 43 boxes, include Minutes from 1941–86, membership and financial records, reports on aspects of Jewish youth work in Manchester and correspondence, much of this material written by Rowe himself. I was unable to consult more than a fraction of this archive owing to the fact that it only became available when this book was almost complete. Time simply did not permit.

The small collection of *David Mellows Papers* (MS 147), also kept at the Hartley Library, proved useful. Like Rowe, Mellows was a youth work professional who was secretary of the Association for Jewish Youth in the 1950s.

The national Brigade has kept Press Cuttings books, including the published Brigade Orders, fairly continuously since 1908. For the very early period, the *Jewish Chronicle* proved invaluable. There are also press cuttings files in both the Rowe and Manchester collections. Copies of Brigade journals *The Reveille* and *The Advance*, from the 1920s and 1930s, in addition to the various post-war publications, are to be found in the national archive. The Manchester Jewish Museum holds two copies of *The Advance*.

I was fortunate in being able to draw upon the Brigade's extensive photographic collection for illustrations for this book. Other pictorial material includes portraits of Brigade Commandants Ernest Halsted and Harold Lion by Flora Lion and cartoons by Phineas May. Little correspondence such as personal letters seems to have survived, but Brigade memorabilia – brochures, flyers, plaques, trophies, colours, insignia, medals and even movie footage (some dating from the 1930s) – abounds in the national archive (especially in the GENeral Box File series compiled by Motel Robins), at the Manchester Jewish Museum and the Scottish Jewish Archives in Glasgow.

Outside Manchester, little material pertaining to provincial Companies has survived, other than that which has been deposited in the national archive in London in the past (two Provincial Box Files marked P/O). Material dating from the 1960s on the Glasgow

Companies is now in the Scottish Jewish Archives but, owing to its recent vintage, was not consulted, given the constraints of time. Joe Wolfman, Archivist to the Merseyside Jewish Representative Council, kindly sent me xeroxes of key documents regarding the JLB in Liverpool, but nothing pre-1960 seems to have been kept at Harold House. *CAJEX*, the magazine of the Cardiff Jewish ex-servicemen's organisation, was useful on the Brigade in Wales. No archives of the turn of the century JLB in Ireland, or overseas in Canada and South Africa, have turned up as yet – but one never knows . . .

Oral history interviews with prominent Brigaders were conducted by Anne Kershen and myself between 1989 and 1993 as set out below (p.194). The tapes have been deposited at the Hartley Library. Other oral history material exists in the Manchester Jewish Museum. With more time at my disposal, I would have liked to compile more memories from ordinary members for inclusion in the book.

Useful secondary sources, both published and unpublished, are listed in the bibliography.

NOTES

1. JLB Minutes, 6 Nov. 1939
2. JC 16 April 1993 (obituary).

Bibliography

Books

Encyclopaedia Judaica
Jewish Year Book

Adler, Michael, *British Jewry Book of Honour* (London 1922)
Alderman, Geoffrey, *The Federation of Synagogues 1887–1987* (London 1987)
——, *Modern British Jewry* (Oxford 1992)
Bentwich, Norman, *They Found Refuge* (London 1956)
Bermant, Chaim, *The Cousinhood* (New York 1971)
Black, Eugene C., *The Social Politics of Anglo-Jewry* (Oxford 1988)
Black, Gerry, *Lender to the Lords: Giver to the Poor* (London 1992)
Bunt, Sidney, *Jewish Youth Work in Britain: Past, Present and Future* (London 1975)
Bush, Julia, *Behind the Lines: East London Labour 1914–19* (London 1984)
Cohen, Stuart, *English Zionists and British Jews* (Princeton 1983)
Collins, Kenneth, *Second City Jewry* (Glasgow 1990)
Emden, Paul H., *Jews of Britain : A Series of Biographies* (London 1943)
Gilner, Elias, *War and Hope: A History of the Jewish Legion* (New York 1969)
Ginsberg, Fay, *Our Beloved Rabbi* [Morris Ginsberg] (privately printed, Surrey 1976)
Henriques, Basil, *The Indiscretions of a Warden* (London 1937)
Henriques, Ursula, *The Jews of South Wales* (Cardiff 1993)
Holmes, Colin, *Anti-Semitism in British Society 1876–1939* (London 1979)
Jabotinsky, Ze'ev, *The Story of the Jewish Legion* (New York 1945)
Jeal, Tim, *Baden-Powell* (London 1989)

Kadish, Sharman, *Bolsheviks and British Jews* (London 1992)

—— (ed.), *Building Jerusalem: Jewish Architecture in Britain* (London 1995)

Lacqueur, Walter Z., *Young Germany: A History of the German Youth Movement* (London 1962)

Loewe, Lionel L., *Basil Henriques: A Portrait* (London 1976)

Lowenthal, Marvin (ed.), *The Diaries of Theodore Herzl* (New York 1956)

Magnus, Charles L., *EMJ: The Man and his Work* (London 1962)

Morris, Henry, *We will Remember them : A Record of the Jews who died in the Armed Forces of the Crown 1939–45* (London 1989)

Rosenthal, Michael, *The Character Factory: Baden-Powell and the Origins of the Boy Scout Movement* (New York 1986)

Schechtman, Joseph B., *The Vladimir Jabotinsky Story: Volume I: Rebel and Statesman* (New York 1956)

Silman-Cheong, Helen, *Wellesley-Aron: Rebel with a Cause* (London 1992)

Sokolow, Nahum, *History of Zionism*, 2 volumes (London 1919)

Springhall, John, *Youth, Empire and Society: British Youth Movements 1883–1940* (London 1977)

—— (*et al.*), *Sure & Stedfast: A History of the Boys' Brigade* (London 1983, 2nd edn 1991)

Stern, Malcolm, *First American Jewish Families: 600 Genealogies 1654–1977* (Cincinnati, Ohio and Waltham, MA *c.*1978)

Stroud, Oswald M., *The Story of the Stroud Family* (privately printed, Bradford 1970–74)

Umansky, Ellen M., *Lily Montagu and the Advancement of Liberal Judaism: From Vision to Vocation* (New York and Toronto 1983)

Booklets, Pamphlets and Articles

Bentwich, Norman, 'The Wanderers and other Jewish Scholars of my Youth', *TJHSE*, Vol.20, pp.51–61

Brodie, Israel, 'British and Palestinian Jews in World War II', *American Jewish Year Book*, Vol.48 (1946–47), pp.51–72

Cesarani, David, 'An Embattled Minority: The Jews in Britain during the First World War', *Immigrants and Minorities*, Vol.8, Nos 1 and 2 (March 1989), pp.61–81.

Eisen, George, 'Zionism, Nationalism and the Emergence of the Judische Turnerschaft', *Leo Baeck Year Book*, Vol.28 (1983), pp.246–62

Emden, Paul H., 'The Brothers Goldsmid and the Financing of the Napoleonic Wars', *TJHSE*, Vol.14 (1940), pp.225–46

Fraenkel, Josef, 'Colonel Albert E.W. Goldsmid and Theodor Herzl', in Patai, Raphael (ed.), *Herzl Year Book*, Vol.I (New York 1958), pp.145–53

Goodman, Ronald A., *The Maccabaeans: The Founding Fathers and Early Years* (London 1979)

Hyamson, Albert M., 'An Anglo-Jewish Family' [the Goldsmids], *TJHSE*, Vol.17 (1951–52), pp.1–10

Kershen, Anne (ed.), *150 Years of Progressive Judaism 1840–1990* (London 1990)

Livshin, Rosalyn, 'The Acculturation of the Children of Immigrant Jews in Manchester, 1890–1930', in Cesarani, David (ed.), *The Making of Modern Anglo-Jewry* (Oxford 1990), pp.79–96

Rinott, Chanoch, 'Major Trends in Jewish Youth Movements in Germany', *Leo Baeck Year Book*, Vol.19 (1974), pp.77–95

Roth, Cecil, 'The Jews in the Defence of Britain: Thirteenth to Nineteenth Centuries', *TJHSE*, Vol.15 (1939–1945), pp.1–28

Shimoni, Gideon, 'The Non-Zionists in Anglo-Jewry, 1937–1948', *Jewish Journal of Sociology*, Vol.28 (1986), pp.89–115

—— 'Poale Zion: A Zionist Transplant in Britain (1905–45)', in *Studies in Contemporary Jewry, Vol.II* (Indiana 1986), pp.227–69

Summers, Anne, 'Militarism in Britain before the Great War', *History Workshop*, Issue 2 (1976), pp.104–23

Tydor-Baumel, J. 'The Kitchener Transmigration Camp at Richborough', *Yad Vashem Studies*, Vol.14 (1981), pp.233–46

Voeltz, Richard A., '"A Good Jew and a Good Englishman": The Jewish Lads' Brigade, 1894–1922', *Journal of Contemporary History*, Vol.23 (1988), pp.119–27

Warren, Allen, 'Sir Robert Baden-Powell, the Scout Movement and Citizen Training in Great Britain, 1900–1920', *English Historical Review*, Vol.101 (1986), pp.376–98

Wilkinson, Paul, 'English Youth Movements, 1908–30', *Journal of Contemporary History*, Vol.4, No.2 (1969), pp.3–23

Wilcock, Evelyn, 'The Revd. John Harris: Issues in Anglo-Jewish Pacifism 1914–18', *TJHSE*, Vol.30 (1987–88), pp.163–77

Unpublished

Bernstein, Simon, ' "Ironing out the Ghetto Bend": A History of the Jewish Lads' Brigade, its aims and influences up to 1914', Oxford BA Dissertation, 1984. Copy in National Brigade Archives

Hein, Virginia Herzog, 'The British Followers of Theodor Herzl: English Zionist Leaders 1896–1904', Georgia State University PhD, 1979

Kalman, Matthew, ' "Young Zionism" and Jewish Youth in London between the Wars', Cantab BA History Tripos, 1983

Kosmin, Barry with Grizzard, Nigel, 'The Jewish Dead in the Great War as an indicator for Anglo-Jewish Demography and Class Stratification in 1914', Mimeo. London, Board of Deputies of British Jews, 1974 (subsequently published in *Immigrants and Minorities*)

Livshin, Rosalyn, 'Aspects of the Acculturation of the Children of Immigrant Jews in Manchester 1890–1930', Manchester MEd., 1982

Mendelsson, David, 'The Development of the Pioneering [*Hechalutsi*] Youth Movements from 1929–48', Hebrew University of Jerusalem MA, 1987

Srebrnik, Henry F., 'The Jewish Communist Movement in Stepney: Ideological Mobilization and Political Victories in an East London Borough 1935–45', Birmingham PhD, 1983–84

Oral History Tapes

Beatrice Harris (Sharman Kadish) 22 Dec. 1993
Gordon Hyams (Anne Kershen) 27 April 1990
Charles Kay (Sharman Kadish) 26 Aug. 1993
Charles Magnus (Anne Kershen) 30 Aug. 1989
Josh Manches (Sharman Kadish) 22 Dec. 1993
Sol Marks (Anne Kershen) 6 Dec. 1989
Phineas May (Anne Kershen) 19 Dec. 1989
Motel Robins (Sharman Kadish) 26 Aug. 1993
Ernest Woolf (Anne Kershen) 19 Dec. 1989
'Phone-in' on Spectrum Radio's Jewish Programme (Sharman Kadish, London) 26 July 1993 (in possession of author)

Glossary

The following terms, unless otherwise indicated, are transliterations from the Hebrew.

Aliya   Zionist motivated emigration to Israel. Literally 'going up'.

Arba Kanfot   Four-cornered fringed vest worn by Orthodox Jewish males. Also known as *Tsitsit*.

Barmitzva   The age of religious majority, reached by a Jewish boy at 13.

Bensching (anglicised Yiddish)   Grace after meals.

Beth Din   Jewish ecclesiastical court.

Chalutsiut   Zionist pioneering effort, specifically rural settlement of Israel.

Chanuka   Jewish festival commemorating the story of the Maccabees; 'Festival of Lights'.

Cheder   Traditional elementary class for instruction in Judaism.

Chevra, Chevrot   Prayer circle, religious fraternity.

Dayan, Dayanim   Judge in a Jewish ecclesiastical court.

Din   Jewish Law, ruling.

Eretz Yisrael   The Land of Israel.

Frum (Yiddish)   Pious.

Gedud   Troop, patrol. Term used by *Habonim*, based on Boy Scouts.

Hachshara   Zionist agricultural training in preparation for settlement on farms in Israel.

Haftara, Haftarot   Portion from Judges, Kings or Prophets read at the Sabbath morning service in the synagogue.

Haham   Chief Rabbi of the Spanish and Portuguese community in Britain.

195

Halakha   Orthodox Jewish law

Hatikva ('The Hope')   The anthem of the Zionist Organisation and now the national anthem of the State of Israel.

Ivrit   Modern Hebrew, as spoken in Israel.

Kashrut   The Jewish dietary laws.

Kehilla, Kehillot   A self-governing religious community of Jews.

Ketuba   Jewish religious marriage certificate.

Kibbutz   Collective farm in Israel.

Kiddush, Kiddushim   Blessing made over wine on Sabbaths and festivals.

Kosher   Fit for consumption or use according to Jewish dietary laws.

Mashgiach   Catering supervisor who ensures that food is prepared according to Jewish dietary laws.

Melamed, Melamdim   Male teacher of traditional Judaism to children.

Merkaz Limmud   'Study centre', programme or resource centre for Zionist education.

Mikva, Mikvaot   Ritual bath used for performance of ritual immersion.

Mincha   Afternoon service.

Minhag   Religious custom.

Minyan, Minyanim   Quorum of ten males, over the age of 13, required for collective worship.

Parnas   Lay leader in the Spanish and Portuguese Synagogue.

Purim   'Lots', Jewish festival commemorating the events described in the Book of Esther.

Rav, Rabbanim   Rabbi, plural pronounced *Rabbonim* by Yiddish-speaking Jews.

Sedra   Weekly portion from the Five Books of Moses read in the synagogue.

Shabbat   The Jewish Sabbath, from sunset on Friday until nightfall on Saturday, pronounced *Shabbes* by Yiddish speaking Jews.

Shacharit   Morning service.

Shaliach, Shlichim   Emissary, specifically from the Zionist Organisation, Jewish Agency or the Israeli Government to encourage Jews in the Diaspora to settle in Israel.

Shechita   Ritual slaughter.

Shema   Central prayer in Jewish liturgy, beginning 'Hear O Israel: the Lord our God, the Lord is One' (Deuteronomy, 6:4).

Shoah   The Nazi holocaust.

Shomer   See *Mashgiach*.

Shtetl (Yiddish)   Jewish village in pre-Second World War eastern Europe.

Shtiebel, Shteiblakh (Yiddish)   Small synagogue often in a private house.

Siddur   Weekday and Sabbath prayerbook.

Talmud Torah   Traditional school for Jewish boys, often attended on a part-time basis.

Tephillin   Phylacteries, used by Orthodox Jewish men at weekday morning services.

Yeshiva, Yeshivot   Traditional religious academy for young men.

Yiddishkeit (Yiddish)   Judaism, the traditional Jewish way of life.

Yom Kippur   Day of Atonement, holiest day in the Jewish religious calendar, a fast day.

Index

199

Index